GOTTSCHALK AND A MEDIEVAL PREDESTINATION CONTROVERSY: TEXTS TRANSLATED FROM THE LATIN

MEDIÆVAL PHILOSOPHICAL TEXTS IN TRANSLATION
NO. 47

GOTTSCHALK AND A MEDIEVAL PREDESTINATION CONTROVERSY: TEXTS TRANSLATED FROM THE LATIN

EDITED AND TRANSLATED
BY
VICTOR GENKE &
FRANCIS X. GUMERLOCK
WITH AN INTRODUCTION
BY
VICTOR GENKE

MARQUETTE
UNIVERSITY
PRESS

MEDIÆVAL PHILOSOPHICAL TEXTS IN TRANSLATION
NO. 47

ROLAND J. TESKE, SJ, SERIES EDITOR

LIBRARY OF CONGRESS CATALOGING-IN-PUBLICATION DATA

Gottschalk, of Orbais, ca. 803-ca. 867.
[Selections. English. 2010]
Gottschalk & a medieval predestination controversy : texts translated from the Latin / edited & translated by Victor Genke & Francis X. Gumerlock ; introduction by Victor Genke.
p. cm. — (Mediæval philosophical texts in translation ; no. 47)
Includes bibliographical references (p.) and indexes.
ISBN-13: 978-0-87462-253-9 (pbk. : alk. paper)
ISBN-10: 0-87462-253-0 (pbk. : alk. paper)
1. Predestination—History of doctrines—Middle Ages, 600-1500—Sources. I. Genke, Victor, 1976- II. Gumerlock, Francis X. III. Title. IV. Title: Gottschalk and a medieval predestination controversy.
BT810.3.G73213 2010
234'.9094'09021—dc22

2010032853

∞The paper used in this publication meets the minimum requirements of the American National Standard for Information Sciences—Permanence of Paper for Printed Library Materials, ANSI Z39.48-1992.

Association of American University Presses

MARQUETTE UNIVERSITY PRESS
MILWAUKEE

The Association of Jesuit University Presses

CONTENTS

ILLUSTRATIONS

Cover photo: Holy Cross chapel in Nin. Photo courtesy Ralph Mitterbauer.

INTRODUCTION

GOTTSCHALK AND THE CONTROVERSY OVER HIS TEACHING

BY

VICTOR GENKE

Tous les passés n'ont pas eu d'avenir.
Maurice Godelier

Gottschalk was an important figure in the social and political history of Germany, France, Italy and the Balkans. He was the first to use the expression *gens teudisca,*[1] which is equivalent to *deutsche Volk.*[2] Moreover, he is among the major witnesses for the formation of the independent Croatian state in Dalmatia. However, his place in the history of ideas is even more eminent. Between the Council of Orange in 529 and the sixteenth century, very few people dared to apply so radically the predestinarian theology of Augustine as Gottschalk did.[3]

This introductory essay will briefly review current scholarship on Gottschalk, present the need for this book, and give an overview of Gottschalk's life. It will then trace the course of events of the theological controversy over twofold predestination that he sparked, introducing the key persons involved the controversy and the literature they produced. Finally, it will summarize Gottschalk's doctrine of predestination and offer suggestions for further study.

SCHOLARSHIP ON GOTTSCHALK

In the aftermath of the Reformation James Ussher (1581-1656), the archbishop of Armagh, wrote the first significant account of Gottschalk's life and teaching.[4]

---

1 Lambot, 195.

2 German people.

3 Others include Thomas Bradwardine (c. 1290-1349), Gregory of Rimini (d. 1358) and John Wycliffe (c. 1330-1384). However, they are separated from Gottschalk by almost five hundred years.

4 James Ussher, *Gotteschalci, et praedestinatianae controversiae ab eo motae, historia* (Dublin: ex typographia Societatis Bibliopolarum, 1631; Hannover: Lasche, 1662).

This task was later continued by Gilbert Mauguin (d. 1674),[5] a French Jansenist, who in turn tried to show Gottschalk's orthodoxy, which caused a rather hostile reaction by Louis Cellot (1588-1658),[6] a Jesuit, who, on the contrary, endeavored to reaffirm the rebellious Saxon's condemnation. The predestination controversy in the Carolingian era was also treated by Jacques Sirmond (1559-1651),[7] a Jesuit as well, and by Jacques Basnage de Beauval (1653-1723),[8] a Reformed theologian.

The eighteenth century was less fascinated with Gottschalk, although the works by Johann Jakob Hottinger,[9] Enrico Noris,[10] Domenico Bernino[11] deserve to be mentioned. But in the 19th and the first few decades of the 20th century the interest in this eminent theologian grew more intense, while Latin gradually ceased to be the language in which one had to write about him. Indeed, the current state of research on Gottschalk would be hardly imaginable without the contributions of Gustav Friedrich Wiggers,[12] Heinrich Schrörs,[13] Albert Freystedt,[14] Lüdwig Traube,[15] Norbert Fickermann,[16] Benoit Lavaud,[17] Frédéric

---

5 Gilbert Maugin, *Veterum auctorum, qui IX saeculo de praedestinatione et gratia scripserunt, opera et fragmenta plurima nunc primum in lucem edita, etc.*, 2 vols. (Paris: Apud Ioannem Billaine, 1650).

6 Louis Cellot, *Historia Gotteschalci praedestinatiani et accurata controversiae per eum revocatae disputatio in libros V distincta* (Paris: Sébastien Mabre-Cramoisy, 1655).

7 Jacques Sirmond, *Historia praedestinatiana* (Paris: Sébastien et Gabriel Cramoisy frères, 1648).

8 Jacques Basnage de Beauval, *Histoire de l'Eglise*, Vol. 1 (Rotterdam: Reinier Leers, 1699), Chs. 8-9.

9 Johann Jakob Hottinger, *Diatribe historico-theologica, qua praedestinatianam et Godescalci pseudohaereses commenta esse demonstratur* (Zurich: Typis Heideggeri et Rahnii, 1718).

10 Enrico Noris, *Historiae Gothescalcanae synopsis*. In *Opera*, Vol. 4 (Verona: Tumermaniana, 1729), 681ff.

11 Domenico Bernino, *Historia di tutte l'heresie* (Venice: Stamperia Baglioni, 1724).

12 Gustav Friedrich Wiggers, "Schicksale der augustinischen Anthropologie von der Verdammung des Semipelagionismus auf dem Synoden zu Orange und Valence 529 bis zur Reaction des Mönchs Gottschalk für den Augustinismus. Fünfte Abteilung: Der Mönch Gottschalk," *Zeitschrift für die historische Theologie* 29 (1859):471-594.

13 Heinrich Schrörs, *Der Streit über die Prädestination im IX. Jahrhundert* (Freiburg: Herder, 1884).

14 Albert Freystedt, "Studien zu Gottschalks Leben und Lehre," I-III, *Zeitschrift für Kirchengeschichte* 18 (1897/1898):1-22, 161-82, 529-45, and other articles.

15 Lüdwig Traube, *Prooemium* to *Godescalci Carmina*. In MGH, Poetae 3:707-22.

16 Norbert Fickermann, "Wiedererkannte Dichtungen Gottschalks," *Revue bénédictine* 44 (1932):314-21.

17 Benoit Lavaud, "Précurseur de Calvin ou témoin de l'augustinisme? Le cas de Godescalc," *Révue thomiste* 15 (1932):71-101.

J. Gaudard,[18] Dom Maïeul Cappuyns[19] and many others who wrote on various aspects of the controversy before 1931, when Dom Germain Morin discovered a rich collection of Gottschalk's theological texts in the library of Bern.[20] Before that time only his poetry and his two confessions were known to be extant. Soon other discoveries followed, including Gottschalk's grammatical treatises. The largest part of these materials was published in 1945,[21] yet other texts by the rebellious Benedictine appeared until 1958.[22] Thus, studies published after World War II are the most important, when the body of available writings by this medieval partisan of double predestination grew considerably. Quite surprisingly, these works are not as many as one would expect. Among others, Otto Herding,[23] Frederic J. E. Raby,[24] Bernhard Bischoff,[25] Marie-Luise Weber[26] commented on Gottschalk's poetical works; Jean Jolivet[27] and George H. Tavard[28] explored his trinitarian teaching; Klaus Vielhaber[29] gave a general overview of his life and doctrine; David Ganz[30] and Peter R. McKeon[31] showed the importance of the

---

18 Frédéric J. Gaudard, *Gottschalk moine d'Orbais ou le commencement de la controverse sur la prédestination au IXe siècle* (Saint-Quentin: Moureau, 1887).

19 Maïeul Cappuyns, *Jean Scot Erigène. Sa vie, son œuvre, sa pensée* (Louvain: Abbaye du Mont César, 1933).

20 Germain Morin, "Gottschalk retrouvé," *Revue bénédictine* 43 (1931):303-12.

21 Cyrille Lambot, ed., *Oeuvres théologiques et grammaticales de Godescalc d'Orbais* (Leuven: Spicilegium Sacrum Lovaniense, 1945).

22 Lambot, "Lettre inédite de Godescalc d'Orbais," *Revue bénédictine* 68 (1958):41-51.

23 Otto Herding, "Über die Dichtungen Gottschalks von Fulda" in *Festschrift Paul Kluckhohn und Hermann Schneider gewidmet zu ihrem 60. Geburtstag* (Tübingen: Mohr, 1948).

24 Frederic J. E. Raby, *A History of Christian-Latin Poetry* (Oxford: Clarendon, 1953).

25 Bernhard Bischoff, "Gottschalks Lied für den reichenauer Freund," in *Mittelalterliche Studien: ausgewählte Aufsätze zur Schriftkunde und Literaturgeschichte*, II (1967):26-34.

26 Marie-Luise Weber, *Die Gedichte des Gottschalk von Orbais*. Lateinische Sprache und Literatur des Mittelalters 27 (Frankfurt: Lang, 1992).

27 Jean Jolivet, *Godescalc d'Orbais et la trinité: la méthode de la théologie à l'époque carolingienne* (Paris: Vrin, 1958).

28 George H. Tavard, *Trina Deitas: The Controversy between Hincmar and Gottschalk* (Milwaukee, WI: Marquette University Press, 1996).

29 Klaus Vielhaber, *Gottschalk der Sachse* (Bonn: Röhrscheid, 1956).

30 David Ganz, "The Debate on Predestination," in Margaret T. Gibson and Janet L. Nelson, eds., *Charles the Bald; Court and Kingdom* (Oxford: British Archeological Reports, 1981), 353-73; Second, rev. ed. (Burlington, VT: Variorum, 1990), 285-302.

31 Peter R. McKeon, "The Carolingian Councils of Savonnières (859) and Tusey (860) and their Background," *Revue bénédictine* 84 (1974):75-110.

political side of the controversy; for Jean Devisse[32] Gottschalk was significant in the life of Hincmar, whose excellent biography he authored. Very important for Gottschalk studies is also a book by Bernard Boller[33] that recently appeared in France, since it pays more attention than usual to the Dalmatian period of the wandering monk's life.

This brief overview demonstrates that very little has been written on Gottschalk's thought, particularly his doctrine of predestination. In this respect, the great discoveries of the 1930s resulted in almost no considerable progress. One reason has been nearly a complete absence of modern translations of the theological treatises of this great Carolingian thinker, quite overshadowed by other important figures of his time. Indeed, although in 1996 Croatia printed a postage-stamp commemorating the 1150th anniversary of Gottschalk's coming to the court of the prince Trpimir, only two treatises of Gottschalk on predestination have been heretofore published in English.[34]

As for English translations of primary texts related to the predestination controversy by others in the Carolingian age, Henry Newland provided Florus of Lyons' *Sermon on Predestination* (*Sermo de praedestinatione*) in his 1860 commentary on Ephesians, and a large portion of Florus' *Book on Three Letters* (*Liber de tribus epistolis*) appeared in a 1957 compilation of early medieval theological texts.[35] In 1977 Timothy Roland Roberts contributed a translation of Ratramnus of Corbie's *On the Predestination of God* (*De praedestinatione Dei*) in his dissertation, and in 1998 Notre Dame University Press published Mary Brennan's translation of John Scot Erigena's *On Divine Predestination* (*De divina praedestinatione*).[36] However,

---

32 Jean Devisse, *Hincmar: archevêque de Reims 845-882* (Geneva: Librairie Droz, 1975-1976).

33 Bernard Boller, *Gottschalk d'Orbais. De Fulda à Hautvillers: une dissidence* (Paris: Société des écrivains, 2004).

34 The treatises were the *Shorter Confession* (*Confessio brevior*) and *Longer Confession* (*Confessio prolixior*) in Ronald Hanko, "Gottschalk's Doctrine of Double Predestination" *Protestant Reformed Theological Journal*, 12:1 (1978):42-61. I have not discovered any references to this article in later literature on Gottschalk. English translations of a few poems by Gottschalk were published in Peter Godman, ed., *Poetry of the Carolingian Renaissance* (Norman, OK: University of Oklahoma Press, 1985), 228-46.

35 Henry Newland, *A Practical and Exegetical Commentary on the Epistle of St. Paul to the Ephesians* (Oxford and London: J. H. and James Parker, 1860), 15-20; George E. McCracken, ed., *Early Medieval Theology*. Library of Christian Classics 9 (Philadelphia: Westminster, 1957), 148-75.

36 Timothy Roland Roberts, "A Translation and Critical Edition of Ratramnus of Corbie's De Predestinatione [sic] Dei," Diss. (University of Missouri-Columbia, 1977); Mary Brennan, trans., *John Scottus Eriugena. Treatise on Divine Predestination* (Notre Dame, IN: University of Notre Dame Press, 1998). A few letters of Lupus of Ferrières related to the controversy are in Graydon W. Regenos, trans., *The Letters of Lupus of Ferrières* (The Hague: Martinus Nijhoff, 1966), a letter of Rabanus Maurus

until now no English-language collection of translated texts by Gottschalk and others on this theological controversy has been published.

Truly, "all things past have not had a future."[37] The present book tries to change this for the better. It is my hope that the availability in English of the twenty-one texts herein by Gottschalk and his contemporaries related to the ninth-century predestination controversy will result in a revival of research on Gottschalk, whose role in the history of ideas is still to be fully discovered and appreciated.

GOTTSCHALK'S EARLY LIFE AND EDUCATION (C. 804-822)

One of the earliest records of Gottschalk in history reads as follows: "Gottschalk, son of Bernus, a Saxon count."[38] Gottschalk's date of birth is uncertain. However, in connection with the inheritance that had been offered to the abbey along with Gottschalk, Rabanus Maurus[39] wrote to Hatto the same year: "It is, as you know, a possession of the monastery and the church of Fulda, a dominical property belonging to it, that has rightfully come to the lord emperor through succession to his father as consistent with the law of inheritance."[40] The point is that Louis I the Pious had inherited this property from Charlemagne, which means that Gottschalk must have entered Fulda in the latter's lifetime, thus before 28 January 814.

The annexation of Saxony was a long and painful process of deportations, slaughters, and forced conversions. It is not long before Gottschalk's birth that counties began to be organized in the area, so his father was perhaps among the first counts appointed.[41] But he did not swear fidelity on a formal level, as most others did. In handing over Gottschalk and his legacy to a monastery, he was acting according to Frankish customs, which were not in accord with those of his fatherland.

---

related to Gottschalk in Paul Edward Dutton, *Carolingian Civilization. A Reader* (Petersborough, Ontario: Broadview, 1993), 49-50; and the *Chapters of the Council of Quierzy* (*Capitula conventiculi Carisiaci*) and *Canons of the Council of Valence* (*Concilii Valentini canones*) in Henry Denzinger, *The Sources of Catholic Dogma* (Saint Louis: Herder, 1957), 126-32.

37 See the epigraph.

38 Hatto of Fulda, *Letter to Otgar* (*Epistola ad Otgarium*). Cited in MGH, Epist. 5:529: *Gottescalcus, filius Berni comitis Saxonis.* In contemporary literature, the spelling of "Bernus" varies; it may also read Bern, Berno or Bernon. Hatto was abbot of Fulda, 842-856, Otgar archbishop of Mainz, 826-847.

39 C. 780-856, abbot of Fulda 822-842, archbishop of Mainz 848-856.

40 "*Sunt, ut nostis, possessiones Fuldensis monasterii et ecclesiae ad eam pertinentes proprietas dominicalis, quae domino imperatori ex paterna successione hereditario iure provenit.*" Cited in Traube, *Prooemium*, 709. In the present Introduction translations are mine unless otherwise indicated.

41 See Boller, *Gottschalk d'Orbais*, 21, n. 31.

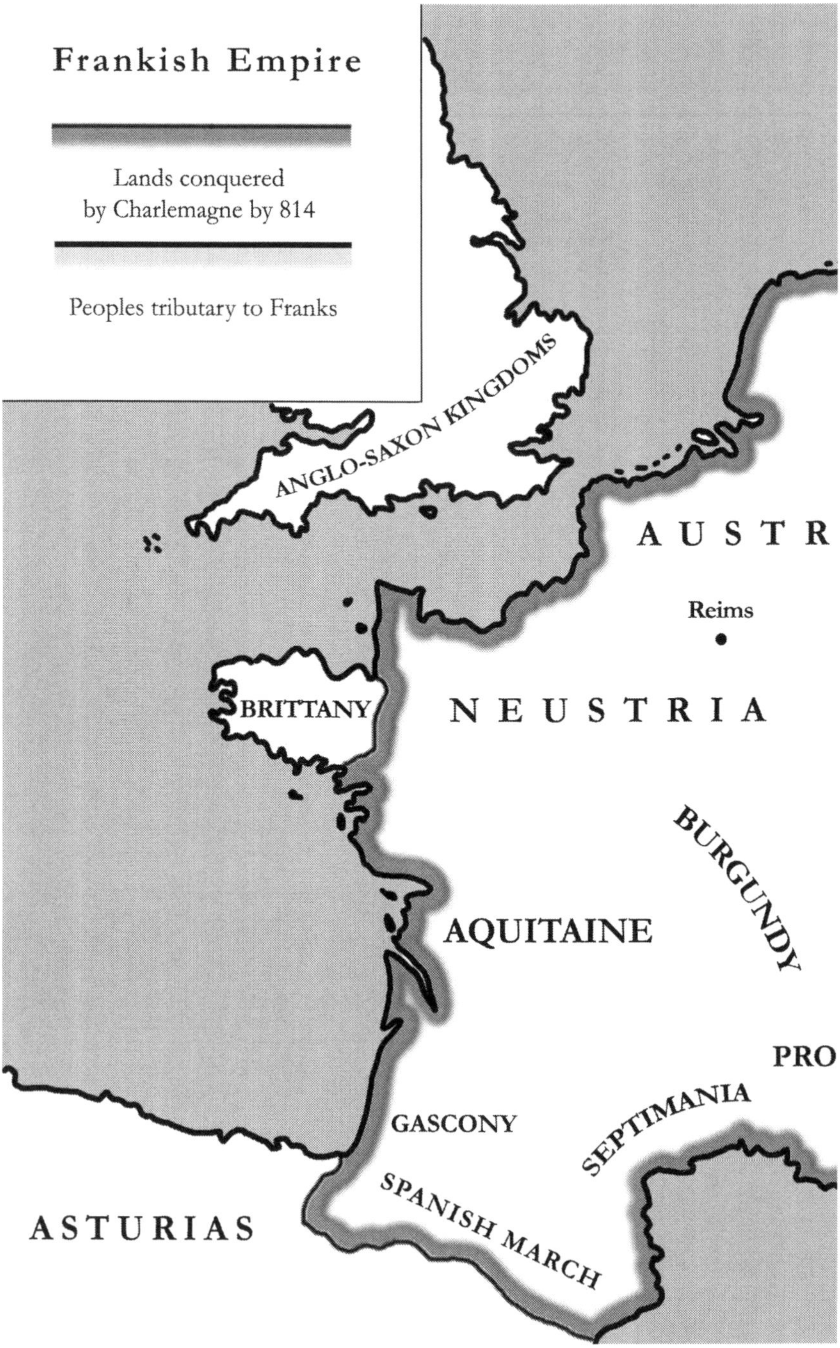

Illustration 1. Carolingian lands

Danes
Obodrites
Slavic Peoples
SAXONY
Wilzians
Sorbs
Fulda
ASIA
Mainz
Bohemians
Moravians
Reichenau
BAVARIA
Avars
ALAMANNIA
CARINTHIA
FRIOUL
Pannonians
LOMBARDY
Croatians
VENCE
ITALY
BENEVENTO

Summarizing the essence of the elementary course of an oblate, Rabanus wrote: "There are certain boys, who from their cradle have been studying sacred literature and have long been fed by the nourishment of the holy church, until, educated enough, they are promoted to the lofty state of holy orders."[42] Founded in 744 by Sturmi, a disciple of Boniface, Fulda was an important center of learning and education, especially since 803, when Rabanus became the director of its school. There Gottschalk would have studied Latin, the fathers, and the Bible, as well as elements of classical literature. Perhaps he did well, because after a while they sent him to Reichenau, a monastery no less renowned for its training.[43]

In this school, located on an island in the Untersee,[44] our oblate met his lifelong friend, Walafrid Strabo.[45] Younger than Gottschalk, perhaps with impaired eyesight[46] and born of humble parents, Walafrid used to call his fellow student Fulgentius,[47] as well as, eventually, his "father and brother."[48] Of Reichenau tutors, "my teacher Wettin" is the only one that Gottschalk would ever mention in his extant works[49]; so we may suppose, in view of his own later mystical experience, that the great visionary, Wettin, was a major influence in his early years. However, a few other names are to be mentioned in this connection. Abbot Haito,[50] who traveled to Constantinople in 811, did much for the classical training of the monks. The librarian Reginbert made the local library one of the most important

42 Rabanus Maurus, *On the Oblation of Children (De oblatione puerorum)*. PL 107:419B-C: "*Sunt ergo quidam qui a cunabulis suis sacras litteras didicerunt, et sanctae Ecclesiae nutrimento tandiu aliti sunt, quousque satis educati in sublime sacrorum ordinum proveherentur.*"

43 Founded in 724 by missionary bishop Pirmin (abbot 724-727), the monastery was located on the highway to Italy and frequented by pilgrims. In Latin Reichenau was called *Augia Dives*. Its vernacular name until the 10th century was Sintlas-Au.

44 Western arm of Lake Constance (Bodensee).

45 C. 808-849, abbot of Reichenau 838, 842-849.

46 Strabo in Latin means "squint-eyed."

47 Walafrid Strabo, *Poem for the Monk Gottschalk, Who is Also Fulgentius* (*Versus Gotescalcho monaco, qui et Fulgentius*). MGH, Poetae 2:362-4; PL 114:1115D. Traube (*Prooemium*, 708, n. 2) subtly remarks: "I believe that Gottschalk was called so after Fulgentius Planciadus, a translator of Virgil, not after the bishop of Ruspe, a disciple of Augustine; it is much more probable that both [Gottschalk and Walafrid] eagerly read Virgil at the period, than meditated upon the doctrine of predestination."

48 Strabo, *Poem for the Monk Gottschalk*. PL 114:1116D: "*Pater fraterque.*"

49 Gottschalk of Orbais, *Answers on Various Questions* (*Responsa de diversis*). Lambot, 170: "*Magistro meo Vuectino.*" Thus Gottschalk was transferred to Reichenau before 824, when the death of Wettin occurred. Before leaving this life, Wettin saw hell, purgatory, and paradise. Haito set forth the vision in prose. Afterwards Walafrid, then about 18 years old, put it into verse in the famous *Vision of Wettin* (*Visio Wettini*) at Grimald's request.

50 Also spelled Heito or Hatto, 762/763-836, head of monastic school under Waldo (abbot 786-806), abbot of Reichenau and bishop of Basle 806-823.

of the age. Also Grimald, future royal chancellor and, later, abbot of St Gallen (841-872), studied and taught at Reichenau at that time.[51]

However, the life of the young oblates at the school was not cloudless. Walafrid would recall in a poem dedicated to his friend: "In how much poverty our youth has passed!"[52] To be sure, the interpretations of Gottschalk's famous poem, "Why Are You Demanding? (*Ut quid jubes*),"[53] are multiple;[54] but if one of the most convincing is correct, it was composed during this period and expresses the young man's deep home-sickness during his at least two-year stay in the island monastery.[55] Whatever the case, Gottschalk, together with Walafrid, finally came back to Fulda,[56] where they probably met deacon Lupus, future abbot of Ferrières.[57]

GOTTSCHALK THE MONK AT FULDA (823-829)

Some time before 829 Gottschalk was forced to take the monastic vows. Traube wrote: "We do not know whether he was tonsured forthwith or, as Heiric, some years after the oblation."[58] Now Hatto, in a *Letter to Otgar*, remarked that Rabanus "compelled Gottschalk to accept monastic life in childhood (*pueritia*)."[59] Regardless of how one translates *pueritia*,[60] it is clear that this had happened quite long before 829 when the letter was written. Some time after his return

---

51 Under abbots Haito (806-823) and Erlebald (823-838).

52 Strabo, *Poem for the Monk Gottschalk*. PL 114:1116C: "*In pauperie passa est quam nostra juventus.*"

53 Gottschalk, *Poems* (*Carmina*): "Why Are You Demanding?" MGH, Poetae 3:731-2.

54 To mention a few, Giuseppe Ludovico Perugi, *Gottschalc* (Rome: Bazzocchi, 1911), 56; Hans von Schubert, *Die Geschichte des deutschen Glaubens* (Leipzig: Quelle & Meyer, 1925), 55; Herding, "Über die Dichtungen Gottschalks von Fulda," 53-4. See also Raby, *A History of Christian-Latin Poetry*, 191.

55 Vielhaber, *Gottschalk*, 85-7.

56 Presumably about 827.

57 In a *Letter to Eginhard*, Lupus mentions that he was sent to Fulda by Aldric, archbishop of Sens 829-836, before Wenilo. PL 119:433B. Traube (*Prooemium*, 708, n. 3) assumed that this happened when Aldric was still the abbot of Ferrières (after Adalbert), so before 829.

58 Traube, *Prooemium*, 707, n. 2: "*Confestimne attonsus sit an, ut Heiricus, aliquot annis post oblationem, ignoramus.*" At any event, if it was Rabanus who forced Gottschalk to become a monk, he was not able to do this immediately after Gottschalk entered the monastery, if it happened about 814. In an historical essay on Rabanus, Jean Mabillon indicates that in 814-817 Rabanus left Fulda on account of disagreement with Ratgar and, presumably, visited the Holy Land (PL 107:17A-B). Rabanus alludes to this trip in his commentary on Joshua (PL 108:1000A).

59 Hatto, *Letter to Otgar*. Cited in MGH, Epist. 5:529: "*Godeschalcum in pueritia coegit (Rabanus) monasticam vitam suscipere.*"

60 Be it "childhood," "boyhood," or "youth," the term is rather vague as a designation of age.

Illustration 2. St Michael's church in Fulda

to Fulda, Gottschalk "disturbed abbot Rabanus, asserting that he had been both tonsured against his will and forcibly installed into monastic life by the same."[61]

Gottschalk's attempt to be released from the monastery was no easy task. With Rabanus, who had been given the name Maurus by his teacher Alcuin after Saint Benedict's dearest disciple, Fulda became a center of missionary work throughout Germany. A strict disciplinarian, Rabanus saw his main task as upholding order at any price in a time when disintegration grew to be one of the most characteristic features of society. He had an immense authority among the ecclesiastics of the age. Nevertheless, Hatto, future abbot of Fulda, supported the rebellious monk. It is unclear whether Gottschalk had been keeping in touch with his relatives in Saxony earlier,[62] but at this point they came to his side, too. In June 829, in Mainz, a synod was convened, where the case had to be determined. Hatto, in a *Letter to Otgar*, described its outcome as follows: "By their judgment he was restored in the fatherly freedom, but so that, should it be acceptable to the abbot, this controversy in which they both[63] as well as his[64] relatives are involved may end with an oath."[65]

61 Hatto, *Letter to Otgar*. Cited in MGH, Epist. 5:530: "*Interpellavit Rabanum abbatem... asserens se et invitum fuisse attonsum et violenter ab eo monasticę vitae mancipatum.*"

62 As suggested by Gaudard, *Gottschalk moine d'Orbais*, 19.

63 Rabanus and Gottschalk.

64 Gottschalk's.

65 Hatto, *Letter to Otgar*. Cited in MGH, Epist. 5:530: "*Eorum iudicio paternae restitutus est libertati: ea tamen ratione, ut, si abbati ita placeret, controversiae eorum finis inter eos*

The refractory Benedictine left the monastery,[66] but the compromise did not satisfy either of the parties. In August of the same year a new synod was convened, at Rabanus' request, this time at Worms. However, before it took place, the abbot of Fulda composed a treatise entitled *On the Oblation of Children,* a document most revealing concerning the details of the controversy.[67]

First of all, he strongly intimated that the whole affair was for him primarily that of *faith.*[68] Having described the upbringing of the oblates, he says in the very next sentence:[69] "But, ungrateful for such a favor, they have opinions that are contrary to the faith of the orthodox fathers, and daily attack the mother of all faithful by the weapons of their iniquity."[70] Such are the ways of the "heretics" and "schismatics."[71] They act with their hearts "blinded through earthly cupidity."[72] These "misguided defenders of genuine freedom"[73] ventured to "set the worldly and temporal law before the divine and eternal law."[74] What exactly irritated the abbot so much? "They say that those who become monks become slaves."[75] Actually, the whole treatise is conceived to militate against this statement or, more correctly, against its implications: monks do become slaves, but God's slaves, which brings no dishonor; on the contrary, "the holy fathers deemed it a great honor to be called slaves of God."[76] First, quoting the examples of Abraham and Jephthah, Rabanus insists that it is good on the part of the parents to sacrifice their children to God; second, that it is good on the part of the children to renounce the world and to serve God. Those who say otherwise

istius ac propinquorum suorum esset iuramentum."

66 See Traube, *Prooemium,* 709.

67 Rabanus, *On the Oblation of Children* (PL 107:419-40).

68 Even though in his correspondence he considers the problem of Gottschalk's legacy as an important factor in it, see above.

69 Rabanus gives no names, but there is no doubt at all that he means Gottschalk and those supporting him.

70 Rabanus, *On the Oblation of Children* (PL 107:419C): *"Sed ingrati tanto munere, contraria orthodoxorum Patrum fidei sentiunt, ac matrem universorum fidelium telis iniquitatis suae quotidie impugnant."*

71 Rabanus, *On the Oblation of Children* (PL 107:420C).

72 Rabanus, *On the Oblation of Children* (PL 107:429C): *"Obcaecato corde per cupiditatem terrenam."*

73 Rabanus, *On the Oblation of Children* (PL 107:423A): *"Importuni defensores genuinae libertatis."*

74 Rabanus, *On the Oblation of Children* (PL 107:423B): *"Legem mundanam et temporalem legi divinae atque aeternae... praeponunt."*

75 Rabanus, *On the Oblation of Children* (PL 107:431C): *"Dicentes eos servos fieri qui monachi fiunt."*

76 Rabanus, *On the Oblation of Children* (PL 107:420B): *"Hoc pro magno honore sancti patres habuere, quod servi Dei nuncuparentur."*

"do not understand that they wage war against the Lord."[77] They actually "have opinions that are contrary to the catholic faith and, the end of the world being near, introduce new sects into the church."[78]

The technical side of the question is described like this: the abbot's opponents asserted that the oblation of children "must be confirmed by suitable witnesses."[79] In Gottschalk's case, such witnesses could be only Saxons: "They say that the law of their race does not allow that a man of a different race should be called to witness to make void the law of their freedom."[80] Rabanus' answer is very straightforward. How do they dare to despise a nation that is superior to them? Everybody knows that Franks came to Christ earlier, and, moreover, they conquered the Saxons and turned them away from idolatry.[81]

Towards the end of the treatise, the abbot of Fulda expressed himself very clearly with respect to the rebellious monk, calling him "this our adversary."[82] The die was cast.

GOTTSCHALK'S TRAVELS AND RELOCATION IN ORBAIS (829-835)

Here begins one of the most enigmatic periods of Gottschalk's life. We do not know what happened at the synod of Worms, presided over by Louis the Pious. First of all, was the rebellious Benedictine compelled to remain a monk against his will? Most researchers have been inclined to think so. Indeed, this would explain much of Gottschalk's later biography. Having returned to the monastery under compulsion, he never stopped struggling against those who oppressed him. Thus, the permission to change monasteries (Fulda to Orbais) would be a kind of concession made to the monk in view of his conflict with the abbot.

However, after 829 Gottschalk never gave any sign of being discontent with his monastic status. If Rabanus had gained the upper hand at Worms and exposed Gottschalk as a deviant, he would perhaps use this argument in the polemics that followed. But this never happened. It is possible that all this points to the

77 Rabanus, *On the Oblation of Children* (PL 107:431C): "*Non intellegunt se contra Dominum pugnare.*"

78 Rabanus, *On the Oblation of Children* (PL 107:429C): "*Contraria fidei catholicae sentiunt, atque sectas novas, appropinquante fine mundi, in Ecclesiam introducunt.*"

79 Rabanus, *On the Oblation of Children* (PL 107:431A): "*Testibus idoneis confirmari debere.*"

80 Rabanus, *On the Oblation of Children* (PL 107:431B): "*Hoc enim, aiunt, legem gentis suae pati non posse, ut alterius gentis homo in testimonium citetur ad infringendam legem libertatis suae.*"

81 Rabanus, *On the Oblation of Children* (PL 107:432A).

82 Rabanus, *On the Oblation of Children* (PL 107:438B-C): "*Iste adversarius noster.*"

fact that the refractory monk came back to the monastery of his own accord.[83] It could be added that the young man's rebellion might have been inspired by his relatives in Saxony, who were irritated by the donation made by Gottschalk's father to Fulda. As it seems, for them the whole affair was basically that of the Benedictine's legacy, not his monkhood.[84]

Anyway, at some later point Gottschalk was canonically affiliated with the monastery of Orbais,[85] near Château-Thierry, in the diocese of Soissons. However, it is admitted that before his installation at Orbais, Gottschalk visited the monastery of Corbie[86] in Picardy, near Amiens. Indeed, it is known that he was acquainted with at least two monks from that cloister, Gislemar and Ratramnus.[87]

Now some time before 835,[88] Ebbo, archbishop of Reims, commissioned Peter,[89] then abbot of Hautvillers[90] (Ebbo's country residence, where he established a famous scriptorium), to produce a magnificent manuscript largely known as Ebbo Gospels.[91] Written with golden ink on vellum, it contained, along with the texts of the four Gospels and prologues by Jerome, a dedicatory poem addressed to Ebbo.[92] Already Fickermann[93] pointed to the fact that the poem's author was Gottschalk. This statement was later brilliantly corroborated in a careful philological analysis of the poem by Vielhaber,[94] and recently reaffirmed by Boller.[95]

Thus, before Orbais, Gottschalk also undoubtedly visited Hautvillers. This explains well why in 849, at the synod of Quierzy, the abbots of the three mon-

---

83 For more details see Vielhaber, *Gottschalk*, 16-7.

84 It is highly improbable that the legacy was given back. It is important to note that being "free" but without the inheritance was a rather shaky social status. On the contrary, monastic life offered a possibility of a stable career.

85 Founded in 677 by Reol (Regulus), bishop of Reims 669-695.

86 Founded in 657 by Bathilde, widow of Clovis II.

87 He also might have known personally Paschasius Radbertus (who was a monk at Corbie under Adalhard and Wala, and himself elected abbot of Corbie about 843) whose understanding of the Eucharist Gottschalk would later criticize in his treatise *On the Body and Blood of the Lord* (*De corpore et sanguine domini*). Lambot, 324-37.

88 The year of Ebbo's deposition. Or even before 833, See Vielhaber, *Gottschalk*, 90.

89 Abbot 820-841.

90 A monastery founded about 662 by Bercharius (636-696), its first abbot.

91 The manuscript is preserved in the *Médiathèque municipale* of Épernay. Another work of art produced at Hautvillers' scriptorium around the same time is the Utrecht Psalter, preserved in the *Bibliotheek der Rijksuniversiteit*.

92 MGH, Poetae 1:623-4. For a facsimile reproduction see Boller, *Gottschalk d'Orbais*, 226-31.

93 MGH, Poetae 6:88.

94 Vielhaber, *Gottschalk*, 88-9.

95 Boller, *Gottschalk d'Orbais*, 65-70.

asteries were present: Bavo of Orbais, Paschasius Radbertus of Corbie, and Halduinus of Hautvillers.[96]

In a poetical letter to Ratramnus, written by Gottschalk during his incarceration after the synod of Quierzy (849), the imprisoned monk says that he spent a year at a school of a teacher of versification,[97] which must have taken place after he had stayed at Corbie.[98] Moreover, in a letter to Ebbo,[99] Gottschalk mentions a period of time when he lived in his house,[100] and when the archbishop, his benefactor, gave him an opportunity to study.[101] It is most likely that in both passages Gottschalk writes about one and the same period. His teacher might have been Dunchad, Irish poet and erudite, who lived at Reims around the same time.[102] It is also very important that Hincmar would later write to the monks and simple folk of his diocese that they knew his prisoner very well before he went to Italy,[103] which remark would be inconceivable if Gottschalk did not stay for rather long periods of time in Reims and its neighborhood.[104] No less important is Gottschalk's own testimony concerning his dispute with a certain "Faustus the Manichean" (*Faustus manichaeus*) about the latter's teaching that supposed the existence of the "blood of the Holy Spirit," which took place in

96 These three are the only abbots that Hincmar mentions by name. Hincmar of Reims, *On Predestination* (*De praedestinatione*), 2; (PL 125:85C). Hincmar might have planned beforehand for Hautvillers to be the monastery of Gottschalk's imprisonment, and that is why the abbot of Hautvillers was invited. However, Vielhaber believes (*Gottschalk*, 90) that the idea of Hautvillers as Gottschalk's prison came to Hincmar's mind during the synod itself. See also Lambot, 379.

97 Gottschalk, *Letter to Ratramnus* (*Epistola ad Ratramnum*) in MGH, Poetae 3:735; PL 121:370A.

98 Since Ratramnus was supposed to ignore this episode of his life.

99 Gottschalk, *Unedited Letter* (*Epistola inedita*) in Lambot, "Lettre inédite," 42-4. Written before 835.

100 Lambot, "Lettre inédite," 42, 44. As a "*vernaculus*" or "*cliens*."

101 Lambot, "Lettre inédite," 43: "*Dedistis operam ut lumen scientiae addiscerem verenter.*"

102 As suggested by Traube, *Prooemium*, 710-11.

103 Hincmar, *Letter to the Monks and Simple Folk of his Diocese* (*Epistola ad reclusos et simplices suae dioeceseos*), Wilhelm Gundlach, ed. "Zwei Schriften Hinkmars von Reims," *Zeitschrift für Kirchengeschichte* 10 (1889), 261: "*Gotescalcus... antequam ex ista parrochia contra leges ecclesiasticas excommunicatus pergeret... auribus et aspectibus vestris commendans... venena pessima auditibus simul et cordibus vestris infudit.*"

104 Thus definitively outside Orbais which he ought not to have left, if he were a monk there at the period.

Reims at the same period.[105] Gottschalk might also have visited Châlons, as it may follow from his *Letter to Lupus*, bishop of that city.[106]

As for Gislemar, another of Gottschalk's Corbie acquaintances, Traube identified him as a co-worker of Anskar in his missionary activities in Scandinavia.[107] Proceeding, as it seems, from Traube's remark that Gislemar left the monastery to evangelize Denmark at Harald's request in 830,[108] Vielhaber suggested that if Gottschalk had met Gislemar before the latter's departure, he would have come to Corbie as early as in 830.[109] But in fact it is already in 826 that Harald Klakk, an exiled Danish king, appealed to Louis the Pious for support. The same year the Dane was baptized in Mainz and came back to his homeland together with Frankish military forces and missionaries, among whom were Anskar, Autbert, and Gislemar. However, in 827 Harald was exiled again and Anskar had to leave Denmark. Of Gislemar's role in this episode we know only what Rimbert,[110] Anskar's biographer, wrote,[111] namely, that Wala[112] arranged that "the most devoted father Gislemar, a man approved by faith and good works, as well as by his fervent zeal for God, should stay with Harald," when Anskar had to come back to the court of Louis.[113] In 829 this "Apostle of the North" was already going to Sweden to establish a mission there,[114] this time with Witmar[115] as a

---

105 Gottschalk, *On Various Topics* (*De diversis*), 2 in Lambot, 298-301. This text of Gottschalk is not to be confused with his *Responsa de diversis* in Lambot, 130-79, excerpts of which are translated as *Answers to Various Questions* in the present volume.

106 Gottschalk, *Letter to Lupus* (*Epistola ad Lupum*) in MGH, Poetae 3:723-4. Very little is known about Lupus of Châlons beside the fact that he was present at the synod of Quierzy in 853. See Hincmar, *On Predestination*, 2 (PL 125:85B).

107 To Gislemar Gottschalk, in the words of Hincmar, sent a tome (*thomus*) in which he set forth his teaching. Hincmar, *Letter to the Monks* in Gundlach, 261.

108 Traube, *Prooemium*, 710.

109 Vielhaber, *Gottschalk*, 17, n. 38.

110 This Rimbert also authored a letter to Ratramnus addressing the question about *cynocephali*, dog-headed men, in which he wondered whether they were in need of Christian witness. See Ratramnus' answer in MGH Epist. 6:155-7.

111 Between 869 and 876.

112 A cousin of Charlemagne, abbot of Corbie 826-831 and abbot of Bobbio in Italy since 834.

113 Rimbert of Hamburg, *Life of Saint Anskar* (*Vita Sancti Anscharii*) in PL 118:971B: "*Porro cum Herioldo esse disposuit Patrem devotissimum Gislemarum, fide et operibus bonis probatum, atque in zelo Dei ferventissimum.*"

114 He returned in 831 to become the abbot of Corvey and bishop of newly established diocese of Hamburg, both of which were in Saxony.

115 Later on a prior at Corvey.

co-worker. It is not known whether Gislemar accompanied him in 829-831. It is also unclear when Gislemar finally left Denmark to return to the monastery.[116]

GOTTSCHALK'S PREPARATION FOR MISSIONARY WORK

Even though the whole story does not help us to determine the exact date when Gottschalk came to Corbie, it does help to clarify some other relevant circumstances. Indeed, missionary work in Scandinavia was among the most important as well as most characteritic features of the new policy begun by Louis the Pious, whose ideal for the empire was that it be profoundly Christian.[117] The era of great conquests by fire and sword ended with Charlemagne; the tasks of his only surviving son were to keep the unity of the empire and to preach the gospel to heathen nations.

Evangelization of the Norsemen was started by no other than Ebbo who, appointed apostolic legate by Pope Paschal I in 821 with this special purpose, worked as a missionary in Denmark for one year in 823. The primary goal was to secure the Danish frontier, but the mission proved unsuccessful. Monks involved in further effort were associated with Corbie and Corvey, its daughter monastery, since 822 the chief Saxon cloister.

When Gottschalk traveled to Corbie he could not have been ignorant of these developments. It is very likely that he was attracted by a certain ideology that stood behind the missionary movement. Indeed, the whole undertaking was seen as a fulfillment of the eschatological scriptures such as Is 49:5-7 and Mt 24:14 that play so great a role in the *Life of Saint Anskar*. Scandinavia was the end of the known earth; when Christ is proclaimed there, the end of the world will come. Besides, the overall approach was deeply mystical: missionaries were guided by visions and miracles. It is in this circle that Gottschalk was received warmly. James T. Palmer's reading of Rimbert's hagiographical work led him to state:

> Rimbert was notably sympathetic to Gottschalk's ideas and there is a strong predestination theme in the *Vita Anskarii*. With his concern to illustrate mission in relation to prophecy and salvation, especially in the context of creating a new Christian society in the north, it was natural for Rimbert to include such themes in the *Vita*.[118]

---

116 For further details see Konrad von Maurer, *Die Bekehrung des Norwegischen Stammes zum Christentume*, Vol. 1 (Münich: Kaiser, 1855), 19-22.

117 Its other important trend was the establishment of the Benedictine rule in all of the Frankish monasteries under the leadership of Benedict of Aniane. For a detailed account of this reform see, for example, Rosamond McKitterick, *The Frankish Kingdoms under the Carolingians, 751-987* (New York: Longmans, 1983), 108-24.

118 James T. Palmer, "Rimbert's *Vita Anskarii* and Scandinavian Mission in the Ninth Century," *Journal of Ecclesiastical History*, 55 (2004):235-56 at 243.

It is significant that Rabanus and Hincmar were notable for their "more sober, historical evaluation of the northmen" and the missionary work in Scandinavia.[119]

POLITICAL UNREST OF THE TIME

Tragically, the year 829, when Gottschalk left Fulda, became the turning-point in the reign of Louis the Pious. Previously he had done virtually everything in his power to keep the unity of the empire. In 817, soon after Louis' imperial coronation in 816, it had been decreed that the succession would be as follows: his only heir had to be his eldest son, Lothair I, but the empire would include three dependent kingdoms, that of Aquitaine for Pippin, that of Bavaria for Louis, and that of Italy for Louis the Pious' nephew, Bernard. However, in 818 Louis' wife, Ermengard of Hesbaye, the daughter of count Ingramn, died. Four months later the emperor married Judith, the daughter of a mighty count Welf. In June 823 they had a son, future king Charles the Bald (Walafrid Strabo became both Charles' tutor and Judith's private chaplain[120]). This "biological and dynastic fact" (Laurent Theis) unchained a whole series of events that dominated Carolingian politics for the next few decades. Indeed, in 829 Louis the Pious allotted to Charles the region of Alemannia, Rhaetia and part of Burgundy, which led to an open rebellion of his elder sons in 830.[121] Pippin, with Lothair's consent, was able to depose his father, and imprison his step-mother (accused of adulterous liason with count Bernard) in the monastery of St Radegund in Poitiers. However, by October of the same year Louis was reinstalled.

In 833 Louis' sons managed to form a coalition against their father, and the emperor's own army deserted him on the Field of Lies. They seized and sent to Italy Judith and imprisoned Charles in the monastery of Prüm. Lothair assumed control over the imperial office and many magnates as well as churchmen allied with him. Both Wala, the abbot of Corbie, and Ebbo of Reims joined the rebels.

Charlemagne himself observed Ebbo, born as a serf. When Charlemagne's son Louis governed Aquitania, Ebbo served him as a librarian, and in 814, when Louis came to power, Ebbo accompanied him to the royal palace, and two years later[122] was raised to the episcopal see of Reims.[123] In 833 he was among the leaders of

119 Palmer, "Rimbert's *Vita Anskarii*," 244.

120 McKitterick, *Frankish Kingdoms*, 166. See also Walafrid's two poems to Judith in PL 114:1095C-1096D, and the one about her and her son Charles in PL 114:1093D-1094C.

121 That same year another significant event took place, perhaps even more important for Gottschalk's biography. In 829 the synod of Paris was convened, where the necessity of good works for salvation was emphasized as an inalienable part of orthodox doctrine.

122 In 816.

123 Frankish aristocracy was deeply displeased by this nomination, because of Ebbo's obscure origin, as well as by the elevation of Agobard, who was a Visigoth, to the archiepiscopal see of Lyons.

Illustration 3. Frankish kingdoms between 843-855.

the nobility who allied with Lothair's rebellion. Moreover, it was Ebbo who took the responsibility of convicting the emperor of his "crimes" (partly fictitious) and in the fall of the same year he imposed penance on the emperor at the church of Notre-Dame at Compiègne, which was something unheard of. Many ecclesiastical leaders, among others Rabanus, remained faithful to Louis, and acutely disapproved of Ebbo's proceedings. The requital came in due time. As early as 834 Louis was restored, and the next year Ebbo was deposed at Thionville and incarcerated. In 840, after Louis' death, he was freed and restored to his see for a short time, but soon lost this position. He tried to regain it for the rest of his life, thus creating serious complications for his successor, Hincmar of Reims.[124] Ebbo died in 851, having been sheltered by Louis the German, who had made him bishop of Hildesheim.

Now the question is to what extent these vicissitudes affected Gottschalk personally. Even a brief overview of his travels immediately after August 829 shows how improbable the idea is that he remained in the orders at that time. For beside the vows of poverty, chastity and obedience, every Benedictine monk took an oath of "stability of place" (*stabilitas loci*), which meant that he would by no means leave the monastery, with which he was affiliated, without a special dispensation. It is virtually impossible that a monk already denounced by his abbot as deviant, would be allowed to travel so much without any specific mission.[125] It is also very significant that in 849, at the synod of Quierzy, the sentence signed by the bishops contained the following phrase: "Because you have presumed to disturb both ecclesiastical and civil[126] affairs."[127]

Even more important is Gottschalk's own witness in his letter to Ebbo. According to Lambot's interpretation,[128] not long before he wrote that letter Gottschalk had been separated from his patron[129] and suffered all kinds of tribulations. It was painful for our Benedictine to learn that some calumniators were charging

124 In the 850s this struggle against Hincmar was continued by the bishop of Grenoble, Ebbo's nephew and namesake. See McKeon, "Carolingian Councils," 100-1.

125 Besides, it is difficult to conceive any such mission entrusted to Gottschalk at this time, in view of the two synods where he had shown quite a disobedient attitude towards his abbot.

126 "*Civilia negotia*" may be translated as "public affairs," which at all events presupposes Gottschalk's rather deep involvement, at least at some point, in social and political life of his day.

127 Hincmar, *Sentence against Gottschalk at the Synod of Quierzy* (*Ecclesiastica sententia in pertinacissimum* Gotescalcum) in Gundlach, 309: "*Quia et ecclesiastica et civilia negotia... conturbare... praesumpsisti.*" Translated by Francis X. Gumerlock in the present volume.

128 Lambot, "Lettre inédite," 45.

129 It is probable that at the time of its writing Gottschalk was already a monk at Orbais, since he speaks about the accusations of the "secular people" (*saeculi homines*) and describes himself as enjoying "fellowship of the brethren" (*fratrum consortium*),

him with scheming against the archbishop of Reims. Gottschalk asked to receive him as soon as possible and hear out his own explanations as he had never done so. The monk had enemies who sought to destroy him by accusing him of "the crime against the name of the emperors."[130] His only refuge was Ebbo's protection to which he appealed.

Gottschalk was of noble birth, but bereft of his inheritance. This might be the reason why Ebbo, his fellow coutryman, advised him to enter a monastery so as to facilitate his further promotion in the church. On the other hand, it might have been Gottschalk's own decision, choosing to distance himself from the archbishop, at whose house he lived, and whose actions might have seemed increasingly questionable. Indeed, Gottschalk's best friend, with whom he probably kept in touch, was patronized by Judith, and Gottschalk's patron was plotting agaist her.

Even though the young monk might have planned to stay at Orbais for a long time, that plan was less and less feasible, especially after Ebbo's deposition in 835. The only way out was seeking the patronage of a powerful magnate and fleeing from the monastery. The first goal might well have been achieved by Gottschalk with his friend's help. The appearance of the monk from Orbais at the court of Eberhard, margrave of Frioul,[131] is probably a result of Walafrid's mediation. Indeed, about 835/836 Eberhard married Gisela, Judith's daughter by Louis the Pious. The empress' chaplain had a good chance to arrange Gottschalk's benevolent reception by Judith's son-in-law in Frioul.

However, leaving calm Orbais on the Surmelin river was no easy thing, because of the same *stabilitas loci*. Gottschalk knew well that Anskar's prolonged wanderings, which contradicted the above-mentioned principle, aroused too many questions.[132] As it seems, in connection with the Scandinavian mission, the problem was resolved on the basis of permission to leave the monastery granted to monks by Pope Gregory the Great (d. 604), in case they were active as missionaries.[133] The same pope also indicated that if monks were needed as priests for a long time, they had to be ordained and could break their ties with

---

Lambot, "Lettre inédite," 44. Thus he entered the monastery before 835, the year of Ebbo's deposition and imprisonment.

130 Gottschalk, *Unedited Letter* (*Epistola inedita*). Lambot, "Lettre inédite," 44: "*Contra imperatorum nomen... crimen.*" The phrase is mysterious. What might be the nature of this supposed crime and whether it was connected to Ebbo's own conspiracy against Louis the Pious is unclear. Whatever the case, this passage gives further attestation of Gottschalk's involvement in politics.

131 Died in 867.

132 Rimbert would have to explain on what grounds monks could ignore the vows of stability for years in case they were involved in missionary work.

133 Cuthbert Butler, *Benedictine Monachism: Studies in Benedictine Life and Rule* (London: Longmans, Green & Co, 1924), 327.

the monastery.[134] This explains well why Gottschalk sought ordination before he left the cloister. To all appearances, this was done in haste. Rigbold, the interim bishop of Reims (835-845), ordained the monk without the knowledge of Rothad, bishop of Soissons, to which diocese Orbais belonged.[135]

Thus, between 835/836 (Ebbo's deposition and Eberhard's marriage) and 840 (the first witness of Gottschalk in northern Italy) our Benedictine, presumably leading a group of monks,[136] went to the southeast of the empire, perhaps authorized by Bavo, his abbot, for missionary work. In all likelihood Gottschalk never planned to come back.

GOTTSCHALK'S PREACHING OF PREDESTINATION IN ITALY (836-845)

Eberhard of Frioul was a remarkable figure.[137] Thanks to his marriage to Gisela, grand-daughter of Charlemagne, he acquired enormous political influence. Louis' sons (Eberhard's brothers-in-law) sought his friendship and advice. He played an important role in negotiations that preceded the treaty of Verdun (843), designed to bring to an end the strife between Lothair and his brothers. Moreover, the march of Frioul was a key territory in the defense of the empire. It is also known that Eberhard, whom Sedulius Scottus called a defender of the church,[138] possessed a great library and corresponded with the leading theologians of the age.[139] Protection under such a magnate allowed Gottschalk's rare gifts and abilities to reach full bloom. Indeed, in Italy Gottschalk first preached his doctrine on a large scale and became an eminent teacher of double predestination. Unfortunately, this period of almost ten years, from about 836 through 846, is the least known in Gottschalk's life.

It has been often alleged that Gottschalk left Orbais to make a pilgrimage to Rome. The only source for this assertion is a poem by Walafrid, written as an answer to a now lost letter of Gottschalk, where he alludes to his friend's visit to that city.[140] Scholars who assert this also assumed that this poem had been written before Gottschalk was ordained, which led to the idea of two supposed visits of his to Italy: one before and one after ordination. However, as early as in 1886, Traube argued convincingly that the poem in question was written in

134 Palmer, "Rimbert's *Vita Anskarii*," 245.

135 Hincmar, *On Predestination*, 2 (PL 125:85C): "*Gothescalcus... honore presbyterali, quem per Rigboldum Rhemorum chorepiscopum, cum esset Suessonicae parochiae monachus, inscio civitatis suae episcopo, usurpaverat potius quam acceperat....*"

136 See Traube, *Prooemium*, 711, n. 2.

137 See Tavard, *Trina Deitas*, 31.

138 MGH, Poetae 3:202: "*tutor ecclesiae*."

139 Among whom, beside Rabanus, was Lupus of Ferrières.

140 Strabo, *Poem for the Monk Gottschalk* (MGH, Poetae 2:362-4).

December 848.[141] Consequently, there are no substantial reasons to speak about two visits of Gottschalk to Italy. It is also likely that soon after Ebbo's deposition he did not travel to Rome, but directly to the court of Eberhard. He may have gone "to the tombs of the apostles" (*ad limina apostolorum*) at any time during his prolonged stay in Frioul.

Two basic sources for the Italian period are letters of Rabanus addressed to Noting[142] and Eberhard.[143] The first one was written in May 840.[144] In its first lines Rabanus says that, when he accompanied Louis the Pious in a military expedition and passed through Logana,[145] he had a conversation with Noting, during which they discussed "a heresy that some people are wickedly defending concerning the predestination of God."[146] As a result of this meeting Rabanus wrote to his interlocutor the present letter, having joined a treatise on predestination to it.[147] The identity of Noting is indicated by Rudolph of Fulda: "[Rabanus] also wrote to Noting, bishop of Verona, concerning the foreknowledge and predestination of God, concerning grace and free will."[148] As in the case of his *On the Oblation of Children*, Rabanus does not mention his former subordinate by name either in the letter or in the subjoined treatise, but there is no doubt that the uneasiness of Noting was occasioned by Gottschalk's preaching, whose activity in Italy and Noricum[149] is attested in the *Annals of St Bertin*.[150]

It is possible that Rabanus would act more energetically against what he thought was a pernicious heresy, but very soon his own affairs preoccupied him more than anything else. Louis the Pious, with whom he invariably sided, died on 20 June 840, on his way back from a military expedition against his son, Louis the German. Rabanus supported Lothair, who was before long defeated by Louis.

141 Traube, *Prooemium*, 712.

142 Rabanus, *Letter to Noting* (*Epistola ad Notingum*) in MGH, Epist. 5:428-9; PL 112:1530C-31A. Translated by Gumerlock in the present volume.

143 Rabanus, *Letter to Eberhard* (*Epistola ad Eberhardum*) in MGH, Epist. 5:481-7. Excerpts translated by Gumerlock in the present volume.

144 As suggested by Ernst Dümmler in MGH, Epist. 5:332, n. 2.

145 Probably modern Lahngau. See Karl Josef von Hefele, *Histoire des conciles d'après les documents originaux*, Vol. 4.1 (Paris: Letouzey et Ané, 1911), 142, n. 2.

146 Rabanus, *Letter to Noting*. Translation by Gumerlock.

147 Rabanus, *On Predestination* (*De praedestinatione*) in PL 112:1531-53.

148 *Ad Notingum quoque episcopum Veronensem de praescientia ac praedestinatione Dei, de gratia et libero arbitrio scripsit*. Cited by Dümmler in MGH, Epist. 5:428, n. 2.

149 A region north of Italy, comprising central Austria and parts of Bavaria.

150 *Annals of St Bertin*. Georg Waitz, ed., *Annales Bertiniani*. MGH, Scriptores rerum Germanicarum in usum scholarum separatim editi, 5:36. See English translation in Tavard, *Trina Deitas*, 33. The same source indicates that Gottschalk propagated his ideas not only orally, but also through his writings. However, no extant treatise of the Benedictine can be attributed to that period with certainty.

The same year the abbot of Fulda fled from the monastery and returned in 841, only to resign his abbacy in 842. It is in 845 that he was finally reconciled with his new king, Louis.[151]

RABANUS MAURUS OPPOSES GOTTSCHALK (846)

It was now time for Rabanus to deal seriously with Gottschalk. About 846[152] Rabanus composed a lengthy missive to Eberhard. At that time, it seems, the charismatic preacher from Saxony reached the climax of his popularity;[153] his teaching spread not only in Italy, but also in the realm of Louis the German.[154] Eberhard's protection, granted to such a man, deeply troubled Rabanus, who maintained friendly relations with the margrave of Frioul. He wrote:

> Also, about the other things that have been reported in these regions, they say that a certain know-it-all named Gottschalk is staying with you, who is teaching that the predestination of God binds all men in such a way that even if someone would want to be saved and would struggle for this by the correct faith and good works in order to come to eternal life by the grace of God, he would labor in vain and for naught, if he has not been predestined to life, as if God, who is the author of our salvation and not of our perdition, forces a human being to perish by his predestination. And from there this sect has led many into despair over themselves so that they say: "Why is it necessary for me to work for my salvation and eternal life? For if I do good but I have not been predestined to life, it profits me nothing. But if I do evil, it is in no way an obstacle to me. For the predestination of God causes me to come to eternal life." This teaching is a scandal to many in these regions, and makes people disobedient to the preachers of the gospel. For your teacher is said to have excerpted many testimonies from the works of the most blessed and learned father, Augustine, from which he tries to strengthen his sect. However, the previously mentioned father and catholic teacher, writing against the Pelagians who were preachers opposed to the grace of God, was a defender of his grace not a destroyer of the correct faith.[155]

Further, Rabanus sets forth his own understanding of the teaching on predestination. The letter is concluded by the following request:

> Therefore, I have written these things to you, dearest friend, that you may know the sort of scandal that this opinion coming from those regions has generated

151 To succeed Otgar as archbishop of Mainz in 847.

152 Thus Schrörs, *Hinkmar Erzbischof von Reims. Sein Leben und seine Schriften* (Freiburg: G. Olms, 1884), 100, and Traube, *Prooemium*, 712. Freystedt ("Studien," 179-80) believed the letter was written in 847. Vielhaber (*Gottschalk*, 20) dated it by 845/846. Dümmler (MGH, Epist. 5:481) attributed it to 846-847.

153 In his *Letter to Eberhard*, Rabanus uses at least three times the word "*secta*" (MGH, Epist. 5:481, 482, 487), which presupposes the multiplicity of the followers.

154 In Noricum, as the *Annals of St Bertin* say. See above.

155 Rabanus, *Letter to Eberhard*. Translation by Gumerlock.

> in this people and that, if anyone staying with you is impudently teaching things that are contrary to the correct faith, you may forbid him so that he desists from this sect.[156] And tell him: "See to it, brother, lest your liberty in preaching should become a cause of offence for weak people, and lest by your doctrine you should destroy one for whom Christ has died, for his blood will be required at your hand."[157] I do trust confidently that you, O venerable man, are a Christian, and that you do not want to be in communion with anything that is contrary to the gospel of Christ, but rather with that which is pleasing to God and pertains to the salvation of souls.[158]

It is noteworthy that in these two texts, *On Predestination* to Noting and the *Letter to Eberhard*, Rabanus fully expounded what he had to say concerning the issue. Later he would repeatedly point to these documents as a complete statement of his position.

It is not known how Eberhard reacted to Rabanus' message. Since the *Annals of St Bertin* state that Gottschalk was "shamefully ejected"[159] from Italy, it has been assumed that he went to Dalmatia after the margrave of Frioul expelled him from his realm. However, there are reasons to believe that this idea is incorrect.

The confidence with which Gottschalk went to Mainz shows that he was altogether convinced that his ideas were orthodox, and he attacked rather than defended himself. To some extent blinded by the popularity and security he had enjoyed for more than ten years, he rushed to Austrasia (instead of escaping), sure of an easy victory he would gain over Rabanus. Moreover, Gottschalk's trip to Dalmatia and Pannonia, of all places, did not resemble a flight, but rather a long planned operation in a strategic region, for which the margrave of Frioul was personally responsible.[160] Since Rabanus asked Eberhard to prevent Gottschalk's teaching from further spreading, letting a person denounced as a heretic by the most authoritative churchman of the age to evangelize[161] the Slavs (in a mission very much parallel to that of Anskar) would be a rather strange reaction. Thus, it is more likely that Eberhard (whatever his own reaction might have been) received Rabanus' letter and showed it to Gottschalk only upon the latter's return from

156 Up to here translation by Gumerlock.

157 See Ez 3:20.

158 MGH, Epist. 5:487: "*Dicasque ei: Vide, frater, ne hac licentia tua in predicando offendiculum fiat infirmis, et tuo dogmate ne perdas eum, pro quo Christus mortuus est, quia sanguis eius requiretur de manu tua. Confido enim te, vir venerabile, bene esse christianum, nec aliquid te habere velle in tua communione quod evangelio Christi adversetur, sed agis hoc quod placeat Deo, et ad salutem pertinet animarum.*"

159 *Annals of St Bertin*. MGH, Scriptores rerum Germanicarum, 5:36: "*Turpiter ejectus.*"

160 In 827 Baldrich, then margrave of Frioul, was deprived of his office because of his failure to prevent undesirable activity of the Bulgars in Pannonia.

161 See Florus, *Book on Three Letters*, 1 (PL 121:987C): "*... postquam eum dixit ultro sibi praedicatoris nomen assumpsisse, atque ad barbaras et paganas gentes velut evangelizaturum perrexisse....*"

his Balkan mission,[162] and the preacher of twofold predestination immediately assumed the measures against what he thought was a calumny. Prudentius of Troyes, then editor of the *Annals of St Bertin*, lived too far from Frioul to be well informed about the affairs of Eberhard's court. He might have set forth the version of events originated within Rabanus' coterie.

GOTTSCHALK'S MISSION TO THE BALKANS (846-848)

Pannonia passed under Frankish sovereignty about 795, when the Croatian chieftain Vojnomir accepted baptism. Charlemagne established control in the area between the Sava, Drava and Danube rivers. In 799 Franks invaded Dalmatia, and by 803,[163] after a lengthy war, suppressed Byzantine influence in the region.[164] The area became a Carolingian march under the jurisdiction of the margrave of Frioul, with the city of Aquileia as its center of ecclesiastical authority. By 814 Pannonian Croats were led by Ljudevit, and Dalmatian Croats by Borna. That year both of them affirmed their loyalty to Louis the Pious.

Borna (ruled 810-821) was a remarkable leader. If he is identical to Πορίος from the 30th chapter of *On the Administration of the Empire* (*De administrando imperio*) by Constantine VII Porphyrogenitus,[165] it is during his rule that bishops, sent from Rome, baptized many Croats. In the *Annals of the Kingdom of the Franks* (*Annales regni Francorum*) by Einhard, under the year 818, Borna is described as "*dux Guduscanorum et Timocianorum*," that is, the duke of the Gačani (the inhabitants of Gačka, which region corresponds to present-day Lika and Krbava) and the Timočani (who had lived in the lowlands of the Timok river). Borna always remained faithful to the Franks. When in 819 Ljudevit revolted,[166] it was Borna who won the most important battles against him, though Franks sent their troops there in 820, 821 and 822, until Ljudevit finally fled to the Serbs and was murdered in 823. In his recent research Boller set forth an interesting supposition.[167] He suggested that duke Borna was no other than Bernus, Gottschalk's father. Indeed, the etymology of the Dalmatian ruler's name seems to be Germanic. Moreover, Boller pointed to the fact that Charlemagne consciously resettled much of Saxon nobility. Besides, the assumption explains

---

162 See Vielhaber, *Gottschalk*, 21.

163 At the time Dalmatian Croats were led by Višeslav, whose seat was in the city of Nin (Aenona).

164 As a result, Byzantium kept the city-states Zadar (Diadora), Trogir (Tragurium) and Split (Aspalathos) as well as the islands of Krk, Rab and Osor, while Charlemagne controlled Istria and the inland Dalmatia (Treaty of Aachen of 812).

165 Byzantine emperor 913-959.

166 After Charlemagne's death Frankish influence in the area considerably decreased.

167 Boller, *Gottschalk d'Orbais*, 43, n. 90.

Illustration 4. Croatia at the time of Trpimir, 845-855.

well Gottschalk's interest in the region, where he may have had relatives.[168] This theory deserves further research, but if correct, it makes a considerable contribution to our understanding of medieval Croatian history.

It is generally accepted that Gottschalk visited Dalmatia and Pannonia in 846-848. At the time Croatia was ruled by Trpimir (845-864), who came to power after Vladislav (duke of the Croats and Dalmatians 821-830) and Mislav (830-845),[169] and founded his own dynasty.

In Gottschalk's extant writings there are several passages where he alludes to his Balkan mission. The most important of them is found in his *Answers to Various Questions*, in the section entitled "Whether Sibyls and other Foretellers of the Heathens ever Deserved to Merit or Have the Holy Spirit."[170] Having pointed out that birds of prey can predict the outcome of a battle, Gottschalk goes on to say:

---

168 Tavard (*Trina Deitas*, 31) believed that Gottschalk's companion in his Balkan travels, his "little son" (*filiolus*), equally called Gottschalk, was his nephew. However, it is also possible that he was his pupil and godson, whom the Saxon christened with his own name.

169 It is not known whether any of them were Borna's descendants.

170 Gottschalk, *Answers to Various Questions* in Lambot, 162-71: "*Si Sibillae et ceteri vates paganorum spiritum sanctum umquam meruerint vel habere.*"

> Likewise, also horses are cheerful in the battle array on that side which, when God gives it, must be victorious. This I myself have certainly proved by experience through Gottschalk, my little son, with respect to our horse. For when Trpimir, king[171] of the Slavs, was going against the people of the Greeks and their governor, and our villa was in the very neighborhood of the future war, I told him to go and take care of everything that would be necessary for the king and his army, which he, by all means, had to do. However, I have terribly adjured him by the Lord God that he should neither take up arms nor go with the army, but, following them astride with full attention, consider which attitude this our horse would have or take. Indeed, I most certainly knew for a long time that victory would come and be on the side of the people, whose horses would tread cheerfully and show their cheerfulness with their triumphant attitude.[172]

Lovre Katić interpreted this passage as follows.[173] "Our villa" (*villa nostra*), which Gottschalk mentions, must be one of Trpimir's known residences: that of Klis, Podstrana or Bijači (all located near Split). The phrase "people of the Greeks" (*gens Graecorum*) designates Byzantine power in general, not the actual population of the coastal city-states. "Their governor" (*patricius eorum*) must be the imperial governor,[174] a representative of the civil and military power of Byzantium, who had his residence in Zadar. The one with whom Trpimir was at war might be a certain Bryenius, whose name is found on a seal[175] that may be dated either about 840 or after 842.[176] The military conflict probably took place near Split and was

171 Even though Gottschalk designates Trpimir as "king" (*rex*), he was in fact a *knez*, that is, a prince.

172 Gottschalk, *Answers to Various Questions* in Lambot, 169: "*Sic nihilominus et equi sunt in acie laeti ex ea parte quam deo dante debet uictoria sequi. Quod prorsus ego ipse per Gottesscalcum filiolum meum de equo nostro probaui. Cum enim Tripemirus rex Sclauorum iret contra gentem Graecorum et patricium eorum et esset in ipso confinio futuri belli uilla nostra, dixi illi ut iret et quicquid regi et eius exercitui necessarium esset sicut omnino deberet impenderet. Adiuraui tamen terribiliter eum per dominum deum ut nec arma sumeret nec cum exercitu pergeret, sed tamen studiose post eos equitans attenderet quemnam gestum equus ille noster ageret atque gereret. Ex olim siquidem certissime sciebam illi parti hominum uenturam et futuram esse uictoriam quorum equi incederent laeti monstrarentque gestu triumphando laetitiam.*"

173 Lovre Katić, "Saksonac Gottschalk na dvoru kneza Trpimira," *Bogoslovska smotra* 20 (1932), 415-23.

174 According to a lengthy commentary on that word given by Charles du Fresne du Cange, *Glossarium ad Scriptores Mediae et Infimae Latinitatis*, Vol. 6 (Paris: Librairie des sciences et des arts; Stockholm: G. Rönnell, 1938), 214-18.

175 Its inscription reads: Κύριε βοήθει τῷ σῷ δούλῳ Βρυεν[ίῳ] β[ασιλικῳ] σπαθ[αρίῳ] σ[τ]ρ[α]τ[εγῷ] Δαλματίας ("O Lord, help your servant Bryenius, the king's court dignitary, governor of Dalmatia"), quoted in Katić, "Saksonac Gottschalk," 420.

176 Ferdo Šišić, *Povijest Hrvata u vrijeme narodnih vladara* (Zagreb: Nakladni zavod Matice hrvatske, 1925), 327.

about the frontier between the Croatian and Byzantine lands. The context of *Answers to Various Questions* shows that Trpimir gained the upper hand.

Another passage shows that Gottschalk was well acquainted with the usual manner of speech in the coastal cities. In his *On Predestination* he writes:

> Likewise Dalmatian people, that is, likewise Latin people, but subject to the empire of the Greeks, call the king and emperor by an expression common throughout the whole of Dalmatia, which is a most spacious region, I mean, they call the king and emperor kingdom and empire. For they say: "We were at the kingdom," and: "We stood before the empire," and: "The kingdom has told us so," and: "The empire spoke in that way."[177]

It is possible that the linguistic abilities of the Benedictine helped him to become a mediator and an interpreter between Trpimir and the Byzantine army.[178]

Gottschalk also visited Bulgaria, as is evident from his remark in *On the Body and Blood of the Lord*:[179] "For once a certain noble and powerful heathen in the land of Bulgarians humbly begged me to [give him to] drink in the love of that God who makes his blood out of wine."[180]

Katić wrote that Gottschalk might have originated the idea of building a monastery in Rižinice that was realized by Trpimir about 850.[181] Boller even conjectured that

Gottschalk himself might have built a church in Croatia. Indeed, in a funerary chapel,[182] on the lintel of the chapel door, one may read the following inscription: **GODE.SAV.IVP.PANO [...] IS.TO DOMO.CŌ.**[183] The first part of the inscription has long been interpreted as containing the name Godeslav (or Godečaj, Godežav), whereas Boller suggested to read it as follows: **GODES[CALC] AV[CTORE] IVPPANO [...] ISTO DOMO CŌ[STRVXIT]**, that is: "Gottschalk, under the authority of a župan,[184] has constructed this edifice."

---

177 Gottschalk, *On Predestination*, 3.6 in Lambot, 208.

178 As Katić suggests, "Saksonac Gottschalk," 415. This also may point to a strict neutrality on the part of Gottschalk, who forbids his companion to take arms and go into battle. See above.

179 This treatise was for a long time attributed to Rabanus.

180 Gottschalk, *On the Body and Blood of the Lord* in Lambot, 325: "...*Nam quondam in terra Vulgarorum quidam nobilis potensque paganus bibere me suppliciter petiuit in illius dei amore qui de uino sanguinem suum facit.*"

181 Katić, "Saksonac Gottschalk," 423.

182 It is the Holy Cross (Sveti Križ) chapel at Nin, 17 km to the north-west of Zadar. It is reputed to be "the smallest church in the world," even though one may find even smaller church buildings in Greece.

183 Boller, *Gottschalk d'Orbais*, 44, n. 93, and p. 247.

184 Each Croatian clan occupied a certain territory, subdivided into *župe* or counties. Each of them was ruled by a *župan*. The ruler of several *župe* was a *knez* or prince.

Illustration 5. Holy Cross Chapel in Nin.

Another interesting supposition of Katić deserves special attention.[185] He wrote that a certain Martin, mentioned by Constantine VII Porphyrogenitus in the 31st chapter of his *On the Administration of the Empire* is no other than Gottschalk. The actual text of Porphyrogenitus reads as follows:

> After a long time, in the days of the king Trpimir, king Krešimir's father, a certain man, one of those who are very pious, named Martin, came from Francia, from the region between Croatia and Venice, clothed with worldly shape, who, as Croats themselves say, has performed many miracles. Such a pious man was

185 Katić, "Saksonac Gottschalk," 430-2.

weak and his legs were cut off[186] so that four people took him up and carried him wherever he wanted.[187]

It is evident that the only feature that Gottschalk has in common with Martin is that they both came from the lands between Croatia and Venice, that is, from Frioul. First of all, Porphyrogenitus' text speaks about king Trpimir II (928 - c. 935), father of Krešimir I (c. 935 - c. 945), and not prince Trpimir I, whose guest Gottschalk was. Furthermore, even though Boller suggested that the report of Martin's mutilation is explained by the punishment Gottschalk endured at Quierzy,[188] it does not account for the fact that Martin was unable to walk while in Croatia, should he really have been our Benedictine. Finally, it is rather difficult to explain why Gottschalk's name would be changed to Martin.[189] Identification of Martin mentioned by Porphyrogenitus as St Martin of Podsused seems to be more plausible.[190]

Upon the completion of his mission, Gottschalk came back to Frioul, but left it as soon as he learned what Rabanus wrote to Eberhard concerning himself and his teaching.[191] The same year he came to Fulda, where he was received by Hatto, who had supported him in 829 and since 842 was the abbot of the monastery which Gottschalk had entered as an oblate child. The great circle of his wanderings was now closed. Catastrophe was imminent.

GOTTSCHALK AT THE SYNOD OF MAINZ (848)

Gottschalk's behavior at this point is mysterious. Even though upon leaving Frioul he might have had illusions of being victorious over Rabanus, back in Fulda he could not ignore that Rabanus, the archbishop of Mainz since 847 and still the most respected theologian of the age, acquired enormous political influence. Gottschalk's own status was incommensurable with that of his

186 The other possible translation is: "His legs were mutilated."

187 Μετὰ δὲ χρόνους πολλοὺς ἐν ταῖς ἡμέραις Τερπημέρη τοῦ ἄρχοντος, τοῦ πατρὸς τοῦ ἄρχοντος Κρασημέρη, ἐλθὼν ἀπὸ Φραγγίας, τῆς μεταξὺ Χρωβατίας καὶ Βενετίας, ἀνήρ τις τῶν πάνυ μὲν εὐλαβῶν, Μαρτῖνος ὀνόματι, σχῆμα δὲ κοσμικὸν περιβεβλημένος, ὃν καὶ λέγουσιν οἱ αὐτοὶ Χρωβάτοι θαύματα ἱκανὰ ποιῆσαι· ἀσθενὴς δὲ ὢν ὁ τοιοῦτος εὐλαβὴς ἀνὴρ καὶ τοὺς πόδας ἠκρωτηριασμένος, ὥστε ὑπὸ τεσσάρων βαστάζεσθαι καὶ περιφέρεσθαι, ὅπου δ' ἂν καὶ βούλεται.

188 Boller, *Gottschalk d'Orbais*, 54, n. 119.

189 Katić's idea ("Saksonac Gottschalk," 432) that it happened because for Croatians Martin was a typical Frankish name, while the name Gottschalk sounded too strange for them, does not seem convincing.

190 On St Martin of Podsused, see Antonija Zaradija Kiš, *Sveti Martin: Kult sveca i njegova tradicija u Hrvatskoj* (Zagreb: Intistut za etnologiju i folkloristiku, 2004). On Porphyrogenitus' text, see page 159 of that work.

191 See above.

former abbot. Besides, the general context was that of social unrest,[192] and any pronouncement against the authorities, as Gottschalk was about to make, had very little chance of being treated tolerantly. If the rebellious monk had gotten the upper hand at Worms in 829, was he encouraged by this fact to appeal to a king against Rabanus once again? Was he too naive? Was he too arrogant? Nothing or almost nothing helps us to solve these riddles.

Whatever the case, on the 1 October 848[193] the synod or rather the diet (*placitum generale*),[194] presided over by Louis the German, was opened in the presence of many bishops and abbots of the East Frankish Kingdom, including Einhard, bishop of Seligenstadt, Charlemagne's famous biographer. What happened next is very chillingly stated in the *Annals of St Bertin*[195] as well as those of Xanten.[196] Gottschalk, together with some of his followers, appeared before the assembly and presented two writings that he authored, namely, a treatise[197] in which he answered Rabanus' accusations[198] and a confession of faith (*chartula suae professionis*).[199] Since our Benedictine and his companions refused to acknowledge their views as heretical, they were publicly flogged. Gottschalk had to swear that he would never come again into the kingdom of Louis the German and was sent to Hincmar of Reims, his metropolitan, accompanied by a letter,[200] in which Rabanus explained the case as he saw it. As one might

---

192 In that connection anti-sacerdotalist preaching of the chiliast Thiota should be mentioned (See McKeon, "Carolingian Councils," 89), as well as the council of Paris (which condemned those teaching that Christians are at all events saved, even in case they persist in evil, and that the pagans are automatically punished) that took place around the same time (See Devisse, *Hincmar*, 121, n. 26). Perhaps in the perspective of Rabanus, Gottschalk's teaching was something very similar.

193 Hefele, *Histoire des conciles*, 148.

194 *Annals of Fulda*. Friedrich Kurze, ed. *Annales Fuldenses*, ad ann. 848. MGH, Scriptores rerum Germanicarum, 7:37-8. Wiggers, ("Schicksale der augustinischen Anthropologie," 475) designates it *ein Reichstag*; Lavaud ("Prédestination. IV. La controverse sur la prédestination au IXe siècle," in *Dictionnaire de la théologique catholique*, Vol. 12 [Paris: Letouzey et Ané, 1935], 2903) calls it *la diète de Mayence*; Hefele (*Histoire des conciles*, 137) defines it as *moitié diète, moitié concile*.

195 *Annals of St Bertin*. MGH, Scriptores rerum Germanicarum, 5:36-7.

196 *Annals of Xanten*. Bernhard von Simson, ed. *Annales Xantenses*, ad ann. 848. MGH, Scriptores rerum Germanicarum, 12:16.

197 Fragments preserved by Hincmar. PL 121:365-8. Translated by Gumerlock as *Reply to Rabanus Maurus* in the present volume.

198 Probably those expressed in Rabanus' *Letter to Noting*.

199 Preserved by Hincmar in PL 125:89D-90A. Translated by Victor Genke as *Confession of Faith at Mainz* in the present volume.

200 Rabanus, *Letter to Hincmar on the Council of Mainz* (*Epistola ad Hincmarum Remensem*) in PL 112:1574-6. Translated by Gumerlock in the present volume.

expect, the archbishop of Mainz, who was then 72 years old,[201] did not change his own views in the least.

HINCMAR'S SUBSEQUENT TREATMENT OF GOTTSCHALK (SINCE 849)

Flodoard of Reims, in his *History of the Church of Reims*, mentions a letter that Hincmar wrote to Rothad of Soissons concerning his reception of Gottschalk,[202] revealing that after the Synod of Mainz the monk was first sent to Orbais, where he awaited what was to follow, while the archbishop of Reims twice wrote to Rabanus asking for instructions.[203] Rothad grew notably sympathetic with the condemned Benedictine's ideas,[204] and Gottschalk there in Orbais used the opportunity to prepare himself for what he might have expected would be a more serious investigation of his case.

However, Hincmar, as it seems, only aspired to bring the case to a conclusion. A small synod that took place in February or March 849[205] at the royal *villa* of Quierzy (Carisiacum) presented his chance to do so. It was not convened by Hincmar to examine Gottschalk's teaching, but by the order of the king to deal with the king's affairs.[206] The canons of this synod where fifteen bishops were

201 Devisse, *Hincmar*, 133, n. 84.

202 Flodoard of Reims, *History of the Church of Reims* (*Historia Remensis ecclesiae*), 21 (PL 135:204D): "*Rothado Suessonico, quem saepe ad synodum venire differentem vel negligentem vocabat, scribit... pro recipiendo et adducendo ad judicium Gothescalco, quem domnus Rabanus ad dioecesim Remensem remiserat: qui profectus fuerat ex parochia Suessonica, scilicet Orbacensi monasterio.*" The letter is now lost.

203 Flodoard, *History of the Church of Reims*, 21 (PL 135:200A-C): "*Diversis etiam tam episcopis quam archiepiscopis multimoda utillima dedit scripta... Hrabano Moguntiae praesuli, super ejusdem Gothescalci (quem idem pontifex a parochia sua ob haeresum semina, quae spargebat, repulsum, ad eumdem cum quibusdam complicibus suis direxerat) susceptione vel discussione; item de hac eadem re, et quid post susceptionem ipsius de eodem egerit, qualemve invenerit ipsius vesaniam, consilium ab eo rationabilius, quid sibi adversus eum agendum sit, expetens.*" See Devisse, *Hincmar*, 126, n. 56.

204 As Hincmar would later write to Pope Nicholas. Hincmar, *Letter to Pope Nicholas* (*Epistola ad Nicolaum papam*) in PL 126:43C-D. An excerpt of that letter is translated by Genke in the present volume.

205 The synod must have taken place a few weeks before the Easter (April 14), since in the letter, in which Hincmar informs Prudentius of Troyes concerning Gottschalk's condemnation, he also asks, "*si in coena Domini vel in Pascha debeat illum admittere ad audiendum sacrum officium vel accipiendam communionem.*" Flodoard, *History of the Church of Reims*, 21. PL 135:206A.

206 "*Regio mandato pro negotiis regis,*" as Hincmar says in his *Letter to the Church of Lyons* (*Epistola ad ecclesiam Lugdunensem*), lost but cited by Florus, *Book on Three Letters*, 24 (PL 121:1027C).

Illustration 6. Royal villa in Quierzy.

present[207] are lost. What actually happened there is reported in the *Annals of St Bertin*.[208] Gottschalk presented to the assembly presided over by Charles the Bald a collection of scriptural and patristic quotations, designed to prove the orthodoxy of his doctrine,[209] but it was found heretical. Gottschalk was again publicly flogged and compelled to throw into the fire "the books that contained his teachings," which apparently was this same scriptural and patristic florilegium.[210] Found guilty of disobedience to his monastic status because of his wanderings, Gottschalk was also deposed from priesthood, since he had been uncanonically

207 Beside Hincmar, there were his nine suffragans and his interim bishop, the archbishop of Sens, bishops of Langres and Rennes, as well as the interim bishop of Cambrai. Hincmar, *On Predestination*, 2 (PL 125:85A-B): "*Indeque a synodali conventu in Carisiaco palatio iterum auditus ab episcopis, et caeteris quam plurimis viris ecclesiasticis atque religiosis, qui eidem synodo interfuerunt, videlicet Wenilone Sennensium archiepiscopo, Hincmaro Rhemorum episcopo, Folcoino Morinensium episcopo, Teuderico Camaracensium episcopo, Rothado Suessonicae civitatis episcopo, Ragenario Ambianensium episcopo, Immone Noviomagensium episcopo, Erpoino Silvanectensium episcopo, Lupo Catalaunensium episcopo, Yrminfrido Belvacensium episcopo, Pardulo Laudunensium episcopo, Teutboldo provinciae Lugdunensium et Lingonicae civitatis episcopo, Gernobrio Turonensium provinciae episcopo, Rigboldo Rhemorum chorepiscopo, Witao Camaracensium chorepiscopo*." In his *Letter to the Monks* (Gundlach, 308) the archbishop of Reims affirms that the sentence was pronounced by twelve bishops, which means that three persons abstained from subscribing it.

208 *Annals of St Bertin* (MGH, Scriptores rerum Germanicarum, 5:36-7).

209 The disastrous experience in Mainz perhaps compelled him to think about the presentation of his ideas. If previously Gottschalk had produced only his own writings (as we may assume from what is extant), this time he took into account his adversaries' custom of relying on authorities, even though it did not help him much.

210 Perhaps Section 2 of Gottschalk's larger *On Predestination* entitled "Testimonies of the Gospels and the Pauline Epistles" (Lambot, 197-201) in the present volume was a copy or a later reconstruction by Gottschalk of the scriptural part of this florilegium.

ordained by the interim bishop Rigbold, without informing Rothad of Soissons, in whose diocese Orbais belonged. Not only did Gottschalk's being a former protégé of Ebbo not endear him to the new archbishop of Reims, he probably also fell victim to Hincmar's longstanding sentiment against the institution of interim bishops, whose prerogatives were altogether unclear.[211] However, Hincmar's trust in Rothad, even though the latter was not an interim bishop, was not much better.[212] Gottschalk was not let back to Orbais to be confined there, but was sent to the abbey of Hautvillers, which lay in the archdiocese of Reims. The text of the sentence reducing the deposed priest to perpetual silence, translated by Francis X. Gumerlock, can be found in the present volume.[213]

The synod and its proceedings give rise to several questions. First of all, was Hincmar so dreadful as depicted in Florus'[214] dramatic account[215] in his *Book on Three Letters* (*Liber de tribus epistolis*), containing the words *pene emoriens* ("almost dying") and *inauditum crudelitatis exemplum* ("an example of unprecedented cruelty") so often quoted in modern literature on Gottschalk? As Devisse rightly notes, Florus' work was written at least six years later and was based on the descriptions of bishops whose remorse over that which they had done to Gottschalk was quite belated.[216] One may add that the nature of the *Book on Three Letters* as a covert personal attack against the archbishop of Reims does not permit such statements to be taken literally. Florus' emotional description and cold account of Hincmar aroused suspicion in the witness of the *Annals of St Bertin* then edited by Prudentius of Troyes.[217]

211 See Vielhaber, *Gottschalk*, 22 and n. 56.

212 In 863 he would depose Rothad for contesting his authority.

213 Hincmar, *Sentence against Gottschalk at the Synod of Quierzy* in Gundlach, 308-9.

214 Theologian and poet of Burgund or Spanish origin, d. c. 860.

215 Florus, *Book on Three Letters*, 25 (PL 121:1030B-C): "*Quapropter illud prorsus omnes non solum dolent, sed etiam horrent: quia inaudito irreligiositatis, et crudelitatis exemplo, tandiu ille miserabilis flagris et caedibus trucidatus est, donec (sicut narraverunt nobis, qui praesentes aderant) accenso coram se igni libellum, in quo sententias Scripturarum sive sanctorum Patrum sibi collegerat, quas in concilio offerret, coactus est jam pene emoriens suis manibus in flammam projicere, atque incendio concremare: cum omnes retro haeretici verbis, et disputationibus victi, atque convicti sunt. Et sic pravitas, quae videbatur hominis, fuerit coercenda, ut nulla divinis rebus inferretur injuria. Maxime cum illi sensus, qui ipso continebantur libello, excepto uno qui extremus ponitur, non essent sui, sed ecclesiastici: nec ignibus damnandi, sed pia et pacifica fuerint inquisitione tractandi. Sed et illa ejusdem miserandi hominis tam longa, et inhumana in ergastulum per tot annos damnatio, aliqua ut credimus, compassionis benignitate, et consolatione fuerat temperanda, vel etiam removenda, ut frater pro quo Christus mortuus est, per charitatem, et spiritum mansuetudinis potius lucraretur, quam abundantiori tristitia absorberetur.*"

216 Devisse, *Hincmar*, 129.

217 Prudentius was probably a Basque whose parents came to the Frankish side of the Pyrenees at the beginning of Louis the Pious' reign. See Tavard, *Trina Deitas*, 17.

Were the proceedings of the synod later falsified by Hincmar? There are no substantial grounds to believe so. On the other hand, even though Hincmar indeed applied chapter 27 of the Rule of St Benedict regarding the treatment of obdurate monks, i.e., flogging, and followed the example of Rabanus given at Mainz, softer measures in the same Rule had hardly been exhausted.

Other charges against Hincmar by modern scholars include his unwillingness to let Gottschalk's case be treated by Rothad, to whose diocese the monk from Orbais formally belonged, as well as his unwillingness to convene a large council to investigate the matter. In fact, it was Rabanus who infringed upon canon law; the monk was to be judged first by a provincial synod in his own province, that of Reims, which, as Devisse indicated,[218] is commanded in the canons preserved in the so-called *Dionysian-Hadrian Collection* (*Collectio Dionysio-Hadriana*).[219] As for general councils, they had not been convened since 794 to treat the issues of dogmatic theology. The archbishop of Mainz did not realize the extent of the problem; the archbishop of Reims blindly acted upon the instructions of Rabanus, in whom he confided without reserve; the kings merely let the prelates accomplish their duties. Who else in 848-849 would be able to grasp the essence and scope of Gottschalk's teaching?

GOTTSCHALK'S IMPRISONMENT AND WRITING AT HAUTVILLERS (849)

In contrast to the many discussions about why Rabanus or Hincmar did or did not do this or that, another question has not been investigated, namely, why a simple monk like Gottschalk, backed by only a few followers who were common people, would present himself before kings and archbishops and let them know that all their ideas about God and the Church were nonsense, and that they were in fact heretics unless ready to agree with him at once. There is no doubt that Gottschalk was a great theologian, but his unusual manner of confronting the whole world with his doctrine may be explained in light of what a few witnesses wrote concerning his behavior in Hautvillers. Hincmar reports:

> He also wrote, addressing himself to God and telling him, that he had commanded him not to pray about me, and that first the Son had entered him, then the Father, and afterwards the Holy Spirit who, entering him, scorched his beard around the mouth. And, since he refused to receive clothes from the vestiary of the brothers who were in communion with me unless he purchased them for a price that he did not have, he preferred to walk as Adam walked

---

His original name was Galindo.

218 Devisse, *Hincmar*, 127, n. 59.

219 Book of canon law sent by Pope Hadrian I to Charlemagne at the latter's request in 774.

> before he sinned. However, soon, when cold began to seize him, he took pains about procuring himself both a fur coat and a fire-place.[220]

Farther on he continues:

> Indeed, a few years ago he wrote to one of his friends that in three and a half years I, as Antichrist who usurped the power, would at once die, and he himself would become the bishop of Reims, and seven years later would perish being poisoned, and thus should reach the glory of a martyr. ... He did not see the accomplishment of the prophecy inspired by his spirit.[221]

This was written after the council of Soissons that took place in 853, to which Hincmar's *On the One and Not Trine Deity* elsewhere alludes. In connection with Quierzy Hincmar wrote that Gottschalk behaved "like one possessed" by a demon.[222] Little had changed over a decade later, when about 866 Hincmar came to the same sad conclusion in a letter to Egilo:[223]

> Lastly, I would be able to write much about this Gottschalk to you, how destructive he is, and how very harmful he would be to others if he were released from this custody; for assuredly he says and does such things by which he is certainly recognized as either one possessed by a demon or mad, and you know that madness does not usually occur without a demon.[224]

---

220 Hincmar, *On the One and Not Trine Deity* (*De una et non trina deitate*), 18 (PL 125:613A-B): "*Scripsit quoque ad Deum loquens, et dicens ei quod ipse illi praeceperit ut pro me non oraret, et quia primum Filius in eum intraverit, postea Pater, deinde Spiritus sanctus, qui in illum intrans ei circa os barbam adussit: et quia nollet vestimenta de vestiario fratrum communicantium mihi accipere, nisi pretio compararet qui pretium non habebat, sed sic vellet ire, sicut Adam ibat antequam peccaret. Mox autem ut frigus eum coepit constringere, cum vestimentis etiam pelliciam et focum studuit quaerere.*"

221 Hincmar, *On the One and Not Trine Deity*, 18 (PL 125:613B-C): "*Ante hos siquidem annos revelatum sibi quibusdam familiaribus suis scripsit, quod ego statim post tres semis annos suae revelationis, sicut Antichristus usurpans sibi potestatis potentiam mori, et ipse Rhemorum episcopus fieri, et post septennium veneno interfici, et sic gloriae martyrum adaequari deberet.... Prophetiam a spiritu suo inspiratam impleri non vidit.*"

222 Hincmar, *Letter to the Church of Lyons*, cited in Florus, *Book on Three Letters*, 24 (PL 121:1027D): "*ut arreptitius.*" Other spellings of the term are "*arreptivus*" and "*arrepticius.*" See Alexander Souter, *A Glossary of Later Latin* (Oxford: Clarendon, 1949).

223 Hincmar, *Letter to Egilo* (*Epistola ad Egilonem*); PL 126:68-71. This is the letter that preceded another one to the same addressee, translated by Genke in the present volume.

224 Hincmar, *Letter to Egilo* (PL 126 :70D): "*Plura denique vobis de ipso Gothescalco scribere poteram, quam perniciosus sit, et multo magis noxius erit multis, si ab ipsa custodia fuerit absolutus: quia pro certo talia dicit et talia facit, in quibus evidenter cognoscitur aut daemoniacus esse, aut maniaticus: et scitis quoniam mania esse non solet absque daemone.*"

Attempts to explain all this as senile dementia or prison psychosis[225] do not seem convincing. Gottschalk wrote almost all the time that he spent at Hautvillers, and his treatises do not resemble in the least the thoughts of a feeble-minded person. Becoming psychotic in the rather mild conditions, in which he was kept in Hautvillers, would be unlikely: "Whatever food or drink the brothers have, they serve him with it daily without any negligence; he is offered sufficient clothes if he wants to accept them; he is given enough wood to make a fire. In the lodge where he lives he has a fireplace and a toilet."[226] And, quite characteristically, Hincmar adds: "Baths are not denied to him, but since he entered this lodge he has not only been unwilling to wash his body, but even his hands and face. In fact, those with whom he used to keep company witness that he has been most filthy formerly and thus far remains in his filthiness as much as he can."[227]

Strangely enough, despite the "perpetual silence" imposed upon him at Quierzy, Gottschalk managed to send his treatises and letters to many influential people, arousing public interest to his case. Within the year 849 alone three of his writings fell into Hincmar's hands:[228] *Tome to Gislemar*,[229] *Reply to Rabanus Maurus*

---

225 Vielhaber, *Gottschalk*, 27; Dennis E. Nineham, "Gottschalk of Orbais: Reactionary or Precursor to the Reformation?" *Journal of Ecclesiastical History* 40 (1989), 5.

226 Hincmar, *Letter to Egilo* (PL 126:70D): "*Quidquid fratres in cibo et potu habent, hoc ei quotidie sine ulla negligentia ministratur; vestimenta illi ad sufficientiam offeruntur, si vult ille accipere: ligna ad focum faciendum illi sufficienter dantur. In mansione in qua degit caminatum habet, et necessarium.*" There is also no doubt that Gottschalk had access to the library of the abbey. See Devisse, *Hincmar*, 132, n. 82.

227 Hincmar, *Letter to Egilo* (PL 126:70D): "*Lavacra illi non denegantur: sed postquam in eamdem mansionem intravit, non solum corpus lavare noluit, verum nec manus, nec faciem. Antea enim, sicut illi testantur inter quos conversatus erat, turpissimus et adhuc quantum potest in sua turpitudine manet.*" This interesting report about Gottschalk being "most filthy" (*turpissimus*) even before Mainz, Quierzy and Hautvillers, as well as the sharp inconsistency between how he behaved and how he wrote, led us to draw a parallel, namely, with the type of holiness, which was represented by *yurodivys* in medieval Russia. Indeed, a *yurodivy* was an eccentric figure outside the conventional society, whose madness might be either factual or feigned. They were sure of their divine inspiration and thus were able to say things that others would never dare to utter. The Russian Orthodox Church numbers 36 *yurodivys* among its saints.

228 Hincmar, *Letter to the Monks* in Gundlach, 261-2: "*De quibus perversitatibus scilicet suis et scripta illius suscepi: unum quidem thomum a confratribus nostris oblatum, scripsit...; alterum autem quem contra Rabanum... ; tertium quoque thomulum quantitate parvum, sed impietate maximum ab illo ipso mihi oblatum suscepi.*"

229 Extant fragments are translated by Genke in the present volume. There is almost no doubt that this is the same as "*pitacium ad quemdam monachum*" (PL 125:369C-D) and the writing addressed "*ad quemdam complicem*" (PL 125:291A).

(which had been presented at the diet of Mainz[230]), and *Shorter Confession*.[231] These (except, perhaps, the *Tome*, though the date of its composition is unclear) had been written earlier.[232] Even more surprising is that the archbishop of Reims wrote in reply,[233] establishing a written dialogue with Gottschalk, who, in his turn, sent him his *Longer Confession*,[234] a copy of which was probably delivered to Amolo.[235] Amolo wrote to Gottschalk: "Afterwards a certain writing of yours was brought to us by the zeal of men of the church in which you set forth what you taught and were teaching very openly and in a lengthy discussion and, as you thought, with testimonies of the scriptures and holy fathers." The bishop of Lyons continued: "We have now also received other long treatises of yours that you seem to have written or published for the bishops or even against the bishops who had been present at the council that condemned you."[236] We know[237] as well that Gottschalk wrote to persons named Matcaud,[238] Lupus[239] and Jonas.[240] He also wrote to the bishop of Ferrières concerning the beatific vision and got quite

---

230 See above.

231 Gottschalk's *Shorter Confession* is translated by Gumerlock in the present volume. "*Thomulum quantitate parvum*" mentioned by Hincmar was identified as the *Shorter Confession* by Cappuyns, *Jean Scot Erigène*, 106, n. 1.

232 Boller (*Gottschalk d'Orbais*, 240) places the date of composition of the *Shorter Confession* as early as in the year 840, which date does not seem to be justified. Vielhaber (*Gottschalk*, 23, n. 60) places it between the synod of Quierzy and Hincmar's *Letter to the Monks*.

233 Flodoard, *History of the Church of Reims*, 18 (PL 135:258D).

234 The date of its composition must be placed between Hincmar's *Letter to the Monks* and Hincmar's letter to Rabanus written in 850. Cappuyns, *Jean Scot Erigène*, 107, n. 3; Devisse, *Hincmar*, 132, n. 80; Vielhaber, *Gottschalk*, 23, n. 60. In the *Longer Confession* Gottschalk requested to be put to an ordeal so as to test the orthodoxy of his teaching.

235 See Devisse, *Hincmar*, 132 and 192, n. 25.

236 Amolo of Lyons, *Letter to Gottschalk* (*Epistola ad Gothescalcum*), Intro. (PL 116:86C-D): "*Deinde perlata est etiam ad nos studio ecclesiasticorum virorum quaedam scriptura tua, in qua apertissime, et prolixo sermone, atque ut tibi visum est etiam testimoniis Scripturarum, sive sanctorum Patrum, quid sentires sive doceres multipliciter exsecutus es. Nunc quoque accepimus et alia scripta tua non parva, quae ad episcopos, vel contra episcopos, qui in concilio damnationis tuae affuerunt, scripsisse vel protulisse videris.*" This was written about 850-851. See Devisse, *Hincmar*, 192.

237 From Hincmar, *On the One and Not Trine Deity*, 19 (PL 125:618C).

238 Hefele (*Histoire des conciles*, 140) seems to identify him as Marquard of Prüm.

239 Traube (*Prooemium*, 717, n. 3) believes that here Lupus of Ferrières is implied. However, it may be Lupus of Châlons (c. 835-c. 857). See Gottschalk's letter to this bishop published by Traube in the same volume of MGH, Poetae, 3: 723-4.

240 Probably Jonas of Orleans, d. 843 or 844.

a cold answer from him,[241] in contrast to Ratramnus, who sent him two poems[242] and a letter[243] full of sympathy, in which he criticized Hincmar's *Letter to the Monks*. In his poetic *Letter to Ratramnus* Gottschalk asserts that he wrote not only to the eminent West Frankish theologians, but also to those who lived in barbarian kingdoms.[244] During this period the majority of the material published by Lambot must have been produced. However, any reliable chronology would hardly be possible.[245]

Rabanus was shocked when he learned that Gottschalk had such a freedom to communicate with the outer world.[246] However, for some mysterious reason, Hincmar never cut short Gottschalk's activity in authoring and sending out letters and treatises. This, nonetheless, did not help the condemned monk much.

SUBSEQUENT POLEMICAL EXCHANGE ON PREDESTINATION (849-850)

As it seems, exchange of texts with Gottschalk engendered doubts in Hincmar's heart. Indeed, it is rather strange that the archbishop of Reims should consult Prudentius of Troyes, a bishop belonging to the jurisdiction of the archdiocese of Sens, about whether he should admit the condemned monk to the sacrament, if he was absolutely sure that his prisoner was nothing more than an unrepentant heretic.[247]

Gottschalk's active correspondence must have given rise to rumors about his case, at least in the outskirts of Reims. That is why in autumn 849 Hincmar published a lengthy pastoral *Letter to the Monks and Simple Folk of his Diocese*,

---

241 Lupus of Ferrières, *Letter to Gottschalk* (*Epistola ad Godescalcum*) in PL 119:491-5.

242 See Traube, *Prooemium*, 717.

243 It is the *Chartula Ratramni monachi* mentioned by Rabanus (MGH, Epist., 5:488). See PL 112 :1522B: "*Ille Corbeiensis monachus in epistola sua vituperavit vos non recte sententiam Fulgentii exposuisse scribendum de vobis ad amicum suum.*"

244 Gottschalk, *Letter to Ratramnus* (*Epistola ad Ratramnum*). PL 121:367-72 at 370B: *Per barbara regna locatos*. See Vielhaber, *Gottschalk*, 24.

245 See Lambot, xxiii.

246 Rabanus, *Letter to Hincmar* (PL 112:1527D): "*Miror enim prudentiam vestram quod istum noxium virum, hoc est Gotescalcum, qui in omnibus vituperabilis inventus est, quia nec monachi votum, nec sacri ordinis ritum, sed neque praedicandi officium legitime observavit, scribere aliquid permisistis, in quo officio magis nocere potuit quam viva voce loquendo.*"

247 In the same letter Hincmar also sought Prudentius' counsel concerning a passage in Ezekiel that he would use in *Letter to the Monks* (Gundlach, 297), as well as wondered why he "deprived him of his presence" (*quare sibi praesentiam suam subtrahat*). Flodoard, *History of the Church of Reims*, 21. PL 135:200C. It is obvious that at the period the opinion of the bishop of Troyes was very important to Hincmar.

where he warned them against the dangerous false prophet.[248] Even though in this work Hincmar did everything to convince his perplexed parishioners that Gottschalk was the devil himself, nevertheless, together with his suffragan of Laon, Pardulus, he resolved to learn the opinion of several noted theologians concerning the issue of predestination—which shows that doubts did not disappear. According to Florus,[249] Pardulus, in a letter to the church of Lyons, mentioned five authorities addressed, including Amalarius of Metz.[250] However, the first to be consulted was again Prudentius, and his answer must have confirmed Hincmar's worst fears.[251] The bishop of Troyes, even though his tone was not at all controversial, affirmed a perfectly Augustinian teaching that clearly contradicted Hincmar's own ideas.

At this point the archbishop of Reims turns to the authority whose judgment had always been unquestionable for him: Rabanus. Having written a letter to the archbishop of Mainz[252] (February or March 850), Hincmar joined to it a dossier that contained the sentence of Quierzy, *Letter to the Monks*, the letter of Prudentius, Gottschalk's *Longer Confession* ("*nugae Gotescalci,*" in the words of Rabanus[253]), as well as Ratramnus' letter to Gottschalk criticizing Hincmar's *Letter to the Monks*. Since the letter of Lupus of Ferrières, who had also been consulted, was not added, it must have come later, afflicting Hincmar no less than Prudentius' reply.[254] How uneasy about Gottschalk Hincmar was at the time is seen in the fact that he again asked advice, this time from Rabanus, concerning administering the Lord's Supper to his prisoner.

At the time, as it seems, the archbishop of Reims was still ignoring the fact that a few months earlier the debate had attracted his king's attention. In December 849, back from his expedition to Toulouse, Charles the Bald spoke at Bourges

---

248 Hincmar, *Letter to the Monks and Simple Folk of his Diocese* in Gundlach, 258-309. Excerpts translated by Gumerlock in the present volume.

249 Florus, *Book on Three Letters*, 39 (PL 121:1052A).

250 No wonder that Florus preferred to repeat only this name: it is as a result of his protests that Amalarius' teaching concerning the symbolism of the Mass, expressed in his treatise *On Ecclesiastical Duties* (*De ecclesiasticis officiis*), had been officially condemned by the council of Quierzy in 838. Amalarius' answer to the request of Hincmar and Pardulus is lost. Among the other four authorities must have been Prudentius, Lupus and Rabanus.

251 Prudentius of Troyes, *Letter to Hincmar and Pardulus* (*Epistula ad Hincmarum et Pardulum*); PL 115:971-1010. This letter probably reached them late in 849.

252 Cappuyns (*Jean Scot Erigène*, 108, n. 2) asserts that it is lost, but see Devisse, *Hincmar*, 142, n. 133.

253 MGH, Epist. 5:488.

254 Lupus of Ferrières, *Letter to Hincmar* (*Epistola ad Hincmarum*) in MGH, Epist. 6:109-10; PL 119:606-8. Lupus answered Hincmar and Pardulus separately, but the letters seem to have been identical.

to the abbot of Ferrières, asking him for instruction concerning the issues of "predestination, and the free will, and the redemption by the blood of Christ."[255] Lupus gave his vision of these issues first orally and later in a treatise entitled *Book on Three Questions*, where he expressed himself more thoroughly than he did in the letter to Hincmar and Pardulus.[256] As it seems, the archbishop of Reims and his suffragan of Laon reacted rather bitterly, since Lupus had to write to the king an explanatory letter and publish a *Collection* of patristic quotations supporting his point of view.[257] Moreover, Charles decided to consult Ratramnus, whose friendly relationship with Gottschalk and critique of Hincmar's *Letter to the Monks* must have been already known. However, in a treatise addressed to the king[258] the monk of Corbie repeatedly asked him to keep it private unless his doctrine should be approved and/or corrected by Charles.[259] Cappuyns believes that this work was handed over to Hincmar only later in 855.[260]

To be sure, the archbishop of Reims was anxious to hear from Mainz in response to the dossier that he had sent in February/March 850. Rabanus let him know that he received it right away (it happened before Easter, that is April 6), but wrote that he would examine the documents later.[261] In summer the real answer came, but it sounded disappointing.[262] Rabanus, now aged, simply acknowledged that he agreed with Hincmar, and that what Ratramnus and Prudentius wrote agreed with Gottschalk's teaching. He himself would not participate in the discussion any more. All he had to say was to be found in his letters to Noting and Eberhard. Now Hincmar had to accomplish what was actually begun by Rabanus without the latter's support, which was obviously a serious loss for his side. As for the sacrament, the archbishop of Mainz was inexorable: Gottschalk was an obdurate heretic and as such could not be given communion.

Simultaneously, a correspondence between Reims and Lyons developed. As it seems, it was Gottschalk himself who began it. As stated above, "by the zeal of men of the church" he sent to Amolo a writing, in which he set forth "in a lengthy discussion" his understanding of "the testimonies of the scriptures and

255 Lupus, *Letter to the lord King* (*Epistola ad dominum regem*) in PL 119:601B: *De praedestinatione et libero arbitrio ac redemptione sanguinis Christi.*

256 Lupus, *Book on Three Questions (Liber de tribus quaestionibus)* in PL 119:619-48.

257 Lupus, *Letter to the lord King* in PL 119:601-5); *Collection on the Three Questions* (*Collectaneum de tribus quaestionibus*) in PL 119:647-66.

258 Ratramnus of Corbie, *On the Predestination of God* (PL 121:13-80). Prefatory letter in MGH, Epist. 6:151-3.

259 Most probably out of fear to do harm to Gottschalk.

260 See Cappuyns, *Jean Scot Erigène*, 111, n. 1.

261 Rabanus, *Letter to Hincmar (VIII)* in MGH, Epist. 5:487-90; PL 112:1574-6.

262 Rabanus, *Letter to Hincmar (IV)* in MGH, Epist. 5:490-99; PL 112:1518-30.

holy fathers" as well as his own position.[263] There is almost no doubt that the *Longer Confession* is implied. However, when exactly did it take place? At all events any correspondence with Amolo would have taken place before March 31, 852, the date of his death. If it is assumed that Gottschalk sent this confession both to Hincmar and to Amolo right after it had been written, then its delivery to Lyons immediately followed the time of its composition, between autumn 849 (*Letter to the Monks*, which ignores it) and February/March 850, when Hincmar joined it to the dossier sent to Rabanus. Thus a reply from Lyons (addressed to Hincmar who was supposed to deliver it to Gottschalk[264]) arrived in 850, possibly as early as in summer of that year.

As it seems, upon the arrival of Rabanus' second letter (written in reply to the dossier containing *Letter to the Monks* and other documents), to which the archbishop of Mainz subjoined his writings concerning predestination (summer 850), Hincmar sent to Lyons another dossier[265] that contained two letters (his own and Pardulus') and Rabanus' *On Predestination*.[266] Fragments of Hincmar's *Letter to Amolo* are preserved in Florus' *Book on Three Letters* and summarized by Flodoard.[267]

ERIGENA'S TREATISE AND THE SYNOD AT QUIERZY (851-853)

A fateful move was made by Pardulus of Laon: "However, since all these [opinions] differed much, we urged the Scot from the king's palace, named John, to write."[268] *On Divine Predestination* by John Scot Erigena that appeared at the end of 850 or early in 851, nearly destroyed Hincmar's cause.[269] Indeed, Erigena's noble mind, not unlike Gottschalk's in its bold singularity, originated ideas that

263 Amolo, *Letter to Gottschalk*, Intro. (PL 116:86C-D).

264 It is not known whether he did it.

265 According to Devisse (*Hincmar*, 195), it happened in December 849/January 850, which seems to be too early, since by that time Rabanus' *Letter to Noting* is unlikely to have reached Hincmar and therefore he would have been unable to send it to Lyons.

266 It follows from what is said in Florus, *Book on Three Letters* (PL 121:985B-987A), as well as from Flodoard's remark in *History of the Church of Reims*, 21 (PL 135:200B-C). See Cappuyns, *Jean Scot Erigène*, 116, n. 2.

267 Hincmar, *Letter to Amolo of Lyons* (Epistola ad Amolonem archiepiscopum Lugdunensem) In Florus, *Book on Three Letters* (PL 121:987C-988B, 1027D-1028A; Lambot, 15-6). Translated by Genke in the present volume. Summary of Flodoard in his *History of the Church of Reims*, 29 (PL 135:260C).

268 *Sed quia haec inter se valde dissentiebant, Scotum illum qui est in palatio regis, Joannem nomine, scribere coegimus*. Pardulus, *Letter to the Church of Lyons*, which is lost but is cited in Florus' *Book on Three Letters* (PL 121:1052A).

269 Erigena, *On Divine Predestination*. CCCM 50; PL 122:355-440. Prefatory letter in MGH, Epist. 5:630-1.

could not but scandalize his contemporaries. Enrolled on Hincmar's side was now a theology that seemed to deny the reality of hell and even the reality of good and evil.

The interference of Erigena had two major consequences. First, Gottschalk ceased to be the focus of the controversy that grew much larger in scope. It would be a mistake to believe that being opponents of Gottschalk's opponents automatically meant becoming his supporters. Second, Hincmar's political rivals now had an opportunity (which they would never lose) to denigrate the archbishop of Reims.[270] Making a beast out of Erigena and a martyr out of Gosttchalk was now the surest way to undermine Hincmar's authority, which was a goal of too many bishops around him.

The first to come into play was Wenilo, the archbishop of Sens and Hincmar's chief competitor in the race for power within the kingdom of Charles the Bald. He took nineteen statements, which John Scot himself had placed at the beginnings of sections into which his treatise was subdivided,[271] and sent them to the bishop of Troyes, commissioning his suffragan to refute them. In autumn 851[272] Prudentius answered with his own *On Predestination*,[273] where he accompanied each of Erigena's statements with "the sign that in Greek is called theta, which some used to put before [the names of] those to be condemned for capital crimes."[274] Moreover, he sent the nineteen statements of Erigena (seemingly together with his own treatise) to Florus, a learned deacon in Lyons, with whom he seems to have been in correspondence earlier.[275] Under Remigius, the new archbishop, Florus authored two works, both in 852: *Book on Three Letters* that treated Hincmar's appeal to the see of Lyons, and a *Book against the Erroneous Definitions of John Scot Erigena*.[276]

---

270 Especially taking into consideration Lothair's tenacious hostility towards Hincmar. See Emile Lesne, "Hincmar et l'empereur Lothaire," *Revue des questions historiques* 34 (1905):5-58.

271 Hincmar would constantly deny his association with these nineteen statements, either saying that they are counterfeit (PL 125:51A) or pretending to be ignorant of their content (PL 125:296A-B).

272 Cappuyns, *Jean Scot Erigène*, 115, n. 1.

273 Prudentius of Troyes, *On Predestination against John the Scot* (*De praedestinatione contra Joannem Scotum*) in PL 115:1009-1366, Preface in MGH, Epist. 5:631-3.

274 Prudentius, *On Predestination*, Preface (PL 115:1012A-B): "*...Illud nota quae graece dicitur theta, quam sententiis capitalibus damnandorum aliqui praescribere solebant.*" Concerning this sign, see George Ronald Watson, "Theta nigrum," *Journal of Roman Studies* 42 (1952): 56-62.

275 See Devisse, *Hincmar*, 153.

276 Florus, *Book on Three Letters* (PL 121:985-1068); *Book against the Erroneous Definitions of John Scot Erigena* (*Adversus Ioannis Scoti Erigenae erroneas definitiones liber*) in PL 119:101-250.

Even though official, these treatises were anonymous, which gave Hincmar the possibility of discarding them as unauthentic, at least until 859. Now that Sens in the kingdom of Charles and Lyons in that of Lothair, obviously united against Hincmar, the archbishop of Reims, resolved to take a radical step and shove back his enemies through synodal decisions.

The first successful move was made in April 853. Clerics, ordained by Ebbo, Hincmar's predecessor, during his brief restoration in 840, and most of whom subsequently left Reims, suddenly reappeared and requested a reconsideration of their status. This demarche was aimed at the weakening of Hincmar's position. Should the ordinations be acknowledged as legitimate, the archbishop's own elevation to the see of Reims would become highly questionable, and Ebbo's deposition in effect illegal. However, at a council of Soissons these ordinations were pronounced null.

Inspired by this manifest political success, Hincmar at once convened another council, this time at Quierzy, where he also triumphed in the matter of the predestination controversy. Four chapters (*capitula*), issued there, affirmed his own understanding of free will, predestination, and Christ's atonement, and were signed by the bishops as well as by the king himself.[277] If Hincmar is to be trusted at this point, Prudentius of Troyes subscribed to the document too.[278]

RESPONSES AGAINST THE CANONS OF QUIERZY (853-857)

The council did not stand a good chance of being applauded in the south. Indeed, during the next few years the church of Lyons produced two more treatises aimed against the four chapters of Quierzy: an emotional *Sermon on Predestination* as well as a *Booklet on Holding Immovably to the Truth of Scripture*, both by Florus.[279] On 8 January 855, at Valence, Lothair convened a council where the bishops of Lyons, Vienne and Arles were present. The six chapters (*capitula*) concerning predestination enacted there openly attacked those of Quierzy and Erigena's nineteen statements.[280]

In August 855 Heribald of Auxerre, during their meeting at Bonneuil, delivered to Hincmar a copy of Florus' *Sermon*.[281] Before September 29th[282] of the same year (the date of the emperor's death) Lothair, retired in the convent of Prüm,

277 *Chapters of the Council of Quierzy* (*Capitula conventiculi Carisiaci*) in PL 125:63-4.

278 Hincmar, *On Predestination*, 21 & 26 (PL 125:182C-D, 268C-D).

279 Florus, *Sermon on Predestination* (PL 119:95-102). Translated by Gumerlock in the present volume; *Booklet on Holding Immovably to the Truth of Scripture* (*Libellus de tenenda immobiliter scripturae veritate*) in PL 121:1083-134.

280 *Canons of the Council of Valence* (*Concilii Valentini canones*) in Mansi, 15:1-15.

281 Hincmar, *On Predestination*, Preface (PL 125:55-6).

282 Devisse (*Hincmar*, 215, n. 115) suggests that it happened in spring 855, possibly after Easter.

received the chapters of Valence through Ebbo of Grenoble,[283] who had taken an active part in their composition, and commissioned him to deliver them to his brother Charles. The chapters were delivered to the latter at Verberie, together with other documents from Lyons, among which was probably the *Booklet* by Florus. It is only in July 856,[284] at Neaufle (diocese of Rouen), that Charles handed over this dossier to Hincmar.

If Cappuyns believes that Hincmar's first *On Predestination* (*De praedestinatione*)[285] was the reaction of the archbishop of Reims to these writings[286] (which probably included Ratramnus' *On the Predestination of God*, since Flodoard mentions it in connection with Hincmar's work[287]), Devisse is sure that by this time it was already written.[288] Whatever the case, the treatise was never published and its text is lost.

A new blow to the chapters of Quierzy was delivered at the ordination of Aeneas.[289] Prudentius, who was ill, sent one of his priests to announce to the assembly a condition for consent to Aeneas' ordination: the bishop of Troyes composed four counter-chapters to those of Quierzy,[290] which Aeneas had to sign if he was to become the successor to Ercanrad at the see of Paris.[291]

The death of the emperor disturbed the fragile balance achieved between Louis, Lothair and Charles at the second Meersen conference in 851. Riots in Aquitaine and Brittany, Viking raids as well as Louis' invasion into Neustria distracted general attention from the debate. However, the need for reconciliation of the brother kings made a very large meeting inevitable, which took place in 859.

THE SYNODS OF SAVONNIÈRES AND TUSEY (859-860)

At a preliminary conference held at Langres, bishops from the south edited the chapters of Valence in order to eliminate that which offended the northern

---

283 A nephew to Ebbo of Reims.

284 Devisse, *Hincmar*, 215 and n.117.

285 Devisse (*Hincmar*, 123, n. 39) and Ganz ("Debate on Predestination," 298) call it Hincmar's second treatise on predestination, counting his *Letter to the Monks* as the first one.

286 Cappuyns, *Jean Scot Erigène*, 123.

287 Flodoard, *History of the Church of Reims*, 15 (PL 135:181A): "*Item collegit atque composuit volumen ingens plures continens libros de praedestinatione Dei et libero arbitrio contra quosdam reprehensores suos atque Ratramnum monachum Corbeiensem.*"

288 Devisse, *Hincmar*, 215.

289 It took place between May 856 and February 857. McKeon, "Carolingian Councils," 92, n. 5.

290 Prudentius, *Letter to Wenilo* (*Epistola tractoria ad Venilonem*) in PL 115:1365-8.

291 Since Aeneas in effect became the bishop of Paris, Prudentius' counter-chapters must have been signed.

party led by Hincmar. Any reference to the chapters of Quierzy was removed. Since the archbishop of Reims was extremely displeased by the association of his name with the unfortunate nineteen statements, it was specified that their author was "a certain Scot."[292] The seventh chapter of Valence, which implied that many bishops were inadequate in their positions (understood by Hincmar as a personal attack[293]), disappeared; and it was replaced by harmless formulas that concerned only the bishops in the realm of Charles of Provence. Despite these conciliatory efforts the final decision was postponed, and the decrees (*decreta*) prepared at Langres were again presented by Remigius of Lyons a few weeks later, at the council of Savonnières,[294] which was opened 14 June 859, in presence of the three kings and representatives of twelve provinces. Since Hincmar and his party raised questions, now concerning contradictions between the decrees of Langres and those presented now, the decision was again postponed.[295]

When Charles the Bald received from Remigius his version of the chapters, he delivered them to the archbishop of Reims, who reacted with the second treatise *On Predestination*,[296] which turned out to be the last one concerning the issue in that controversy. When a new representative meeting was scheduled, Hincmar wrote a synodal letter, which treated a lot of subjects like the Trinity, angels, humans, incarnation, redemption, and the sacraments.[297] As for predestination, it said that God "wants all men to be saved" (which might well be understood in the restrictive sense) and equated "all who are to be saved" with "all those predestined."[298] Such conciliatory formulas became the basis for the

292 *Decrees or Canons of the Synod of Langres* (*Decreta seu canones synodi Lingonensis*), 4 (Mansi, 15:538: "*Quodam Scoto*").

293 Hincmar, *On Predestination*, 36 (PL 125:385A-C).

294 Savonnières, "*villa regia Saponariae*" near Toul, arose as a military station dependent from the governor of Trier. Under Childeric (456-481) it became royal property. After the Treaty of Verdun (August 845) the palace of *Saponariae* passed into the ownership of the Emperor Lothair I, and later was inherited by his son, Lothair II. There are three places called Savonnières in Lorraine: Savonnières-devant-Bar, Savonnières-en-Perthois and Savonnières-en-Woëvre. None of them is the place where the council of 859 was held. Ancient royal *villa* was later called Savonnières or Savonnières-lès-Toul (near Foug, to the west of Toul, Meurthe-et-Moselle département). In 1870 a column was erected there in commemoration of that notable meeting of Frankish princes and prelates (Hefele, *Histoire des conciles*, 217, n. 3). However, the village is now destroyed and not found on maps of modern France.

295 Hincmar, *Letter to Charles the King* (*Epistola ad Carolum regem*) in PL 125:66B-C.

296 Hincmar, *On Predestination* (PL 125:55-474). Devisse and Ganz call it Hincmar's third treatise on predestination.

297 Hincmar, *Letter of the Council of Tusey* (*Epistola concilii Tusiacensis*) in PL 126:122-32.

298 Hincmar, *Letter of the Council of Tusey* (PL 126:123C, 126B): "*Vult omnes homines salvos fieri... Omnes qui salvandi sunt, id est omnes praedestinati.*"

decisions[299] of the council of Tusey[300] that was opened 22 October 860 and put an end to the controversy.

AFTERMATH AND DEATH OF GOTTSCHALK (861-868)

Prudentius of Troyes died in April of the next year. Hincmar, who was to continue the *Annals of St Bertin*, left there a note full of venom concerning his predecessor:

> Galindo, surnamed Prudentius, bishop of Troyes, of Spanish origin, a most erudite person, who during a few years had offered resistance to Gottschalk, but later, moved by bitterness against certain bishops who made a stand with him against the heretic, dies as a most violent defender of the same heresy, having composed since then a lot of things contradicting each other and opposed to faith; thus, even though he was wearied by a lasting illness, he ceased to write only when he ceased to live.[301]

Such acrimony was understandable. Indeed, in the annals, under the year 859, the archbishop of Reims discovered a short but vexing entry: "Nicholas, the Roman pontiff, faithfully confirms and in a catholic manner determines his position concerning grace and free will, as well as concerning the truth of the twofold predestination and the blood of Christ, which was shed for all believers."[302] Even though Hincmar "neither heard about this from anyone else nor read it anywhere else,"[303] in 866 he begged Egilo of Sens, who made his way to Rome, to ask the Pope whether anything like that had indeed taken place,[304] since the

299 Mansi, 15:563-71.

300 Tusey is not to be confused (as it often has been) with Douzy on the Chiers River, near Sedan (Ardennes). An ancient Gallo-Roman settlement, Douzy was one of the boroughs where Charlemagne stayed while visiting Ardennes. In 871 two synods were held there. This is also the place of meeting of Otto I with Louis IV d'Outremer in 947. In Medieval Latin Douzy was called *Duciacum* or *Duziacum*. However, the council of 860 was held at a different place called *Tusiacum*, which is now a small village Tusey near Vaucouleurs (Meuse), southwest of Toul. See also Tavard, *Trina Deitas*, 52, n. 28; and Nineham, "Gottschalk of Orbais," 8, n. 39.

301 Hincmar, *Annals* (*Annales*), ann. 861 (PL 125:1203A): "*Galindo cognomento Prudentius, Tricassinae civitatis episcopus, natione Hispanus, adprime litteris eruditus, qui ante aliquot annos Gotescalco praedestinatiano restiterat, post felle commotus contra quosdam episcopos secum heretico resistentes, ipsius haeresis defensor acerrimus, indeque non modica inter se diversa et fidei adversa scriptitans moritur; sicque, licet diutino languore fatigaretur, ut vivendi ita et scribendi finem fecit.*"

302 *Annals of St Bertin* (MGH, Scriptores rerum Germanicarum, 5:53): "*Nicolaus pontifex romanus de gratia et libero arbitrio, de veritate geminae praedestinationis et sanguine Christi, ut pro credentibus omnibus fusus sit, fideliter confirmat et catholice decernit.*"

303 Hincmar, *Letter to Egilo* (PL 126:70B): "*Quod per alium non audivimus, nec alibi legimus.*"

304 The letter was written because a certain Guntbert, a monk from Hautvillers, escaped the monastery to bring Gottschalk's appeal to the Pope (PL 126:68D-69A).

annals were already accessible to many.[305] Since we are unaware of what Egilo was able to find out, the basis of that statement of Prudentius remains a subject of much controversy until this day.

Whatever the case with regard to the annals, it is certain that Nicholas I was in effect interested in Gottschalk's case. In 863 Hincmar had been ordered to appear together with his prisoner before two papal legates at the council of Metz. The archbishop of Reims did not go there. In a letter to the pontiff he later had to explain that the summons had not reached him in due time.[306] In the same letter he felt compelled to add: "Regarding the aforementioned Gottschalk, if your authority writes to me that I should release him from custody or that I should give him permission to go to you so that you may examine his doctrine for yourself or to travel to anyone designated by name... I will in no way hold back from your orders."[307] However, nothing like that ever happened.

Having several times refused to renounce his views, Gottschalk died in October 868 unreleased.

GOTTSCHALK'S TEACHING ON PREDESTINATION

We do not possess a comprehensive account of Gottschalk's teaching on predestination. Most of his writings dedicated to this subject are very fragmentary (besides perhaps the *Longer Confession*, which is not enough for a conclusive judgment), each presenting only some aspect of his doctrine, almost without any connection to other parts of the system. Accordingly, the temptation is strong to read into his works meanings that he never intended, under the pretext of "reconstructing" the rebellious Benedictine's original teaching. Indeed, the theological vocabulary related to predestination has grown richer since the ninth century, especially after the Reformation, and caution is needed to avoid anachronisms. However, Gottschalk's thought revolves around a few *loci* or points of doctrine that can be detected and described. I have distinguished eight such points in an order that is purely casual, reflecting neither succession in Gottschalk's reasoning or a hierarchy of importance. The idea that predestination is twofold is placed first simply because Gottschalk himself often began with that assertion. Each point will be illustrated with select quotations from writings translated in this book.

1. God predestined both the elect to eternal life and the reprobate to eternal death. Accordingly, predestination is one but twofold.

"The omnipotent and immutable God has gratuitously foreknown and predestined the holy angels and elect human beings to eternal life, and... he equally predestined the devil himself, the head of all the demons, with all of his apostate

305 Hincmar, *Letter to Egilo* (PL 126:70C).

306 Hincmar, *Letter to Pope Nicholas* (PL 126:25-46).

307 Hincmar, *Letter to Pope Nicholas* (PL 126:45C-D).

angels and also with all reprobate human beings, namely, his members, to rightly eternal death"[308] (*Shorter Confession*).

"Just as he truly predestined all of the elect to life through the gratuitous benefit of the his grace alone... so he also absolutely predestined any reprobate to the punishment of eternal death"[309] (*Reply to Rabanus Maurus*, 2).

"Just as immutable God before the foundation of the world immutably predestined to eternal life all his elect through his gratuitous grace, the same immutable God through his just judgment likewise immutably predestined to deservedly eternal death absolutely all the reprobate"[310] (*Confession of Faith at Mainz*). Likewise:

On this Saint Isidore also speaks in this manner:

> Predestination is twofold, either of the elect to rest or of the reprobate to death.' For he does not say that there are two predestinations, because there are not. But he says 'a twofold,' that is, a bipartite one, because you, Lord, spoke once of how by one, but still by a twofold predestination, you both gratuitously justify and eternally save the elect[311] (*Longer Confession*, 10).

"Predestination is said to be twofold so that there are not by any means said to be two predestinations, but one, just as they say that charity is twofold but one"[312] (*Another Treatise on Predestination*, 1).

"Predestination is known to be twofold, that is, one in a general sense because it was established eternally once and for all time, neither—God forbid!—unjust, but both just, but twofold in the special sense, because one is owed and the other is gratuitous"[313] (*Another Treatise on Predestination*, 1).

It is noteworthy that Gottschalk was often charged with teaching that God predestined the reprobate to sin. Since his opponents interpreted the word *evil* in the canons of Orange as "sin," it gave them a basis for accusing Gottschalk of proclaiming ideas contrary to these canons. Gottschalk indeed said that God predestined some people to evil, but he understood "evil" differently:

> What was briefly also said in the *Canons of Orange*, that is, by Saint Caesarius and his fellow bishops, assembled in the city of Orange, namely, 'Let whoever says that God predestined human beings to evil be anathema,' should be understood as 'to the evil of sin, trespass, and crime,' not as 'to the evil of torment, torture, and punishment,' as the truth holds[314] (*On Predestination*, 1.9).

308 Lambot, 52. Translation by Gumerlock.

309 Lambot, 38. Translation by Gumerlock.

310 Lambot, 38.

311 Lambot, 67. Translation by Gumerlock.

312 Lambot, 339.

313 Lambot, 342.

314 Lambot, 189.

Gottschalk makes a distinction between unjust evil which humans commit, i.e., sin, and just evil which God inflicts, i.e., punishment:

> Upon the death of sin that men have inflicted, inflict, and will inflict on themselves, God has inflicted, inflicts, and will inflict bodily death, that is, the separation of the soul from the body, and the death of hell, that is, on account of the one unjust death the twofold just. Such is the difference between the unjust evils that every unjust person has committed, commits, and will commit and the just evils that God has paid back, pays back, and will pay back through present adversities and perpetual torments, as the just one sees fit[315] (*On Predestination*, 1.7).

2. Predestination of the reprobate to eternal death is on the basis of God's foreknowledge of their evil merits.

"He equally predestined the devil himself, the head of all the demons, with all of his apostate angels and also with all reprobate human beings, namely, his members, to rightly eternal death, on account of their own future, most certainly foreknown evil merits"[316] (*Shorter Confession*). Similarly:

> The immortal, eternal, and immutable God did not create the angels, whom he nonetheless foreknew were going to be apostates and deserters, or also human beings, whom he likewise foreknew would be perpetually reprobate, in order that they would sin against God and abandon him. But those whom he foreknew were going to fall and persevere in evil through their own wrongdoing and outrage, offense and vice, he of course rightly predestined through just judgment[317] (*Answers to Various Questions*, 4).

At this point an important observation has to be made. These two texts are the only extant instances when Gottschalk explicitly refers to foreknown evil merits as the *basis* of predestination to eternal death. However, the correct understanding of his assertions concerning evil merits depends on what Gottschalk says about the nature of foreknowledge itself: "You have foreknown and predestined instantly, that is, without any interval, that is, at one and the same time before the ages, each and every one of your works"[318] (*Longer Confession*, 3). And in the following:

> Your same blessed servant, Augustine, also strove to present truthfully, namely, that the reprobate have been condemned by foreknowledge, although here and there he admits that they have been condemned to death by predestination, each of them is of course true, because each of them is true here. For foreknowledge is sometimes put in place of predestination, as he wisely and truthfully admits.

315 Lambot, 183.

316 Lambot, 52. Translation by Gumerlock.

317 Lambot, 155. Translation by Gumerlock.

318 Lambot, 56. Translation by Gumerlock.

> Nor is it contrary to—God forbid!—but is rather seen to agree with truth[319] (*Longer Confession*, 7).

It is in this light that we should understand what Gottschalk says in his *Reply to Rabanus Maurus*: "I say that he [God] foreknew those who were going to have a very bad birth and a worse death, but he predestined them to suffer eternal torment and everlasting destruction," since, at least at times, he does not differentiate predestination and foreknowledge.[320] Indeed, he taught that in this case one word is simply used for the other, according to the rhetorical figure known as *metalepsis*:

> The reprobate have been condemned by foreknowledge and by predestination, who it is absolutely clear were justly predestined to destruction. The aforementioned testimonies prove this sufficiently and beyond, and surely catholics in no way doubt that they are invincible, although if the testimony on this matter has to be from within, it could have regularly and certainly ought to have been, understood by metalepsis, namely, so that what follows would be understood by what precedes[321] (*Longer Confession*, 7).

No less interesting is the formula found in the *Confession of Faith at Mainz*: "The same immutable God through his just judgment likewise immutably predestined to deservedly eternal death absolutely all the reprobate, who at the judgment day will be condemned because of their evil merits," since there is no mention of foreknowledge there.[322] Finally, the following text is most revealing:

> God, who does not know how to err nor can err, be deceived or deceive, never had to, has to, or will have to do any thing—God forbid!—except how he once, simultaneously, and eternally has immutably arranged to carry out his foreknown, predestined, already fixed, already prepared, already determined, and already preordained gratuitous benefit of his grace over the elect and the just judgment of his justice over the reprobate, always *according to the counsel of his will* (Eph 1:11), showing mercy to whomever he wills with great goodness, and hardening, abandoning, and consequently condemning whomever he wills with no injustice, but certainly with highest fairness, as befits a just judge, bestowing grace on the elect and rendering justice, judgment, and punishment to the reprobate[323] (*On Predestination*, 3.1).

Even though Gottschalk does mention foreknowledge here, he clearly states that predestination is always "according to the counsel of his will" and that God condemns "whomever he wills" with no harm to divine justice.[324] Identifying

---

319 Lambot, 63. Translation by Gumerlock.

320 Lambot, 37-8. Translation by Gumerlock.

321 Lambot, 64. Translation by Gumerlock.

322 Lambot, 38.

323 Lambot, 202.

324 At another place Gottschalk says: "For God truly by no means wanted to save with eternal salvation those whom he on that account, as scripture testifies, justly hardens

grace as God, Gottschalk exclaims: "Is not grace God and omnipotent, which gratuitously sets free and saves whomever it wants?"[325] (*On Predestination*, 1.8).

Does it mean that at a certain period of time Gottschalk simply chose formulas that might seem less offensive for his opponents? Or did his views change, and with time he in fact rejected the idea of foreseen demerits (*praevisa demerita*)? Without a reliable chronology of his works no conclusive decision can be made. But it is certain that the condemned Benedictine's views on foreknowledge were not something fixed: they evolved, as also did the formulas which conveyed them.

3. *God does not want to save all people.*

"*All* those whom God *wills to be saved* (1 Tm 2:4), are without doubt saved"[326] (*Reply to Rabanus Maurus*, 6).

"All who are not saved... God does not will to be saved"[327] (*Reply to Rabanus Maurus*, 7).

"Did he will to redeem them by dying, but did not save them, although to redeem by dying is a more burdensome than to save by rising? Or did he will to save them, but they refused? Where then is that omnipotence of God?"[328] (*On Predestination*, 6). And:

> For those who say that God, who generally and universally, equally and without distinction *wills all men to be saved* (1 Tm 2:4), saves the elect because they will to be saved and does not save the reprobate because they themselves do not will to be saved, certainly deny God's grace in the elect and deny, although unknowingly, God's omnipotence in the reprobate[329] (*On Predestination*, 9).

4. *Humankind is divided into two groups, the elect and the reprobate. The elect cannot be lost to God and become reprobate.*

"For there are two bodies: one Christ's and the other antichrist's, and each one consists of the wholeness or plenitude of its members"[330] (*On Predestination*, 3.3).

"The reprobate are not the city of God, but the city of devil"[331] (*On Predestination*, 3.4).

---

because he wills, not because he does not will" (*On Predestination*, 9. Lambot, 238) and: "He hardens with no iniquity" (*On Predestination*, 9. Lambot, 237).

325 Lambot, 185.

326 Lambot, 40. Translation by Gumerlock.

327 Lambot, 40. Translation by Gumerlock.

328 Lambot, 229.

329 Lambot, 239.

330 Lambot, 203.

331 Lambot, 206.

"There are... two kinds of human beings in the one human race"[332] (*On Predestination*, 4.1).

"Those who are redeemed by Christ's death do not perish, but only the reprobate, slain by deadly outrages and crimes"[333] (*On Predestination*, 6).

"And so it is seen quite clearly that no one who has been redeemed by the blood of your cross ever perishes for you"[334] (*Tome to Gislemar*, 5).

"God forbid that I should ever want even to dream or only to whisper that the ancient serpent might be able to carry off with him into eternal perdition any of those for whose redemption such precious blood of our Lord his Son has been poured out to God the Father. Amen"[335] (*Tome to Gislemar*, 1).

5. *Christ redeemed only the elect.*

"Our omnipotent God, the creator and maker of all creatures, has deigned to be the gratuitous repairer and restorer of all of the elect alone, but willed to be the Savior of none of the perpetually reprobate, the redeemer of none, the glorifier of none"[336] (*Reply to Rabanus Maurus*, 9).

"But he who says that the Lord suffered in general for the salvation and redemption of all, that is, of both the elect and the reprobate, contradicts God the Father himself"[337] (*Tome to Gislemar*, 2).

"For he bought them [the reprobate] by the sacrament of baptism, but did not suffer the cross, undergo death, or shed his blood for them"[338] (*Tome to Gislemar*, 3).

"We of course correctly believe, rightly hope and trust that the body and blood of Christ were handed over and shed for the church of Christ alone"[339] (*On Predestination*, 1.9).

"[The psalmist] declares that the reprobate were neither redeemed nor set free by God through the blood of Christ's cross"[340] (*On Predestination*, 1.9).

"For that God did not suffer for the baptized reprobate is clearly seen from the fact that the devil conquers them and subjects them to himself"[341] (*On Predestination*, 5).

"Christ redeemed only his holy church and only the elect, that is, only his body and members, through the blood of his cross; he was certainly crucified

332 Lambot, 213.

333 Lambot, 225.

334 Lambot, 44.

335 Lambot, 41-2.

336 Lambot, 41. Translation by Gumerlock.

337 Lambot, 42. Translation by Gumerlock.

338 Lambot, 43. Translation by Gumerlock.

339 Lambot, 188.

340 Lambot, 190.

341 Lambot, 218.

only for them, and he undoubtedly suffered the death of the cross, which was the most disgraceful, ignominious, and shameful death of that time, only for them"[342] (*On Predestination*, 11).

"Finally, the Lord suffered only for the elect"[343] (*On Predestination*, 6).

6. Since the Fall humans can do only evil. It is only God's grace that enables them to do good. The reprobate do not have that grace.

"For from the time he became *a slave of sin* (Jn 8:34), he is of course shown to have had free choice only for doing evil, as someone completely lost"[344] (*On Predestination*, 10).

"Anticipating the unwilling man, it [mercy] makes him to will in a good way, and it follows the willing man so that he can [continue to will good]"[345] (*On Predestination*, 8).

"The will that God gave to the elect is present for them, but they do not find how to carry out the good."[346] (*On Predestination*, 9).

"It is clear without a scruple, is evident without ambiguity, and is manifest without a cloud that, just as the reprobate do not have it [freedom] for acting well, but for acting wrongly, so they certainly do not have it for speaking the truth, but for lying"[347] (*Answers to Various Questions*, 3).

7. Baptism liberates only from past sins and therefore is of no avail for the salvation of the reprobate.

"Redemption that takes place in baptism is common to the elect and the reprobate, for both are completely redeemed from past sins"[348] (*On Different Ways of Speaking about Redemption*).

"But that redemption that is brought about by the grace of baptism... which is common to the elect and the reprobate, ... washes away past sins, but does not redeem from future sins"[349] (*On Predestination*, 5).

"At the same time know and also say to yourself joyfully that the redemption that takes place in baptism from past sins is common to the elect and the reprobate. ... After this redemption all the reprobate, the members of antichrist, ... perish"[350] (*On Predestination*, 6).

---

342 Lambot, 243.

343 Lambot, 226.

344 Lambot, 241.

345 Lambot, 234.

346 Lambot, 240.

347 Lambot, 151.

348 Lambot, 279-80.

349 Lambot, 221-2.

350 Lambot, 226.

"That redemption of baptism is similarly common, by which both [elect and reprobate] are redeemed from their past original and personal sins"[351] (*Another Treatise on Predestination*, 1).

"He clearly did not redeem, while hanging on the cross, any crime of any reprobate, even if baptized, however small and insignificant a crime, that any of them commit after the redemption of baptism, although he certainly redeemed all the sins of all the elect"[352] (*Another Treatise on Predestination*, 1).

8. The Eucharist that is received by the reprobate is of no avail for their salvation.

"The body and blood of Christ remains unto salvation and prevails as a remedy unto eternal life only in those who are the body of Christ, not in the members of devil and the body of antichrist"[353] (*On Predestination*, 1.9).

"For the bread and wine, that is, the body and blood of the Lord, are eaten and drunk by many unto their judgment,[354] for they do not have the Holy Spirit with which the elect are filled"[355] (*On Predestination*, 1.13).

"For the reprobate world that eats and drinks in an unworthy manner *eats and drinks judgment upon itself* (1 Cor 11:29)"[356] (*On the Body and Blood of the Lord*).

TOPICS FOR FURTHER RESEARCH

Gottschalk and Augustine. Since Gottschalk's teaching is largely based on that of Augustine, questions naturally arise about the correlation of their two systems. Such an examination is beyond the scope of the present introduction, but a few preliminary considerations may be set forth.

If it was anthropology that often constituted the starting point of Augustine's reasoning, this is not the case with Gottschalk. The immutable God fascinated him, very much in line with certain views of Plato, whom the rebellious Benedictine highly esteemed, and he wrote that God's wisdom spoke through this pagan.[357] It is the unalterable creator that stands in the center of Gottschalk's teaching; he indeed cared much less about fluid, variable creatures like human beings.

Gottschalk and Pastoral Theology. It is undeniable that such a break with the previous anthropocentric tradition was outstanding, but it is no less undeniable that Gottschalk's theocentrism ran counter to pastoral theology. It is there that the reasons of the violent reaction of many contemporary church leaders to his

351 Lambot, 342-3.

352 Lambot, 343.

353 Lambot, 189.

354 See 1 Cor 11:29.

355 Lambot, 195.

356 Lambot, 330.

357 Lambot, 476.

teaching are to be found. Amolo of Lyons, whose position towards the condemned monk was one of the most brotherly and compassionate, still wrote to him:

> And you exhort the bishops, to whom you write, as if compassionately, that they should preach to people that since they cannot escape the predetermined condemnation, they should plead with God a little and humble themselves so that he may soften a little and lighten the punishments established for them. I ask, where in the sacred scriptures did you ever read that? Where did you find that in the holy and catholic doctors of the church? ...Or what more do you leave to them whom you say have been similarly condemned to an irrevocable sentence?"[358]

It is very understandable that Gottschalk's teaching would have produced on parishioners in recently Christianized areas the effect described by Rabanus: "Why is it necessary for me to work for my salvation and eternal life? For if I do good but I have not been predestined to life, it profits me nothing. But if I do evil, it is in no way an obstacle to me. For the predestination of God causes me to come to eternal life."[359] Further research comparing Gottschalk's writings with those of Prudentius, Ratramnus, Lupus, and Florus may reveal to what extent our Benedictine disregarded reservations that made the ideas of others who disagreed with Hincmar and Rabanus much less scandalous, if at all, for bishops and abbots.

To a certain extent what bothered people was not so much in *what* actually Gottschalk taught, but *how* he did it. His behavior patterns sometimes bordered on those of a sociopath, and any compromise was abhorrent to him. Only God and his own certitude in God-given truth mattered. Anything else did not, conventionalities of the human society and the visible church included. It was the invisible that led him through his earthly pilgrimage. In some respects Gottschalk's such deep religious subjectivity resembles later Christian mystics like Bernard of Clairvaux or Richard of Saint-Victor.

Gottschalk's Gnoseology and Logic. Gottschalk's gnoseology has also not yet been an object of thorough scrutiny, an investigation which may turn out to be very fruitful. What is indeed striking is that Gottschalk's theology is altogether rational, and his confidence in reason is almost boundless. He uses "inevitably captious" syllogisms throughout, giving Aristotle his due no less than Plato.[360] Actually, formal logic is the basis of his whole system as well as the basis of his nearly unlimited assuredness in its verity.

Indeed, it is *logical* that God should not will all men to be saved. If he willed that, he would not be omnipotent, since in fact all men are not saved. But he is omnipotent, ergo he does not will all men to be saved. Here are a few more striking examples of Gottschalk's method of reasoning:

358 Amolo, *Letter to Gottschalk*, 5 (PL 116:92A-B).

359 Rabanus, *Letter to Eberhard* (PL 112:1554B-C).

360 Gottschalk, *On Predestination*, 3.5 (Lambot, 206).

> For if the baptized reprobate were redeemed through the blood of Christ's cross, they were therefore also saved and set free by him. But those who have been quite rightly already judged, already condemned, already predestined to eternal death by Christ himself and, as has been said, rightly hurled down into it, were not saved and set free by him. Therefore, they were not redeemed by the blood of his cross[361] (*On Predestination*, 1.3).

"If Christ redeemed by his blood the baptized reprobate, then he undoubtedly will hand them over to contemplate his Father. But he will not hand them over to contemplate his Father. Therefore, he did not redeem them by his blood"[362] (*On Predestination*, 4.2).

> However, I want also prudently to add this, asking that most wicked scoundrel to which of the two worlds he thinks the baptized reprobate belong according to the just judgment of God, that is, to the reconciled and cleansed world or to the hostile, condemned, and polluted world? If he says that they belong to the reconciled, saved, and cleansed world, you will tell him: Therefore they have been reconciled, saved, and cleansed by the death of the Son of God and for that reason they *will be saved from wrath through him* (Rom 5:9)? If, whether he likes it or not, he sees and says that this is not true and for this reason answers that they rather belong to the hostile, condemned, and polluted world, consequently draw a conclusion and refute him by cornering him, saying cheerfully and confidently: Therefore, whether you like it or not, you finally are forced to believe, understand, and confess that Christ, the Son of God, by no means redeemed by the blood of his cross the baptized reprobate, whom he does not have as reconciled, saved perpetually, and cleansed[363] (*On Predestination*, 6).

Gottschalk's use of logic and rational approach to the issues he treats, as shown in the quotations above, lend support for regarding him as a forerunner of early scholastics together with Anselm of Canterbury and Berengar of Tours.

The details set forth in this essay about the life and thought of Gottschalk, as well as the controversy he provoked, provide context for the texts in this volume, most of which are translated into English for the first time here. The nine treatises of Gottschalk are presented in the order which they appear in Lambot's edition. Providing further context for the predestination controversy of the ninth century, eleven other writings by Rabanus Maurus, Hincmar of Reims, Amolo of Lyons, and Florus of Lyons are included.

Truly "all things past have not had a future." But they surely will. For it is my hope that these translated texts become a wellspring of research for historians and theologians.

361 Lambot, 182.

362 Lambot, 217.

363 Lambot, 230.

PART I:
WRITINGS OF GOTTSCHALK

REPLY TO RABANUS MAURUS

In the late 830s Gottschalk traveled to northern Italy and the Balkans teaching his views on divine predestination. These opinions, or negative implications construed from them, had upset a number of notable Christian leaders, one of whom was Noting, bishop elect of Verona. Noting heard Gottschalk teach on predestination at a hospice of Count Eberhard, and informed Rabanus Maurus, who promised to write him a treatise on predestination. In May of 840 Rabanus, abbot of the monastery at Fulda, wrote *On Predestination* (*De praedestinatione*, PL 112:1531-53) against Gottschalk. Around 846, Rabanus wrote a *Letter to Eberhard* (*Epistola ad Eberhardum*, PL 112:1553-62) against Gottschalk's doctrine. It is unclear against which of these Gottschalk's *Reply to Rabanus Maurus* (*Responsum ad Rabanum Maurum*) is directed. The reply must be dated after 842, when Rabanus became archbishop of Mainz, for Gottschalk calls him "bishop," and before 849, when Hincmar, archbishop of Reims, described Gottschalk's reply in his *Letter to the Monks and Simple Folk of his Diocese* (*Epistola ad reclusos et simplices suae dioeceseos*. Lambot, 9). Most likely among the works that Gottschalk was forced to burn, only nine fragments of it have survived, preserved mainly in Hincmar's *On Predestination* (*De praedestinatione*, PL 125:49-474). According to Hincmar, it collected and brought together teaching on predestination gathered from scripture and the catholic fathers.[1] Editions: Lambot, 37-41; PL 121:365-8. Translated by Francis X. Gumerlock.

1. I have at last, venerable bishop, read your book,[2] in which I found it set forth that the impious or the reprobate are not also divinely predestined to damnation.[3]

---

1 Hincmar's *Letter to the Monks and Simple Folk of his Diocese* (*Epistola ad reclusos et simplices suae dioeceseos*) in Lambot, 9.

2 Either Rabanus' *On Predestination* (*De praedestinatione*, PL 112:1531-53) or his *Letter to Eberhard* (*Epistola ad Eberhardum*, PL 112:1553-62). John Alzog (*Manual of Universal Church History*, Vol. 2 [Cincinnati: Robert Clarke & Co., 1876], 427) thought it was the former.

3 Fragment 12. Lambot, 37.

2. I say that he [God] foreknew that they were going to have a very bad birth and a worse death, but he predestined them to suffer eternal torment and everlasting destruction.[4]

3. Just as he truly predestined all of the elect to life through the gratuitous benefit of his grace alone, as the pages of the Old and New Testaments offer a very clear proof to those who consider them skillfully and soberly, so he also absolutely predestined any reprobate to the punishment of eternal death, that is, through the most just judgment of his immutable justice.[5]

4. Blessed Augustine said: "If [Judas] were created like this, then he would be blameless, and it would be imputed to the work of God, not of Judas, and the condemnation would have been leveled against him unjustly."[6] And Peter said: *For them judgment from long ago is not idle, and their destruction does not slumber* (2 Pt 2:3). And Jude said: *Certain ungodly persons crept in, who long ago were marked out for this judgment* (Jude 4).[7]

5. What is to be held and be believed by the church of Christ, that is, about free will has—thank God!—been clearly discussed by some of the catholic fathers and is known to have been taught more fully and richly, especially by blessed Augustine against the Pelagians and Celestians in his diverse little works and most of all in his *Hypomnesticon*. Hence, I would also have incomparably preferred that you rely on the most fruitful statements of the same most catholic teacher on this rather than on the erroneous opinions of Gennadius of Marseilles, who presumed in many places to resist the most irrefutable authorities of both the catholic faith and the blessed fathers, following the extremely pernicious dogma of the wretched Cassian.[8]

6. *All* those whom God *wills to be saved* (1 Tm 2:4) are without doubt saved, nor can any be saved but those God wills to be saved. Nor is there any one whom God wills to be saved, and is not saved, since our God *has done* all things *whatever he willed* (Ps 134:6).[9] They therefore are all saved—all whom he wills to be saved.

---

4 Fragment 13. Lambot, 37-8.

5 Fragment 14. Lambot, 38.

6 Pseudo-Augustine, *Hypomnesticon against the Pelagians and Celestians* (*Hypomnesticon contra Pelagianos et Caelestianos*), 6.5, 7 (PL 45:1661).

7 Fragment 16. Lambot, 39.

8 Fragment 17. Lambot, 39. Gennadius of Marseilles (c. 495) rejected predestination. See Ralph W. Mathisen, *Ecclesiastical Factionalism and Religious Controversy in Fifth-Century Gaul* (Washington, D.C.: Catholic University of America Press, 1989), 245. John Cassian (d. 435) was a leading Gallic opponent of Augustine's doctrine of predestination.

9 Fragment 18. Lambot, 40.

7. "All" and "every" have to be understood, that is, as all who are saved, about whom the Apostle says: *Who wills all men to be saved* (1 Tm 2:4), and all who are not saved, whom God does not will to be saved.[10]

8. All those impious persons and sinners for whom the Son of God came to redeem by shedding his own blood, those the omnipotent goodness of God predestined to life and irrevocably willed only those to be saved. And again all those impious persons and sinners for whom likewise the Son of God neither assumed a body nor prayed, I say that he did not shed [his] blood nor was in any way crucified for them. In fact, those whom he foreknew were going to be very evil and whom he very justly foreordained unto eternal torments into which they should be cast, he thoroughly does not want them in any way to be eternally saved.[11]

9. Therefore, I very faithfully believe, very confidently speak, and likewise most certainly and fruitfully confess and most truthfully profess that our omnipotent God, the creator and maker of all creatures, has deigned to be the gratuitous repairer and restorer of all of the elect alone, but willed to be the Savior of none of the perpetually reprobate, the redeemer of none, and glorifier of none.[12]

---

10 Fragment 19. Lambot, 40.

11 Fragment 20. Lambot, 40.

12 Fragment 21. Lambot, 41.

CONFESSION OF FAITH AT MAINZ

Upon his return from Frioul, Gottschalk stayed for some time at Fulda, sheltered by abbot Hatto, and then presented himself at the diet of Mainz that was opened October 1, 848. There he produced two writings: a *Reply to Rabanus Maurus* (*Responsum ad Rabanum Maurum*) as well as the present *Confession of Faith* (*Chartula suae professionis ad Rabanum episcopum*), preserved by Hincmar of Reims in his second *On Predestination* (*De praedestinatione*). Editions: Lambot, 38; PL 125:89-90. Translated by Victor Genke.

I, Gottschalk, believe and confess, profess and testify from God the Father through God the Son in God the Holy Spirit, and both affirm and approve before God and his saints that "predestination is twofold, either of the elect to rest or of the reprobate to death."[1] For just as immutable God before the foundation of the world immutably predestined to eternal life all his elect through his gratuitous grace, the same immutable God through his just judgment likewise immutably predestined to deservedly eternal death absolutely all the reprobate, who at the judgment day will be condemned because of their evil merits.

1 Isidore of Seville, *Sentences* (*Sententiae*), 2.6, 1 (CCSL 111:103; PL 83:606A).

TOME TO GISLEMAR

According to Hincmar's *Letter to the Monks and Simple Folk of his Diocese* (*Epistola ad reclusos et simplices suae dioeceseos*. Gundlach, ed., 261-2), in the year 849 three of Gottschalk's writings fell into Hincmar's hands: *Tome to Gislemar* (*Tomus ad Gislemarum*), *Reply to Rabanus Maurus* (*Responsum ad Rabanum Maurum*) and *Shorter Confession* (*Confessio Brevior*). Hincmar referred to the *Tome to Gislemar* in three places as "the accursed writing to Gislemar" (*maledicto scripto ad Gislemarum*, Gundlach, 271), "the tome he had composed to a certain monk" (*pitacio quod ad quemdam monachum composuerat*, PL 125:369) and a writing addressed "to a certain friend" (*ad quemdam complicem*, PL 125:291). Hincmar preserved fragments of it in his *Letter to the Monks and Simple Folk of his Diocese* and his second work *On Predestination* (*De praedestinatione*). Gislemar was a monk of Corbie who accompanied Anskar in his mission to Scandinavia. Editions: Lambot, 9, 41-44; Gundlach, 271; PL 125:370-2. Translated by Victor Genke.

1. God forbid that I should ever want even to dream or only to whisper that the ancient serpent might be able to carry off with him into eternal perdition any[1] of those for whose redemption such precious blood of our Lord his Son has been poured out to God the Father. Amen.[2]

2. But he who says because of these testimonies and other similar to them that the Lord suffered in general for the salvation and redemption of all, that is, of both the elect and the reprobate, contradicts God the Father himself.[3]

3. Nonetheless, because on account of original sin and also every actual sin, the elect and the reprobate were held, are held, and will be held captive under the devil until they have been redeemed and are redeemed by God through baptismal grace, whenever any of us were baptized in the name of the Trinity, we were then undoubtedly whether elect or reprobate, redeemed in common, that is, snatched and set free from the dominion of demonic power, and whenever anyone is baptized and will be baptized thereafter until the day of judgment, they are then redeemed and will be redeemed, that is, are snatched and set free or will be snatched and set free from diabolical captivity. Here belongs what apostle Peter says about the false teachers and those who introduced sects of destruction and bring upon themselves swift destruction: *Denying*, he says,

---

1 Lambot's edition on page 41 has *nullum* "none," but page 44 contains the correct reading *ullum* "any."

2 Fragment 22. Lambot, 41-2.

3 Fragment 23. Lambot, 42.

the Lord who bought them (2 Pt 2:1). For he bought them by the sacrament of baptism, but did not suffer the cross, undergo death, or shed his blood for them. However, the teacher of the Gentiles clearly says that the reception of baptism is called redemption: *Do not grieve the Holy Spirit of God,* he says, *by whom you were sealed for the day of redemption* (Eph 4:30), and he says above in the same *Letter to the Ephesians*: *And believing in him, you were sealed with the Holy Spirit of promise* (Eph 1:13). Concerning this Saint Jerome also speaks, when he says: "He found redemption from the old sins in the waters of baptism,"[4] but such a redemption, which is common to both the elect and the reprobate, redeems only from the past sins.[5]

4. But that which is proper and specific only to all of the elect, which their loving, crucified redeemer imparted only to them, redeemed, rescued, and cleansed those born and going to be born, the living and the dead, that is, all the elect from both past and present sins. These, of course, these[6] are the world for which the Lord suffered, as he himself says: *The bread that I will give is my flesh for the life of the world* (Jn 6:52).[7]

5. And so it is seen quite clearly that no one who has been redeemed by the blood of your cross ever perishes for you.[8]

6. And so when we hear: *Have I not chosen twelve of you, but one of you is a devil?* (Jn 6:71), we ought to understand that they were chosen through mercy, but that he was chosen through justice. Therefore, he chose them to obtain the kingdom, but him to shed his blood.[9]

---

4 Jerome, *Letters* (*Epistolae*), 108.11 (CSEL 55:319; PL 22:886).

5 Fragment 24. Lambot, 42-3.

6 The Latin *ipsi* is repeated.

7 Fragment 25. Lambot, 43-4.

8 Fragment 26. Lambot, 44.

9 Fragment 1. Lambot, 9.

SHORTER CONFESSION

According to Prichard (p. 140-2), the circumstances of Gottschalk's confessions were as follows. Immediately after the council at Quierzy in the spring of 849, Hincmar wrote a letter or treatise showing from the church fathers that predestination does not extend to evil, but only to the good. "Hincmar tried in vain to *persuade* Godeschalcus to subscribe this article of faith and finding him determined in his refusal, wrote to Prudentius, bishop of Troyes, who had been prevented from attending the synod, to beg his advice.... Prudentius...prayed Hincmar to grant him [Gottschalk] the unusual permission to write his own confession of faith, instead of being forced to subscribe the exact words agreed upon by the Council. Hincmar complied with this request, and Godeschalcus accordingly wrote two confessions, one of considerable length, and the other more concise." Gustavsson (p. 33) dated this *Shorter Confession* (*Confessio Brevior*) to the early part of Gottschalk's confinement at Hautvillers about 849. However, Boller (p. 240) assigned this writing of Gottschalk to the year 840 when he was staying with Count Eberhard. It begins with a brief statement of Gottschalk's belief in twofold predestination, followed by a defense of its catholicity through testimonies from scripture and the fathers. Editions: Lambot, 52-4 entitled *Confession of Gottschalk the Condemned Monk* (*Confessio Godescalchi monachi damnati*); Perugi, 86-8; PL 121:347-50 entitled *Confession of the Monk Gottschalk after his Heresy was Condemned* (*Confessio Gotteschalci monachi post haeresim damnatam*); Mauguin, 7; Ussher, 211-3 entitled *Shorter Confession of Gottschalk* (*Gotteschalci confessio brevior*). Translated by Francis X. Gumerlock.

I believe and confess that the omnipotent and immutable God has gratuitously foreknown and predestined the holy angels and elect human beings to eternal life, and that he equally predestined the devil himself, the head of all the demons, with all of his apostate angels and also with all reprobate human beings, namely, his members, to rightly eternal death, on account of their own future, most certainly foreknown evil merits, through his most righteous judgment.

This the Lord himself says in the Gospel: *The prince of this world already has been judged* (Jn 16:11). Explaining this, Augustine spoke plainly to the people on it, that is: "He has been destined irrevocably for the judgment of eternal fire."[1] Again the Truth himself says concerning the reprobate: *But the one who does not believe has already been judged* (Jn 3:18), that is, as the aforementioned author explained: "Has already been condemned."[2] "The judgment," he says, "has not

1 Augustine, *Homilies on the Gospel of John* (*In Iohannis evangelium tractatus*), 95.4 (PL 35:1873).

2 Augustine, *On the Christian Struggle* (*De agone christiano*), 27.29 (PL 40:305).

yet appeared, but judgment has already taken place."[3] Likewise explaining that saying of John the Baptist: *No one receives his testimony* (Jn 3:32), he says this: "'No one' is a certain people, prepared for the wrath of God, to be condemned with the devil."[4] Likewise he refers to the Jews as "those rebellious dead, who are also predestined to eternal death."[5] Likewise he says: "Why did the Lord say to the Jews: *You do not believe, because you are not of my sheep* (Jn 10:26), except that he saw that they were predestined to eternal destruction, not purchased for eternal life with the price of his blood?"[6] Likewise, explaining those words of the Lord: *My sheep hear my voice, and I know them, and they follow me, and I give them eternal life, and they will never perish, and no one will snatch them out of my hand. That which my Father has given to me, is greater than all, and no one is able to snatch them out of the hand of my Father* (Jn 10:27-29), he said this: "What can the wolf do? What can the thief and robber do? They destroy only those predestined to destruction."[7] Likewise, speaking about two worlds, he says: "The whole world is the church, and the whole world hates the church. Therefore, the world hates the world. The hostile world hates the reconciled world. The condemned world hates the saved world. The polluted world hates the cleansed world."[8] Likewise: "There is a world about which the Apostle says: *Lest we be condemned with the world* (1 Cor 11:32). For that world the Lord does not pray,[9] for he is not unaware of that for which it has been predestined."[10] Likewise he says: "Judas, the betrayer of Christ, was called the son of perdition, because he was predestined to perdition."[11] Likewise in the *Enchiridion* he says: "To the damnation of those whom he justly predestined to punishment."[12] Likewise in the book, *On the Perfection of Human Righteousness*, he said: "There was no one who would do this good, which is to seek after God; there was not even one,[13] but in that kind of people which was predestined to destruction. For upon them, the foreknowledge of God looked and passed sentence."[14] Likewise in the books *On*

3 Augustine, *Homilies on the Gospel of John*, 12.12 (PL 35:1490).

4 Augustine, *Homilies on the Gospel of John*, 14.8 (PL 35:1507).

5 Augustine, *Homilies on the Gospel of John*, 43.13 (PL 35:1711).

6 Augustine, *Homilies on the Gospel of John*, 48.4 (PL 35:1742).

7 Augustine, *Homilies on the Gospel of John*, 48.6 (PL 35:1743).

8 Augustine, *Homilies on the Gospel of John*, 87.2 (PL 35:1853).

9 See Jn 17:9.

10 Augustine, *Homilies on the Gospel of John*, 110.2 (PL 35:1921).

11 Augustine, *Homilies on the Gospel of John*, 107.7 (PL 35:1914).

12 Augustine, *Enchiridion on Faith, Hope, and Love* (*Enchiridion de fide, spe, et caritate*), 100.26 (PL 40:279).

13 See Ps 13:13.

14 Augustine, *On the Perfection of Human Righteousness* (*De perfectione iustitiae hominis*), 13.31 (CSEL 42:32; PL 44 :308).

the City of God he says: "What will he who gave these things even to those whom he has predestined to death give to those whom he has predestined to life?"[15]

Likewise blessed Pope Gregory said: "This leviathan with all of his members has been assigned to eternal torments."[16]

Likewise Saint Fulgentius in the third book *On the Truth of Predestination and Grace* says: "God prepared punishments for sinners, for those of course whom he justly predestined to suffer punishments."[17] And blessed Fulgentius composed an entire book on this question alone, that is, *On the Predestination of the Reprobate to Destruction*, for his friend named Monimus.[18]

Hence, Saint Isidore also says: "Predestination is twofold, either of the elect to rest or of the reprobate to death."[19]

So too I believe and confess in every respect with these elect of God and catholics, as I am helped, inspired, animated, and armed by God.

For he is a false witness who corrupts either the meaning or the wording in the statements of any of these.

---

15 Augustine, *On the City of God* (*De civitate dei*), 22.24.5 (CSEL 40.2:649; PL 41:792).

16 Gregory the Great, *Moral Commentary on Job* (*Moralia in Iob*), 34.2.4 (PL 76:719C).

17 Fulgentius of Ruspe, *On the Truth of Predestination and Grace* (*De veritate praedestinationis et gratiae*), 3.5.8 (CCSL 91A:527; PL 65:656A).

18 Fulgentius, *To Monimus* (*Ad Monimum*), Book 1 (CCSL 91:3-33; PL 65:153-78).

19 Isidore of Seville, *Sentences* (*Sententiae*), 2.6.1 (CCSL 111:103; PL 83:606A).

LONGER CONFESSION

If Prichard's narrative (pp. 140-2) of the circumstances surrounding Gottschalk's confessions is correct, this *Longer Confession* (*Confessio prolixior*) may have been a response to Hincmar's disapproval of Gottschalk's *Shorter Confession* (*Confessio brevior*) which asserted twofold predestination. For in this longer confession Gottschalk clarifies that predestination is one, but has two aspects to it. Cross and Livingstone (p. 696) and Gustavvson (pp. 32-3) suggest that Gottschalk wrote this confession in response to Hincmar's *Letter to the Monks and Simple Folk of his Diocese* (*Ad reclusos et simplices suae dioeceseos*). Composed in the form of a long prayer, the *Longer Confession* is essentially an explanation of his doctrine of the predestination of the reprobate to eternal punishment, which, he argues, is a catholic truth. Based upon internal evidence, the date of its composition is generally agreed to be 849 or early in 850, after his imprisonment at Hautvillers. Editions: Lambot, 55-78; Perugi, 89-114; PL 121:349-66; Ussher, 211-33. Its title seems to have been assigned by Ussher. The subheadings and their numbers were added by the present translator, Francis X. Gumerlock.[1]

Opening Prayer

1. Master, Lord, my God, my mercy, all powerful king, incomparably clement, and also patient with inestimable kindness toward the human race and deeply wise with unsearchable depth, whom all of your elect truly always need, that is, in order that they may be able to please you from yourself alone, as branches need a vine so that they can bear fruit or as air and eyes need light in order that it may be bright and they may see. Otherwise, branches without their vine dry up and consequently, having been thrown into fire, are burned. And without light air is dark, and eyes are open in vain. Therefore, as a suppliant, I call upon you, Lord God, most almighty, most merciful, and most glorious, three and one, that you gratuitously may deign to be my most loving helper and hearer and that you may most kindly bestow upon me, who am very needy, through the invincible power of your gratuitous grace, that I may now truthfully and simply *confess with* my *mouth unto salvation* what from you, through you, and in you I have long *believed in* my *heart unto righteousness* (Rom 10:9-10), thanks to you, about your foreknowledge and predestination, as I have already repeatedly

1 I am indebted to Ronald Hanko, whose earlier English translation of this *Longer Confession* in "Gottschalk's Doctrine of Double Predestination," *Protestant Reformed Theological Journal* 12:1 (1978):31-61, was helpful in many places, and to Father Roland Teske of Marquette University, whose expertise in medieval Latin was very helpful.

confessed it through your grace, in order that at long last the truth invincible and blessed without end may on my part be disclosed to your elect and may likewise finally bring it about that falsehood is defeated and also justly accursed, as it ought. Amen.

The Reprobate Are Predestined to Punishment

2. I believe and also confess that you have foreknown before the ages whatever things were going to happen, whether good or bad, but you have predestined only good things. However, the good things have been predestined in a twofold manner, as investigated by your faithful—indeed, it is clearly agreed that they were taught to them through your revelation—that is, the benefits of grace and at the same time the judgments of justice. For as the psalmist offers the surest proof, you, Lord, love both, that is, both both *mercy and judgment* (Ps 32:5). And so you have freely predestined eternal life in all your elect and also predestined them unto everlasting glory. For you would certainly have predestined life for them in vain if you had not also predestined them to it. So also, in nearly the same way, you deservedly predestined everlasting punishment *for the devil and his angels* (Mt 25:41) and also for all the reprobate and similarly predestined the same for it.

For you would of course have predestined the punishment of eternal death for them without reason unless you had also predestined them for it. For they would not go to it unless they were destined, and they would not of course be destined unless they had been predestined, since you always existed before all ages, because you cannot be mutable in any way even for a moment. And you would be shown to be mutable through all ages thereafter, if—God forbid!—any of the reprobate were destined for that, who had not been predestined.

God's Immutable Foreknowledge and Predestination

3. Hence, since you alone, Lord, are who are, as you yourself testify,[2] and as David also says to you: *You are always the same* (Ps 101:27), and as you yourself also say elsewhere: *Lord,* you are *and* you *do not change* (Mal 3:6), and as your outstanding preacher Paul shows that you *alone possess immortality* (1 Tm 6:16), that is, immutability, *with whom,* as is nonetheless asserted by another apostle, *there is neither variation nor shadow of change* (Jas 1:17), it is certainly evident and sufficiently clear and obvious to anyone with sound wisdom that you have foreknown and predestined instantly, that is, without any interval, that is, at one and the same time before the ages, each and every one of your works, for according to what was said by Isaiah: *You have produced the things that will be* (Is 45:11, LXX).

Hence, your most faithful servant Augustine also says this, following and most truly expounding the prophet David: "God," he says, "according to that will of his,

2 See Ex 3:14.

which is everlasting along with his foreknowledge, has already made all things that *he willed in heaven and on earth* (Ps 134:6), not only past and present things, but also those that are future."[3]

Therefore, Lord, since your will is everlasting along with your foreknowledge, as Augustine says here, and since with your omnipotence, to foreknow is the same as to will, at least concerning your works, according to what Orosius writes to the same Augustine;[4] and since for you to will is also the same as to have done, according to what Ambrose says,[5] it is undoubtedly clear that whatever is going to be externally in your works has already been done by you in predestination, according to what Pope Gregory *boldly says* (Rom 10:20), teaches, and writes.[6] God forbid, therefore, that any of your catholics may ever suspect that that there was an interval even of a moment between the foreknowledge and predestination of your works, since one reads or hears and believes that you *have done* at the same time *everything that* you *have willed* (Ps 113:3), especially since you have done nothing whatsoever in effect before you incomparably foreknew that they would be future and arranged them by predestining them in your eternal counsel.

Testimonies of the Prophets with Catholic Explanations

4. But now, Lord, it is time that the truthful testimonies of the divine books be brought forward, in which it is taught without scruple and is declared without ambiguity that the reprobate have been predestined to the flames of eternal torments. And, Lord Jesus Christ, invincible Truth, I think that your words should rightly to be brought forth first: *The one who does not believe*, you say, *has already been judged* (Jn 3:18), that is, as Augustine explained: "Has already been condemned."[7] For "the judgment," he says, "has not yet appeared, but the judgment has already taken place."[8] Likewise you say: *The prince of this world has already been judged* (Jn 16:11), that is, as the same Augustine explained: "He has been destined irrevocably for the judgment of eternal fire."[9]

David also says: *Therefore, the ungodly will not rise up in the judgment* (Ps 1:5). Augustine explains: "Because they have already been destined to most certain punishments."[10] Likewise he says: *You have struck all who are opposed to me without*

3 Augustine, *On the City of God* (*De civitate dei*), 22.2, 1 (PL 41:753).

4 Paul Orosius, *Seven Book of Histories* (*Historiarum libri septem*), 1 (PL 31:1061C).

5 Ambrose, *On the Death of his Brother, Satyr* (*De excessu fratris sui Satyri*), 2.114 (PL 16:1349A).

6 Gregory the Great, *Moral Commentary on Job* (*Moralia in Iob*), 28.5, 14 (PL 76:456B).

7 Augustine, *On the Christian Struggle* (*De agone christiano*), 27.29 (PL 40:305).

8 Augustine, *Homilies on the Gospel of John* (*In Iohannis evangelium tractatus*), 12.12 (PL 35:1490).

9 Augustine, *Homilies on the Gospel of John*, 95.4 (PL 35:1873).

10 Augustine, *Homilies on the Psalms* (*Enarrationes in psalmos*), 1.5 (PL 36:69).

cause (Ps 3:8). He says: "This is correctly said about the devil and his angels in predestination."[11]

And lest it be said that only the devil and his angels have been destined to death, something that is clearly proven to be entirely absurd, namely, that the head should be separated from the body in predestining,[12] David says again: *You have brought me down into the dust of death* (Ps 21:16), that is, "the impious destined to death,"[13] which none of the wise at all doubts was said about human beings, that is, those made from dust and also left for dust.[14]

Solomon also says: *The Lord has made all things for himself, even the impious for the evil day* (Prv 16:4). Also, in the book of Ecclesiasticus, it is said in this manner: *God has prepared for the sword the one who crosses over from righteousness to sin* (Sir 26:27), which clearly should be understood to have been said only about the people of the reprobate.

On this Job also says: *Ask anyone of the travelers; you may learn that he understands these same things, namely, that a wicked person is kept for the day of destruction and is led to the day of wrath* (Jb 21:29-30). Gregory, the expositor of this passage, explains it in this manner: "The divine patience," he says, "often tolerates for a long time those whom it has already condemned to foreknown punishments."[15] Hence, when he explained the passage: *He has counsel and strength* (Jb 12:13), he says among other things:

> That hidden delay of judgment can also be signified by the term 'counsel.' For he sometimes strikes down evil doers more slowly, not because the guilt of the wicked is unseen, but rather so that the sentence of their damnation, which is deferred for doing penance, is ordered to proceed as if slowly and by counsel. Therefore, what was at some time disclosed externally lay hidden with the omnipotent God in his counsel before the ages.[16]

Likewise explaining the passage: *You have determined his limits, which cannot be passed* (Jb 14:5), he says: "Nothing that happens to people in this world comes to pass without the hidden counsel of omnipotent God. For God, foreknowing

11 Augustine, *Homilies on the Psalms*, 3.10 (PL 36:78).

12 The hermeneutical principle of "head and body" had been firmly established in western exegetical tradition, due in large part to the influence of Tyconius' rules of interpretation promoted by and through Augustine. See Augustine, *On Christian Teaching* (*De doctrina Christiana*), 3. R. P. H. Green, ed. and trans. (Oxford: Clarendon, 1995); Pamela Bright, *The Book of Rules of Tyconius: Its Purpose and Inner Logic* (Notre Dame, IN: University of Notre Dame Press, 1988).

13 Augustine, *Homilies on the Psalms*, 21.16 (PL 36:169).

14 See Gn 3:19.

15 Gregory the Great, *Moral Commentary on Job*, 15.56, 68 (PL 75:1116A).

16 Gregory the Great, *Moral Commentary on Job*, 11.8, 11 (PL 75:958C).

all things that are going to follow, decreed before the ages how they would be carried out through the ages."[17]

Likewise explaining the passage about the impious: *They will be like chaff before the face of the wind and like ashes that the whirlwind scatters* (Jb 21:18), he says: "Before the eyes of omnipotent God the life of the iniquitous is ashes. For, although it appears green for a moment, it is nevertheless seen to be already consumed by his judgment, since it has been assigned to eternal consumption."[18]

You yourself, Lord, also say about such people and their crimes through Moses: *Have not these things been stored up with me and sealed in my storerooms? Vengeance is mine, and I shall repay them in time* (Dt 32:34-35). Likewise you say: *The day of perdition is near and the times hasten to be present* (Dt 32:35). Likewise you say:

> *I will lift my hand to heaven and say: I live forever. If I sharpen my sword like lightning and my hands take hold of judgment, I shall take vengeance upon my enemies, and I shall repay those who have hated me. I shall drench my arrows with blood, and my sword will devour the flesh from the blood of the slain and from the captivity of the uncovered head of enemies. Nations, praise his people because he will avenge the blood of his servants and will render vengeance upon their enemies* (Dt 32:40-43).

If anyone presumes to say that all these aforementioned things and many others without limit scattered in many places throughout the breadth of the canonical scriptures, were foretold by you so that they are indeed foreknown, but in no way predestined, make him, please, carefully notice how he is opposed to the immutable truth and how he favors harmful falsity when he rashly subjects you to such varied mutability and does not fear to subject you to such inconstant instability and change. For although it is obvious, according to what Augustine says, that no changeable nature would remain unless you, our Lord God, remained unchangeable,[19] it matters little if you—God forbid!—are thought, believed, and preached by your church to be unchangeable from eternity up to the day of judgment and on the very day of judgment you are changed, as if by not doing what has been predestined, that is, sending the reprobate to torments. And in that way you are shown to have been changed forever thereafter and to have died—God forbid! For one who changes dies in a sense, as the authority of Augustine, Gregory, and other doctors attests.[20] But God forbid, Lord, that you who in no way were ever able, are able, or will be able to be changed, should even for a moment be changeable without any beginning up to the day of judg-

---

17 Gregory the Great, *Moral Commentary on Job*, 12.2, 2 (PL 75:986D).

18 Gregory the Great, *Moral Commentary on Job*, 15.50, 56 (PL 75:1110A).

19 See Augustine, *On the Trinity* (*De Trinitate*), 8.3, 5 (PL 42:950); *Unfinished Work in Answer to Julian* (*Opus imperfectum contra Iulianum*), 5.60 (PL 45:1494-5).

20 See Augustine, *Against Maximinus* (*Contra Maximinum*), 2.12, 2 (PL 42:768); Gregory the Great, *Moral Commentary on Job*, 9.47, 72 (PL 75:899A).

ment, and that for this reason you should appear to have eternally changed only because of the damnation of the reprobate and the torment owed to them.

It would truly have been incomparably better, Lord, if none of the elect had been created, much less saved, than for you to be changeable, much less changed. How much more ought it not be that you should change on account of the vessels of wrath and fury against whom your *face* is set because of the evils that they do, *in order that* you *may destroy their memory from the earth* (Ps 33:17). About these it is also truthfully sung to you far and wide, day and night, by the faithful: *But you, God, will bring them down into the pit of destruction* (Ps 54:24).

Testimonies of the Apostles

5. Of these reprobate the apostle Peter also says: *For them judgment from long ago is not idle, and their destruction does not slumber* (2 Pt 2:3).

And Paul says: *God, wishing to show his wrath and demonstrate his power, has borne with much patience the vessels fitted for wrath* (Rom 9:22) or "fitted for destruction" according to Jerome,[21] or "prepared for destruction" according to Ambrose,[22] or "made for destruction" according to Augustine,[23] that is, without doubt predestined, just as it had already been clearly explained by Augustine. Likewise the same preacher wrote: *In order that they may always fill up the measure of their sins; for the wrath of God has come upon them even to the end* (1 Thes 2:16).

Likewise, Jude, the brother of James, says: *Certain ungodly persons crept in, who long ago were marked out for this judgment* (Jude 4). When he asserted that they were marked out, not "in this judgment" but *for this judgment*, that is, for this condemnation, he wanted to be understood not merely foreknown, but also predestined as well, since you, eternal God, had predestined them before anyone born in time knew that they were foreknown. For those whom you foreknew were going to persevere in damnable sins through their own wretchedness, you, as a most righteous judge, certainly predestined to punishment justly and quite deservedly, and you not only predestined them, but also by predestining them you have of course already destined them.

Hence, David also spoke as if of those already placed in hell by predestination, although they were still to be placed there by your order, after he first said: *And afterward they will delight in their mouth*, he added: *Like sheep they have been placed in hell* (Ps 48:14-15). The apostle John also very clearly agrees with this in every respect, when he says in the Apocalypse: *And the books were opened, and another book was opened which is the book of life, and the dead were judged from those things that had been written in the books, according to their works* (Rv 20:12). Likewise he says: *And each one was judged according to his works* (Rv 20:13), and: *Death and*

21 Jerome, *Letters* (*Epistolae*), 120.10 (PL 22:999).

22 Ambrosiaster, *Commentary on the Letter to the Romans* (*Commentarius in epistolam ad Romanos*), On Rom 9:22 (PL 17:138D).

23 Augustine, *Letters* (*Epistolae*), 186.7, 24 (PL 33:824).

hell were cast into the lake of fire (Rv 20:14). And when he asserts that death and hell were cast into the lake of fire, he says that the devil and his followers *and whoever was not found in the book of life was cast into the lake of fire* (Rv 20:15). Likewise a little before he said: *And the devil, who deceived them, was cast into the lake of fire and brimstone* (Rv 20:9). Likewise a little after he said: *And he said to me: Write, because these words are very faithful and true. And he said to me: It has been done* (Rv 21:5-6).

And lest anyone hearing these things written by John should perhaps be in doubt, you yourself, Lord Jesus Christ, continue and say:

> *I am the Alpha and the Omega, the beginning and the end. To one who thirsts I shall freely give of the fountain of the water of life. One who overcomes will possess these things, and I shall be God to him and he will be a son to me. But as for the cowardly and unbelieving and abominable and murderers and fornicators and sorcerers and idolaters and all liars, their part will be in the lake burning with fire and brimstone, which is the second death* (Rv 21:6-8).

The Destiny of Those Who Resist This Truth

6. Therefore, let the unbelievers and also the liars fear and beware lest their part be with the aforementioned confederates, if they choose to be stubborn by resisting such plain truth.

Likewise you say: *Behold, I come quickly and my reward is with me to render to each according to his works* (Rv 22:12)...[24] except in predestination which you have unchangeably ordered by an irrevocable foreordination. Therefore, you continue and say:

> *I am the Alpha and the Omega, the first and the last, the beginning and the end. Blessed are they who wash their robes so that their power may be in the tree of life and they may enter the city through the gates. Outside are dogs and sorcerers and the unchaste and murderers and those serving idols and everyone who loves and lives a lie* (Rv 22:13-15).

Let all liars in general hear these things, but especially those who in the teaching of religion not only are irreverent or disrespectful, but also do not in any way hesitate to be deceivers. For surely none more serious can ever be found than that kind of lie. In fact, none is found so serious, although it seems slight to some or is even thought to be fine.

But if they consider the preceding insignificant, let them hear the following: *I, Jesus, have sent my angel to testify to you of these things in the churches* (Rv 22:16). And a little after you said:

> *I testify to everyone hearing the words of this prophecy: If anyone adds to these things, God will add unto him the plagues written in this book. And if anyone takes away from the words of the book of this prophecy, God will take away his portion from the book of life and from the holy city and from these things that have been*

24 Something is missing in the text.

> *written in this book. He who gives testimony of these things says: I am also coming quickly* (Rv 22:18-20).

Behold, Lord Jesus, I find in this holy book of yours that the devil and his angels and also all reprobate human beings have already been cast, as you destined them, *into the lake of fire and brimstone* (Rv 20:9), as was mentioned above. I do not dare to deny you, namely, the Truth,[25] because I fear being denied by you, that is, as you yourself testify: *The one who denies me before men, I also will deny before my Father who is in heaven* (Mt 10:33). Hence, Paul also says: *If we deny him, he will also deny us* (2 Tm 2:12). Therefore, as I said above, I do not dare to deny you because I fear being denied by you. But I do not presume to add or take away anything, since I fear either the plagues written in this very book being added to me or my portion in the book of life being taken away from me.

Testimonies of Augustine on God's Foreknowledge and Predestination of the Reprobate

7. Therefore, I pray to you, Lord, in the name of the Father and of the Son and of the Holy Spirit, as far as I am able, that you deign to help me, as I need, and that you not permit that there any longer be doubt on this by any of your elect—God forbid!—but rather you not delay to make known this most salutary truth to this man,[26] as you see that it is of the utmost necessity for him. For according to the most faithful testimony of blessed Augustine, which he openly brought forth to the people, by clearly and faithfully explaining a perplexing passage of the Gospel, he truly says:

> What do they who build a lie in human beings drive out from them but the truth? They let in the devil and shut out Christ; they let in the adulterer and shut out the bridegroom, that is, as bridesmen or rather pimps of the serpent. For they speak in order that the serpent may have possession and Christ be excluded. When falsehood has possession, the serpent has possession. When

---

25 See Jn 14:6.

26 The singular *huic* may indicate that Gottschalk has in mind a particular person whom he believes needs to understand this truth. This is most likely a reference to Hincmar of Reims, who was responsible for Gottschalk's imprisonment and who in 849 wrote a *Letter to the Monks and Simple Folk of his Diocese* (*Epistola ad reclusos et simplices suae dioeceseos*), warning them about Gottschalk's teaching. See Frank Leslie Cross and Elizabeth A. Livingstone, eds. "Gottschalk," in *The Oxford Dictionary of the Christian Church*, 3rd ed. (New York: Oxford University Press, 1997), 696: "Hincmar wrote a pastoral letter in which he warned the simple folk of his diocese against the errors of Gottschalk, who replied with a statement of his views known as the 'Confessio prolixior.'" Louise Reinecke Gustavvson (*Gottschalk Reconsidered: A Study of His Thought as it Bears on the Notion of Predestination*, Ph.D. dissertation [Yale University, 1964], 32-3) similarly suggested: "It is possible that the long confession was Gottschalk's retort to the *Ad reclusos* by which Hincmar wanted to put the folk of his diocese on guard against false teaching such as Gottschalk was accused of having disseminated."

> truth has possession, Christ has possession. For he himself said: *I am the Truth* (Jn 14:6). But about the other he said: *And he did not stand in the truth since the truth is not in him* (Jn 8:44).[27]

Hence, as for that which your same blessed servant, Augustine, also strove to present truthfully, namely, that the reprobate have been condemned by foreknowledge, although here and there he admits that they have been condemned to death by predestination, each of them is of course true, because each of them is true here. For foreknowledge is sometimes put in place of predestination, as he wisely and truthfully admits. Nor is it contrary to—God forbid!—but is rather seen to agree with truth, as that obviously is which the Apostle says: *God did not reject his people whom he foreknew* (Rom 11:2)—although, nevertheless, elsewhere joining both, but distinguishing them from each other by a rational distinction, he wonderfully defined them, saying: By predestination God "foreknew those things that he himself was going to bring about."[28] Hence, it was said: *He produces the things that will be* (Is 45:11). Likewise, connecting what predestination is with foreknowledge more clearly and more fully, he speaks of the Trinity as follows: "To arrange in his foreknowledge, which cannot be deceived or changed, his own future works is absolutely nothing other than to predestine them."[29]

Likewise more briefly, but much more clearly in the above sense—for, although he had first said that the Apostle said: *God has not rejected his people whom he foreknew* (Rom 11:2), and had explained that he wanted to signify predestination in this passage by the term "foreknowledge"— he says a little later: "But to have predestined is the same as to have foreknown what he was going to produce."[30]

Therefore, as I have already said, both are true, that is, that the reprobate have been condemned by foreknowledge and by predestination, whom it is absolutely clear were justly predestined to destruction. The aforementioned testimonies prove this sufficiently and beyond, and surely catholics in no way doubt that they are invincible, although if the testimony on this matter had to be from within, it could have regularly and certainly ought to have been, understood by metalepsis,[31] namely, so that what follows would be understood by what precedes.

Nevertheless, if they[32] still desire to hear more on this, that is, because of their love of the truth, which they think is being attacked too much, let them, I beg, apply their ears to hearing,[33] and let them strive with all their might at this very moment to defend the truth. Let them, I say, still hear Augustine speaking

27 Augustine, *Homilies on the Gospel of John*, 8.5 (PL 35:1453).

28 Augustine, *On the Gift of Perseverance* (*De dono perseverantiae*), 18.47 (PL 45:1023).

29 Augustine, *On the Gift of Perseverance*, 17.41 (PL 45:1019).

30 Augustine, *On the Gift of Perseverance*, 18.47 (PL 45:1023).

31 Metalepsis is the use of one word for another.

32 That is, those who agree with Gottschalk in his interpretation of Augustine.

33 See Mt 11:15.

wonderfully on this through the divine charism that was freely poured out in him quite richly.

He says: "There was no one who would do this good, which is to seek after God; there was not even one,[34] but in that kind of people which was predestined to destruction."[35]

Likewise, speaking about the two cities, he says: "One of them was predestined to reign for eternity with the Lord, the other to undergo eternal punishment with the devil."[36]

Likewise he says: "If the church were to be so sure about some people that she also knew who they are, who although they are still situated in this life, have still been predestined to go with the devil *into everlasting fire* (Mt 25:41), she would not pray for them, as she does not pray for the devil."[37]

Likewise he says: "What will he who gave these things even to those whom he has predestined to death give to those whom he has predestined to life?"[38]

Likewise in the *Enchiridion on Faith, Hope, and Love,* which as an elderly man, with God wonderfully and uniquely helping him, he wrote and published with very keen insight, very experienced genius, very pure eloquence, and a very lucid style, he says: "To the damnation of those whom he has justly predestined to punishment."[39]

Likewise in the same book he says: "They are also called the sons of hell, not born of it, but prepared for it, just as sons of the kingdom are prepared for the kingdom."[40] What clearer is asked for? What more sufficient? He says, "Just as sons of the kingdom are prepared for a kingdom," so also the sons of hell have been prepared for it, which is absolutely nothing other than predestined.

Surely, if such a great author as he had not perceived that all these things above and the many others were entirely true and in agreement with the catholic faith in every respect, he would in no way have left them uncorrected, but rather, when he had reexamined his books, in very carefully reviewing them,[41] he would have made every effort to correct them. Nor would he would have spoken on this to

34 See Ps 13:3.

35 Augustine, *On the Perfection of Human Righteousness* (*De perfectione iustitiae hominis*) 13.31 (CSEL 42:32; PL 44:308).

36 Augustine, *On the City of God*, 15.1, 1 (PL 41:437).

37 Augustine, *On the City of God*, 21.24, 1 (PL 41:737).

38 Augustine, *On the City of God*, 22.24, 5 (CSEL 40.2:649; PL 41:792).

39 Augustine, *Enchiridion on Faith, Hope, and Love* (*Enchiridion de fide, spe, et caritate*), 100.26 (PL 40:279).

40 Augustine, *Enchiridion on Faith, Hope, and Love*, 39.12 (PL 40:252).

41 This is a reference to Augustine's *Revisions* (*Retractationes*), written just a few years before his death. See *Saint Augustine, The Retractations*, trans. by Sr. Mary Inez Bogan. FC 60 (Washington, D.C.: Catholic University of America Press, 1968).

the people so frequently, both fearlessly and intrepidly, so willingly, openly, and freely, so faithfully, confidently, and joyfully, without servile fear and covered with your luminous with love, and with your authority, if he had known that there was some danger in them. Hence, I have already set forth some above and judged that a few should also be added here.

"There is a certain people, prepared for the wrath of God, to be condemned with the devil."[42]

Likewise he says: "There is a certain people born for the wrath of God."[43]

Likewise he says: "Why did the Lord say to the Jews: *You do not believe, because you are not of my sheep* (Jn 10:26), except that he saw that they were predestined to eternal destruction, not purchased for eternal life with the price of his blood?"[44]

Likewise he asks: "What can the wolf do? What can the thief and robber do? They destroy only those predestined to destruction."[45]

Likewise he says: "Those rebellious dead, who are also predestined to eternal death."[46]

Likewise he says: "The world hates the world. The hostile world hates the reconciled world. The condemned world hates the saved world. The polluted world hates the cleansed world."[47]

Likewise he says: "Judas, the betrayer of Christ, was called the son of perdition because he was predestined to perdition."[48]

Likewise he says: "For that world he does not pray,[49] for he is not unaware of that for which it has been predestined."[50]

Testimonies of Fulgentius

8. On this blessed Fulgentius also speaks in this manner: "God also prepared punishments for sinners, for those of course whom he justly predestined to suffer punishments."[51] Here he certainly confesses quite openly both of them, namely, that the punishments were predestined for the reprobate and that they in turn were predestined for the punishments.

---

42 Augustine, *Homilies on the Gospel of John*, 14.8 (PL 35:1507).

43 Augustine, *Homilies on the Gospel of John*, 14.8 (PL 35:1507).

44 Augustine, *Homilies on the Gospel of John*, 48.4 (PL 35:1742).

45 Augustine, *Homilies on the Gospel of John*, 48.6 (PL 35:1743).

46 Augustine, *Homilies on the Gospel of John*, 43.13 (PL 35:1711).

47 Augustine, *Homilies on the Gospel of John*, 87.2 (PL 35:1853).

48 Augustine, *Homilies on the Gospel of John*, 107.7 (PL 35:1914).

49 See Jn 17:9.

50 Augustine, *Homilies on the Gospel of John*, 110.2 (PL 35:1921).

51 Fulgentius of Ruspe, *On the Truth of Predestination and Grace* (*De veritate praedestinationis et gratiae*), 3.5, 8 (CCSL 91A:527; PL 65:656A).

Hence, not surprisingly, he argued in a very catholic manner and at great length in *Seven Books against the Two Books of Faustus* the heretic, who was once a monk at Lérins and afterward bishop of Riez.[52] This same doctor proved him wrong and marvelously crushed the lies of the devil, and with fourteen other holy fellow bishops drove him from the church of Christ and eliminated the lethal poison of antichrist.[53]

He also did this in three other books *On the Truth of Predestination and Grace*[54] and in that one that he is known to have written entirely upon only this question, *To Monimus*, who was asking him about it.[55]

Testimonies of Gregory the Great

9. Glorious Gregory, from whom I have already inserted some things above on this, also spoke in this manner among other things: "The Lord saw the dark doors when he entered the confines of hell and beat down the cruel spirits, and by dying, he condemned the princes of death. This," he said, "is not said of something still

52 Fulgentius' *Against Faustus* (*Contra Faustum*) was mentioned in Fulgentius' *Letters* (*Epistulae*), 15.19 (CCSL 91A:456; PL 65:442C) and in Isidore of Seville's *On Illustrious Men* (*De viris illustribus*), 27 (PL 83:1097B), but it is now lost. It was directed against Faustus of Riez's *On Grace* (*De gratia*) found in CSEL 21. During the Jansenist controversy in the seventeenth century, Jérôme Vignier claimed to have found a manuscript containing this work of Fulgentius against Faustus, but after Vignier's death the manuscript could not be found. See Jean-Louis Quantin, "Combat doctrinal et chasse à l'inédit au XVII siècle. Vignier, Quesnel et les sept livres contre Fauste de Fulgence de Ruspe," *Revue des Études Augustiniennes* 44 (1998):269-97.

53 In actuality, Faustus had been deceased for some twenty or thirty years prior to Fulgentius writing his books against Faustus' *On Grace*. The occasion for Fulgentius' writing against it was a controversy over grace and free will in Constantinople between Scythian monks led by John Maxentius and an African bishop named Possessor living in exile in Constantinople. Possessor was using Faustus' treatise on grace as an authority for his own similar theology, and the Scythian monks lured Fulgentius into their debate to refute it. See Francis X. Gumerlock, *Fulgentius of Ruspe on the Saving Will of God: The Development of a Sixth-Century African Bishop's Interpretation of 1 Timothy 2:4 During the Semi-Pelagian Controversy* (Lewiston, NY: Mellen, 2009), 70-71, 83-105. Gottschalk's statement about Fulgentius driving Faustus from the church is correct only in the sense that, at a time when the orthodoxy of Faustus' teaching on grace was being questioned (See CCSL 85A:153; CSEL 35:695-6), Fulgentius' treatise branded Faustus as a teacher of error and very likely weakened the influence of his books on grace in the church. However, before Fulgentius, the pseudo-Gelasian decree *On Books to Be Received and Not to Be Received* (*De libris recipiendis et non recipiendis*), in PL 59:164A, written about the year 500, pronounced Faustus' literary works apocryphal, not to be received by the faithful.

54 Fulgentius, *On the Truth of Predestination and Grace* (CCSL 91A:458-548; PL 65:603-72).

55 Fulgentius, *To Monimus* (*Ad Monimum*), Book 1 (CCSL 91:3-33; PL 65:153-78).

in the future, but of something in the past, because whatever was going to take place in execution, had already without doubt taken place in predestination."[56]

Likewise he says: "This leviathan with all of his members has been assigned to eternal torments."[57]

Likewise he says that the day of judgment itself has also been predestined. When explaining the passage from the book of Job: *The lamp despised in the thoughts of the rich, is ready for the time appointed* (Jb 12:5), he said: "The time appointed for the despised lamp is the predestined day of the last judgment."[58]

Testimony of Isidore and Explanation of the Term "Twofold"

10. On this Saint Isidore also speaks in this manner: "Predestination is twofold, either of the elect to rest or of the reprobate to death."[59] For he does not say that there are two predestinations, because there are not. But he says "a twofold," that is, a bipartite one, because you, Lord, spoke once of how by one, but still by a twofold predestination, you both gratuitously justify and eternally save the elect and also rightly reject and justly condemn the reprobate, just as the aforementioned Gregory wrote: "Looking upon some, you redeem them; abandoning others, you destroy them."[60]

But such is the fact that predestination is said to be twofold, that is, bipartite for the elect and the reprobate, for although it is one, it is also double. It is much like the way that charity or love is frequently said to be twofold by Augustine and other fathers, although there are certainly not two loves, but one, although it is double for the sake of God and for the sake of the neighbor.[61] This is like that passage of father Augustine, which says that the work of God is bipartite, that is, where he wants it to be understood to be "twofold."[62] And the world is also said by him to be quadripartite, still not four, but one. And because he professes that continence is quintuple, he still does not teach that there are five, but one.[63] Supporting this also, the knowledge of the Jews is said by Saint Gregory to be twofold, and still, although it is double, it is known to be one.[64]

---

56 Gregory the Great, *Moral Commentary on Job*, 19.13, 25 (PL 76:490C-D).

57 Gregory the Great, *Moral Commentary on Job*, 34.2, 4 (PL 76:719B).

58 Gregory the Great, *Moral Commentary on Job*, 10.31, 52 (PL 75:950C).

59 Isidore of Seville, *Sentences* (*Sententiae*), 2.6 (CCSL 111:103; PL 83:606A).

60 Gregory the Great, *Moral Commentary on Job*, 29.2.4 (PL 76:480A-B).

61 See Augustine, *Homilies on the Gospel of John*, 17.6 (PL 35:1531).

62 Possibly a reference to Augustine, *On the City of God*, 7.6 (PL 41:199).

63 See Augustine, *On Eighty-Three Different Questions* (*De diversis quaestionibus octaginta tribus liber*), 59.3 (PL 40:45).

64 See Gregory the Great, *Homilies on the Gospels* (*Homiliae in Evangelia*), 10.2 (PL 76:1111C).

This manner of speaking is also used very much among authors even of secular literature. And since it is altogether correct and perfectly true, it is not irrelevant if some things are set forth here on this that are able to add to the heap for defending the position stated above. For one of them said that a tree was twofold, not wanting two to be understood, but one,[65] and another explained the quality of a name as bipartite[66] and that the condition of all feet is threefold,[67] and a third equally learned man, Priscianus, explained as tripartite what that man had called threefold.[68]

Clearly it should not seem absurd to anyone who is pious and wise, if predestination is believed, known, and is unhesitatingly said to be twofold with you, our Lord, who are indeed naturally one, but also at the same time personally three, who, according to this your twofold predestination, as your Augustine faithfully believes and confidently asserts: "You are good in the benefit of certain ones, just in the punishment of the rest;" and, moreover, as he consequently professes: "You are good in all, since it is good when a debt is paid, and you are just in all, since it is just when a debt is forgiven without cheating anyone."[69]

Fear of Denying the Truth

11. Just as he did, thanks to you, I both believe and confess all these things, thanks to you, as you gratuitously granted this to me. And because in your books, that is, in the books truthfully explained by the labor of your servants, in fact by your grace, I find that these things were said by you, I certainly do not dare to contradict such clear truth—God forbid!—since I certainly fear being denied by you, the Truth, as you threatened,[70] and I also greatly fear that often repeated statement of Paul: *If anyone announces to you something other than that which you have received, let him be anathema* (Gal 1:9).

Since I perpetually owe you, Lord Jesus, invincible Truth, so much love that, as is truthfully shown by your Augustine, I am not turned away from truth—God forbid!—either by the desire to please human beings or by the consideration of avoiding certain difficulties. And as blessed Gregory also teaches: "Inasmuch as we are able to do so without sin, we ought to avoid scandals to neighbors. But

---

65 Publius Vergilius Maro [Vergil], *Aeneid*, 6.203.

66 Vergil the Grammarian, *Epitomes* (*Epitomae*), 5. See Lambot, 67.

67 Perhaps Julius Severus, *Explanation about Feet* (*De pedibus expositio*), which reads: "Threefold is the division of all feet." See Lambot, 68.

68 This seems to be a reference either to Priscianus of Caesarea, a grammarian at Constantinople under Emperor Anastasius, or to Priscianus of Lydia, a non-Christian Neoplatonist philosopher, who also flourished in the Byzantine empire in the early sixth century.

69 Augustine, *On the Gift of Perseverance*, 12.28 (PL 45:1010).

70 See Mt 10:33.

if scandal arises because of the truth, it is better that scandal is allowed to arise than that truth is abandoned."[71]

And the person of no one is in any way an exception to be accepted against this,[72] when an angel or an apostle who is preaching such is stricken with a deserved anathema by the mouth of the Apostle.[73]

For as the aforementioned Gregory truthfully says: "When something is done with the faith preserved, it is the merit of virtue if something prior is tolerated."[74] Otherwise, if it were in any way possible, I should of course and would desire rather to die a thousand times for the truth rather than—God forbid!—to succumb once by yielding to someone speaking otherwise, that is, because I remember that statement of yours: *The one who will confess me before men, I shall also confess before my Father who is in heaven* (Mt 10:32).

Gregory and Cassiodorus on Heretics

12. At the same time I also remember the words: *Do not transgess the ancient boundaries that your fathers have set* (Prv 22:28). The heretics undoubtedly do this, as Gregory explains, "who live outside of the bosom of holy church. They," he says, "change the boundaries because they go beyond the decisions of the fathers by transgressing, because they also ravage and lay waste the flocks, and because they also draw the unlearned to themselves by perverse arguments and feed them with destructive teachings in order to kill them."[75]

Blessed Job also rebukes them, saying: *Does God need your lie that you should speak falsehoods for him?* (Jb 13:7). Gregory explains:

> God does not need a lie, because the truth does not seek to be supported by the help of falsity. But because heretics cannot protect by the truth the things they wrongly understand about God, they require the shadows of falsity in order to establish a ray of light. And for it they speak deceits when they deceive weak minds away from an understanding of the truth by their foolish seduction.[76]

Likewise he says: *Or will it please him from whom nothing can be concealed? Or will he be deceived like a human being by your deceitful dealings?* (Jb 13:9). He explains:

> Heretics offer God a deceit since they construct things which in no way please him for whom they speak, and they offend him when they try as if to defend him, and when they rush into opposition to him whom they seem to serve by their preaching. Hence, it is said by the psalmist: *So that you may destroy*

71 Gregory the Great, *Homilies on the Prophet Ezekiel* (*Homiliae in Hiezechielem prophetam*), 1.7, 5 (PL 76:842C).

72 Gottschalk's chief antagonists at this time, Rabanus Maurus and Hincmar of Reims, were archbishops.

73 See Gal 1:8.

74 Gregory the Great, *Moral Commentary on Job*, 25.16, 36 (PL 76:345A).

75 Gregory the Great, *Moral Commentary on Job*, 16.44, 6 (PL 75:1148C).

76 Gregory the Great, *Moral Commentary on Job*, 11.26, 37 (PL 75:970C).

> *the enemy and defender* (Ps 8:3). Every heretic is certainly an enemy of the omnipotent God and a defender, because he is opposed to his truth in that in which he tries as if to defend him. But because nothing can be hidden from God, he judges in them what they inwardly believe, not what they seem to do outwardly in service. Therefore, because God is not deceived by their deceitful dealings, like a human being, it is correctly added: *He will reprove you because you secretly accept his person. As soon as he rouses himself, he will trouble you, and his dread will fall upon you* (Jb 13:10-11). His words[77] that the person of God is accepted secretly can be understood in two ways. For, there are some who believe the truth in their heart and yet outwardly speak things that are false about God. So that they do not seem to be defeated, they both know the truth inwardly and yet oppose it outwardly. Hence, it is now said well: *He will reprove you because you secretly accept his person,* as if it were plainly said: You have been more reprehended before him because of falsity to the extent that you see in yourselves what is true.[78]

However, so that one may not pretend one is the other, a certain father, as Cassiodorus says, very beautifully defined what a heretic is. "A heretic," he says, "is someone who, carried of by ignorance or contempt of the divine law, either a stubborn inventor of new error, or an adherent of someone else's, wants to oppose catholic truth rather than to be subject to it."[79]

Basil the Great and Gregory of Nazianzus on Falsehood and Truth

13. But I have decided that this should also be added since I have found that many are both deceived and deceive on this matter,[80] namely, those who want, or to speak in a milder way, suspect that those are heretics who by your grace necessarily believe and confess this truth of the catholic faith concerning the predestination of the reprobate against those who resist and speak against it and that those who assert the opposite are catholics, who do not fear to whisper, even to openly preach, the falsity inimical to the clear truth. They regard as worthless the statement of blessed Basil: "They who are fed by the divine words do not allow the corruption of even one syllable of the divine teachings, but they also embrace every form of death for them, if that should happen."[81] And they also hold in contempt that statement of Gregory of Nazianzus: "It is a mark of fortitude to persevere in truth, although someone is beaten down in relation to things that are nothing."[82] But falsehood and deceit are certainly nothing, and

---

77 That is, Sophar's. See Jb 11:1.

78 Gregory the Great, *Moral Commentary on Job*, 11.28-29, 39-40 (PL 75:971A-C).

79 Cassiodorus, *Explanation of the Psalms* (*Expositio psalmorum*), On Ps138, Conclusion (PL 70:994B).

80 See 2 Tm 3:13.

81 Basil of Caesarea cited in Theodoret of Cyrus, *Ecclesiastical History* (*Historia ecclesiastica*), 4.17 (PL 69:1095D).

82 The source of this quotation has not been located.

the hearts of those who are always true certainly avoid, shun, and abhor them beyond all the kinds of bodily deaths, as they ought. Still, they especially avoid in every way in the teaching of religion the precipice of speech containing falsity.

More Apostolic Testimonies: Peter and Jude

14. Thanks to you, Lord, loving Trinity, this is the inviolable faith and my confession, that is, about your foreknowledge and predestination, which the Truth himself preached along with his previously mentioned disciples against lying patrons and, unless they are corrected, sons of falsity and perdition, and against their poisonous venoms and heretical teachings. If sprinkled by your grace, they diligently attend to, weigh, and consider how from the beginning of the fall of the angels, that is, "as the apostle Peter says, *you did not spare* those same *angels that sinned, but reserved for* greater torments on the day of *judgment* (2 Pt 2:4) those handed over by the ropes and prisons of hell to the torments of this air,[83] how also you destroyed the ancient world because of the crimes of evil people,[84] and how you punished both the shameful deeds and also the abominations of the inhabitants of Sodom, destroyed them as they burned with the fire of heaven[85] and cast them down into eternal punishments,[86] and that you hurled *Pharaoh and his army into the sea* (Ex 15:4) and completely wiped them out there like winnowed chaff.[87]

I say, if leaving animosity behind, they look carefully at and wisely attend to these things with your help, they will surely understand very easily that you reserved the aforementioned angels, who, as Jude, the brother of James, writes, *did not keep their principality, but left their habitation for everlasting chains under darkness unto the judgment of the great day* (Jude 6), and you would in absolutely no way without the counsel of your eternal predestination have cast them down into this prison of dark air and reserved them for even greater punishments to be justly tormented throughout the ages, as both aforementioned apostles testify. Nor would you have done those things that were also consequently told about reprobate human beings without—God forbid!—predestination. Otherwise, you would be found to be changeable before all the ages and also, according to the most fallacious teaching of theirs, found to be immediately changed in the beginning of the ages, which is not possible even for a moment, for you alone are certainly believed by all catholics and known more clearly than light by your revelation to be unchangeable.

---

83 See Eph 2:2.

84 See 2 Pt 2:5.

85 See Gn 19:24.

86 See Jude 7.

87 See Ex 15:7.

Prayer for Those Who Oppose Predestination of the Reprobate

15. Bring it about, I also pray, Lord God, that they may not again and again be shameless, stubborn, and obstinate, nor contentious, deceitful, and lying. For people of this kind are certainly not able to defend the truth that they attack, however much they can be naturally sagacious. Rather having become simple lovers of the truth, may they consider with the whole spiritual gaze, not of the eyes, that, if you destined, and afterward destine, and will destine without your coeternal predestination, the souls of the reprobate, which were taken from their bodies from the first of them, namely, Cain, to the last to die before the day of judgment, that is, as often as they died, die, or will die, to the torments owed to them and rightly prepared for them, you are not only changeable before the ages, but also have changed—which you cannot do in any way—from the beginning of the death of the same reprobate, rather from the beginning of the condemnation of the evil angels. You change very many times and by countless changes and through single days and nights, and you will change, and you will remain changed for the ages, that is, on account of the sons of hell alone, whom the enemies of the truth stubbornly and wrongly deny were predestined.

I say, bring about, Lord, I ask, that they attend to, weigh, and consider these things, as they should, and at long last somehow see what they pretend not to have seen up to now, namely, the sort and magnitude of the evil they have in your church long and openly preached and preach, have asserted and assert falsely and destructively concerning you, the ever unchangeable Lord our God, to their own destruction and the destruction of their followers. And I pray that you mercifully call them back to *the way of truth* (Ps 118:30), lest they stubbornly persevere in the error of such a lethal heresy.

Let them see the sort and magnitude of the evil it is that, when all your elect always have done, do, and will do everything with counsel, that is, as they are helped by you by the gratuitous aid of your kindness, they presume, not only by lying, but by swearing falsely, openly to affirm to all that you who are the author of the universe and *fountain of wisdom* (Sir 1:5), in fact eternal wisdom, three and one, will, are able, or ought—God forbid!—to do anything without counsel, not to mention destining without the counsel of predestination the souls of the dying reprobate from the very beginning of the human race or those same souls at the end on the day of judgment, after they have received their own bodies, along with *the devil and his angels* (Mt 25:41).

After, however, these things have been wisely examined and vigorously understood, as they should be, *let them be confounded* in a salutary way *and blush* (Ps 69:3-4), and let them at long last humbly submit to the truth and finally quiet down from me. But if they prefer to persist in falsity, remaining impudently and without any shame, rather than to withdraw from so great an error, as they should, let them see to what those lost people turn themselves.

I ask you, Lord God, to gratuitously protect your church so that they no longer pervert her with their falsity or subvert her any longer with the pestiferous depravity of their heresy, although they unfortunately overthrow themselves and their followers along with themselves.

But I have been gratuitously taught by the very truth that the aforementioned teachers of your church followed and preached as most faithful, most devout, and certainly most renowned ministers of the same truth. Having been freely and piously inspired, quickened, and strengthened by you, and at the same time having been mercifully and wonderfully helped, safely supported and sustained, I—thanks be to you!—firmly believe, truthfully hold, and openly defend the catholic faith here clearly expressed concerning predestination. "And whomever" I "know that teaches contrary to it," I "flee from like the plague and reject as a heretic."[88] And, as I explain with great sadness what follows concerning such people, in accordance with the precept of the most blessed Augustine, whomever I hear "stubbornly opposing" the unconquerable truth and perceive "to be teaching things contrary to it," I of course denounce as "a heretic and an enemy of the Christian faith and as one who, because of this, should be anathematized by all catholics."[89]

Moreover, if, after having read and understood these things, any of them does not want to give up the battle, and hardened like Pharaoh,[90] that is, like a heretic, refuses to submit to such manifest truth, I think that, according to the counsel or rather the commandment of the apostle Paul, he should now be avoided by me, since I see that *such a one is subversive and condemned by his own judgment* (Ti 3:11).

Request for a Public Meeting and Ordeal

16. Nevertheless, on account of those who are less expert and for this reason enticed by them and lost unless they are corrected, I would desire, if it would be pleasing to you, Lord, that there be a public meeting, in order that after the truth has been openly defended and falsity has been completely destroyed, we might in common give thanks to you, who shall have deigned to grant us the favorable outcome that has been so long desired, *even beyond what we ask or think* (Eph 3:20). For I of course suffer an exceedingly great sorrow and endure the greatest grief night and day because I see that the truth has become vile to human beings on account of the vileness of my name and that they do not preserve sincere love for you, as they ought to have. For, in order that they may seem to be victors over me, they have loved or love you none or very little, whom they have not refrained and do not refrain from denying on account of me.

88 Fulgentius, *On the Faith for Peter* (*De fide ad Petrum*), 44.85 (CCSL 91A:760; PL 65:705D).

89 Fulgentius, *On the Faith for Peter*, 44.5 (CCSL 91A:760; PL 65:706A).

90 See Ex 7:13.

And would that it would be pleasing to you, all powerful and equally merciful Lord that, just as I believe and hope in you, with the ability having been gratuitously given me, as you have for a long time deigned and daily deign also to give me the will, this would be granted to me, namely, that before a multitude of people who fear you gathered from everywhere, also in the presence of the prince of this kingdom together with the venerable host of bishops, priests, monks, and canons—if they otherwise refuse to receive this truth of the catholic faith about your predestination by that which I am going to say with your help—I might prove it in the sight of all by means of an ordeal. That is, with four barrels placed one after another, individually filled with boiling water, oil, pitch, and animal fat, and finally heated by most ample fire, may it be permitted me, having invoked your most glorious name, to enter each of them to prove this faith of mine, or rather the catholic faith, and thus to pass through each of them. With you going before me, accompanying me, and following me, and offering your right hand and mercifully leading me, may I be able to come out unharmed, in order that the brightness of the catholic faith may at long last shine forth from this in your church and that falsity may disappear and that faith may be strengthened and disbelief avoided.

Would, Lord, that you would deign to inspire love in those reading and understanding things of this kind, as is necessary, in order that they may beg you as suppliants that you quickly bring to fruition this desire of my soul, as your church needs, and that if, with your help, I shall come forth unharmed from all these things, they would embrace the truth and curse falsity. If, however, I am afraid to begin or fear to finish what I promise in believing, confessing, hoping, and loving you from you, through you, and in you, secure only in you and confident only of your grace, may they immediately throw me into the fire and let me justly perish in it. Nevertheless, I humbly ask you, Lord, in your sweetest name that no catholic rashly reprehend me in his heart—God forbid!—because I certainly do not presume the boldness of asking such things by myself out of my own rashness, as you yourself know better, but rather I receive it from you out of your kindness.

Rather, may whoever, truly fearing you and sincerely loving you, deigns to read these things or to hear them, implore your gratuitous mercy in fraternal compassion and also brotherly love, that you, who alone are *a helper in times of tribulation* (Ps 9:10) may deign to immediately help me, that is, me who, by your gratuitous mercy, believe and hope in you, that you may enrich me with an integral faith for beginning and for finishing this ordeal, that you may strengthen me with a solid hope, endow me with very sincere love, and also always gratuitously adorn me with the truest humility before you.

And after the falsity of such deadly teaching has been driven far away from your orthodox church, may you make me rejoice thereafter with your elect over the truth of the catholic faith disclosed to your faithful ones. And may we hereafter have true and sincere joy, supreme and solid delight, and common glory in you alone, because the populace and people have by your mercy finally become free from such grave disbelief of heretics, since no one ever, no one ever[91] of your elect has been able, is able, or will be able to please you from himself even for a moment, but all of yours have always pleased, do please, and will please you from what is yours.

Therefore, having been gratuitously animated with this faith, also strengthened by hope, and likewise set afire with love, I humbly ask through you yourself, most good God, that, having given me true humility, you may make me always to rejoice with the genuine joy of life.

Finally, [may you receive][92] the glory owed to you and your name through the ages, both on account of justice since you justly humble, bring down, and lay low the proud,[93] and on account of grace since you gratuitously exalt, elevate, and raise up the humble.[94] Through them, namely, both of them, I ask you, all powerful and most clement Trinity and likewise Unity, that you completely forgive all of my enemies—whoever have harmed or wanted to harm you, whether out of hatred for your name, either unknowingly or also knowingly—but they undoubtedly harmed themselves. May you pardon all their transgressions and fully remit and forgive all of their crimes and sins. Amen.

Closing Prayer

17. And I offer you thanks as great as possible, three and one ruler, Lord God, that you have gratuitously deigned, do deign, and will, as I believe and hope, hereafter deign to enlighten me, set me afire, and help me to believe and confess more and more the catholic faith on predestination. Amen.

I pray, to the extent it is given to me by God, with humility before the most present majesty of triune Unity and one Trinity, that whoever reads these things would remember before God Gottschalk, a sinner, not with the malice of a raven but rather with the love of a dove and would with paternal or fraternal affection simply implore his kindest clemency that he may deign with gratuitous piety to give me the excellence of true humility always and everywhere before him and the eminence of perpetually sincere love, and that he may in that way continually *protect* me *in* his *tabernacle from the contradiction of tongues* (Ps 30:21), that is, in the correct faith of the Catholic Church from the false accusations of heretics. And may he grant that in the present I desire incomparably more to endure all the adversities from their persecutions on account of the name of the Lord our God

91 The Latin says: *nullus unquam, nullus unquam electorum tuorum*. The repetition of *nulla unquam* appears in the printed editions of Ussher (p. 231) and Lambot (p. 76), but not in PL 121:363.

92 I have conjectured this addition.

93 See Ps 17:28.

94 See Lk 1:52.

and the love of truth rather than, wavering even for a moment, to deviate—God forbid!—from the love or confession of the truth or from the prescribed faith of catholics, which has been declared above all by the mouth of the Truth himself and also by the most invincible authorities of his ministers. For I certainly owe as much charity to my neighbor as to myself, but to God from the whole of myself, since whatever good there is in us is either God himself or from him.

But whoever you are, who deign to be a pious reader and learned understander of this my faith and confession.....[95] you wisely admit, I respectfully beseech you as a father or I faithfully exhort you as a brother, that if you want to see the Truth for eternity and to rejoice forever over the Truth with the holy angels, chosen and faithful witnesses of that same Truth, you hasten before the death of the body utterly to abhor that most pernicious and most destructive kind of lie that is detestably committed in the teaching of religion. And thus, according to that which was divinely spoken through blessed Augustine: "May the most beautiful and most modest *love poured out in our hearts* (Rom 5:5) joyfully welcome the eye[96] of doves, so that either very cautious humility may avoid or very solid truth may beat back the teeth of dogs."[97] Here he undoubtedly signifies by eye of doves the inspection of the righteous and truthful regarding himself and his teachings, but by the teeth of dogs the malign and mocking censure of the perverse and deceitful. Therefore, pray and beseech the Lord our God and his majesty, I beg, that we may have the truest, sincerest, and kindest love against the barking of heretics and that finally we may beat back their teeth and biting falsity through the most invincible and solid truth, whether they like it or not.

But if anyone is going to be angry at me when I say these things, the statement will be said of him, as another author says.[98]

And therefore, whoever still damnably presumes such things and things of that sort, that is, either not fearing at all or fearing too little the Truth and his judgment, audaciously denies against it that the reprobate have been predestined to everlasting punishment, that is, one who does not fear that same Truth saying to him in the hearing of everyone on the last day: Behold, I now justly deny you since you have unjustly denied me at one time.[99] I say, let such a one, if he wants and dares, deny the Truth, whom he has not feared to offend, and of whom day and night he also stands with us in need. But let us, who hear from the same Truth: *The day of vengeance is in my heart* (Is 63:4) and: *Behold,* our *God will*

95 Something is missing in the text.

96 The Latin in Lambot (p. 77), PL 121:364, and Ussher (p. 232) is *osculum* meaning "kiss;" but I have conjectured *oculum*, that is, "eye," which agrees with the citation from Augustine (PL 42:845) and Gottschalk's explanation of it as "inspection" (*inspectionem*).

97 Augustine, *On the Trinity*, 2, Preface (PL 42:845).

98 See Quintus Horatius Flaccus [Horace], *Satires* (*Sermones*), 1, 69-70.

99 See Mt 10:33.

bring about the revenge of recompense (Is 35:4), trample down this poisonous falsity and preach the truth in order that this same Truth, my *God* and the Son of God, *may have mercy on us* (Ps 66:2) both now and then, when he comes *on the day of vengeance* (Ex 32:34). For if we fear the fury of deceivers...[100] while we can please him who forever rules, protects, and fortifies us against the fury of robbers. Amen.

Lord God, blessed and also invincible Trinity and Unity, pour out upon those reading these things, I beg, the faith for believing them; and upon those believing these things bestow the courage of confessing them. But to those who *believe in the heart unto righteousness and with the mouth confess unto salvation* (Rom 10:9-10), repay to them the amplitude of a copious reward and the blessedness of eternal light with you. Amen.

100 Something is missing in the text.

ANSWERS TO VARIOUS QUESTIONS

After being imprisoned in the monastery at Hautvillers, Gottschalk continued writing and corresponding. These answers to questions that were directed to him about free will and twofold predestination are dated after March 849, since in his answer about twofold predestination he mentions his having been escorted from Quierzy. The title, *Responses of Gottschalk concerning Various Questions Sent by Him to a Certain Objector* (*Responsa Gotteschalci de diversis ab ipsomet alicui censori transmissa*), was given to it by Lambot. Edition: Lambot, 146-58. *On Free Choice* translated by Victor Genke. *On Twofold Predestination* and *On Syllogisms* translated by Francis X. Gumerlock. The subheadings and numbers were added by us.

On Free Choice

1. Free choice, as Saint Augustine says, is "that middle power that can be bent towards faith" by God's grace, "or be turned towards unbelief"[1] through human malice, wickedness, and concupiscence. And this free choice naturally bestowed on the rational creature by God is certainly signified by *the tree of the knowledge of good and evil that is in the midst of the paradise* (Gn 2:9; 3:3), of which the man was forbidden to eat, that is, because one ought not delight in or rely on freedom of choice, but on the grace of God, which is shown to be symbolized by the tree of life. Therefore, whoever eats of it dies miserably right away. And on the contrary, whoever eats of the tree of life, that is, relies on the grace of God as he ought to, lives and is certainly saved, having been brought to life by it. If grace withdraws, offended by the sin of our perversity, a man falls; he is not upright, but hurled down by free choice. Nor as he could fall, can he, rightly abandoned, rise up, once having died, without any grace, but rather he lies slain under a heavy dominion, as the Lord says: *Truly, truly, I say to you, everyone who commits sin is a slave of sin* (Jn 8:34). Blessed Peter also says concerning this: *They promise them freedom although they themselves are slaves of corruption; for one is a slave of him by whom he has been overcome* (2 Pt 2:19), which in another translation has as follows: *For one is enslaved to him by whom he has been conquered.*[2] Likewise he says: *As free and not as using freedom as a cloak for malice* (1 Pt 2:16). Blessed Paul also says on this: *For when you were slaves of sin, you were free from righteousness* (Rom 6:20). Likewise he says: *Do you not know that, if you offer yourselves as slaves to anyone to obey, you are slaves of him whom you obey, whether of sin leading to death or of*

1 Augustine, *On the Spirit and the Letter* (*De spiritu et littera*), 33.58 (PL 44:238).

2 See Augustine, *On Faith and Works* (*De fide et operibus*), 24.45 (PL 40:226).

obedience leading to righteousness? (Rom 6:16). Likewise he says: *You, brothers, have been called to freedom; only do not use freedom as an opportunity for the flesh, but through love serve one another* (Gal 5:13). On this Saint Augustine also says in the books of *Confessions* concerning himself when he was still a pagan: "It was I who willed; it was I who did not will."[3] Likewise he says: "I willed, but I was not able;"[4] for "I was a slave of sensual desire."[5] Saint Ambrose also says in his *Letter to the Verzellians*: "The greedy cannot say: *The Lord is my portion* (Ps 118:57), for greed comes and says: 'He is mine.'"[6] In the same way he also speaks concerning someone given to luxury and concerning another two vices. If you read his letter carefully, as one ought, it will surely benefit you very much through the grace of God. On this, blessed Paulinus[7] says to Licentius, a disciple of Saint Augustine:

> Live, I beg you, but live for God, since to live for the world
> Is death, and the true life is to live for God.[8]

On this Boethius[9] also wrote:

> Let him who wants to be powerful,
> Conquer his wild spirits,
> And let him not submit his neck,
> Overcome by desire, to its foul reins.
> For, although [far off] the land of India
> Trembles at your homeland
> And ultima Thule[10] is its slave,
> Still, to be unable to drive away dark concerns
> And to dispel miserable complaints
> Is not power.[11]

But the authority of blessed Paul declares where there is free choice—or as Saint Augustine says "free will," when he says: *Where the Spirit of the Lord is, there is freedom* (2 Cor 3:17). Having set forth this testimony in the *Letter to the Questions of Hilary*, a monk of Syracuse, Saint Augustine rightly concluded as a consequence and said, as he ought to have: "Therefore, freedom without grace

---

3 Augustine, *Confessions* (*Confessiones*), 8.10, 22 (PL 32:759).

4 Augustine, *Confessions*, 4.7, 12 (PL 32:698).

5 Augustine, *Confessions*, 6.15, 25 (PL 32:732).

6 Ambrose, *Letters* (*Epistolae*) 1.63, 94 (PL 16:1214D-1215A).

7 Paulinus of Nola (353-431), a Christian Latin poet.

8 Paulinus of Nola, *Letters* (*Epistolae*), 8, vv. 107-108 (PL 61:184C-D).

9 Boethius, Anicius Manlius Severinus (d. 524), a Christian philosopher and the author of the famous *Consolation of Philosophy*.

10 In classical antiquity, Thule was the furthest possible place in the world, sometimes identified as Iceland or part of Scandinavia.

11 Boethius, *The Consolation of Philosophy* (*De consolatione philosophiae*), 3, metr. 5, vv. 1-10 (PL 63:744A).

is not freedom but arrogance."[12] On this the glorious Pope Gregory in the third part of his *Moral Commentary* also "is bold," as was fitting, and writes, cries out, "and says" (Rom 10:20): "There is no freedom in sin, for it is written: *Where the Spirit of the Lord is, there is freedom* (2 Cor 3:17)."[13] Here there also belongs what Sedulius,[14] the poet of Christ, says on the end of The Lord's Prayer:

> If we desire to avoid evil, we have to come to
> And to follow after good, for the latter sets free and the former slays,
> The latter nourishes and the former kills.
> For as far as the stars are from the earth,
> Fire from water, light from darkness, peace from wars,
> Life from tombs, so far are the good distant,
> Separated from the evil. It is necessary that everyone walk on either the right
> Or the left road, but the right path of the good
> Summons illustrious just men into its delights
> And into your bosom, O Patriarch, but the left path of the evil
> Tortures with pains and leads to wicked hell.
> Hence, for God's lambs and sheep this is the only will
> And good freedom: to escape the awful mouth of the bloody
> Wolf, and to enjoy life through the pastures of Christ.[15]

2. Christ, beloved Son of God equal to him, sweet Word of God equal to him, sweet utterance of God equal to him, prostrate I beg in your name on account of your Father and you, his Son, and the Holy Spirit, the Father's and your common warmth and love, sufficient, I say, because of both of you, the only splendid Sun,[16] *Holy, holy, holy is the Lord God of hosts* (Is 6:3), the Lord God of armies, the Lord God of powers, the Lord God and the Father of spirits, our Lord God, for the sake of your holy and glorious name—I beg that, gratuitously giving heed, you may now gratuitously give heed to the prayer of my heart willingly, as much as it is necessary for the case, that is, that you be merciful and completely gratuitously be lord now and ever after over his or your ever gratuitously beloved. And because you know him to be my fullest brother, set him free, that is, gratuitously make him completely free from the slavery of sin and also make him a vessel of mercy and a son of the promise.[17] And with all his chains having been broken by your gratuitous mercies and compassions, commend him to your Father and to yourself and to the Holy Spirit, your common love, so that it delights this beautiful young man to die daily[18] more and more from now on for the sake of

12 Augustine, *Letters* (*Epistulae*), 157.3, 16 (PL 33:682).

13 Gregory the Great, *Moral Commentary on Job*, 15.21, 25 (PL 75:1094C).

14 Caelius Sedulius, a fifth century Christian Latin poet.

15 Sedulius, *Easter Hymn* (*Carmen paschale*), 2, vv. 288-300 (PL 19 :631A-34A).

16 See Mal 4:2.

17 See Rom 9:8, 23.

18 See 1 Cor 15:31.

you, three and one beauty, the only one that is always to be adored, worshipped, feared—would to heaven!—to possess and also to be possessed, acquired, and enjoyed face to face and perpetually, but also eternally to please, obey, serve and cling to you, our most loving author, creator, recreator, maker, remaker, former, reformer, redeemer, savior, and deliverer. I beg you that you gratuitously send him the Holy Spirit, *the Paraclete, the Spirit of truth* (Jn 14:16-17), from your Father who begot you from his womb, so that there be done what was written: *The yoke will become rotten by the application of oil* (Is 10:27), that is, the yoke of sin by the presence of the Holy Spirit, and I ask that after his departure out of this world you gratuitously give him eternal life and everlasting blessedness. Amen.

3. However, if after so many and such great or such fine testimonies as these, anyone says that the reprobate have free choice for acting well or even can have it, the Son of God surely refutes him more clearly than light and also more brightly than the sun itself, when he says of the Holy Spirit: *Whom the world cannot receive* (Jn 14:17). Therefore, Saint Augustine rightly says concerning the choice of the reprobate: "O evil choice without God!"[19] Therefore, it is clear without a scruple, is evident without ambiguity, and is manifest without a cloud that, just as the reprobate do not have it for acting well, but for acting wrongly, so they certainly do not have it for speaking the truth, but for lying. Hence, if you want to know more about it, read the *Enchiridion* and the *Hypomnesticon* of Saint Augustine, his three books *On Free Will*, his two *Letters to Valentine*, and the book *On Grace and Free Choice*, where he says among other things:

It is omnipotent God himself:

> who prepares the will so that we will and who completes by working with us what he begins by working. For, in beginning, he works so that we will, who works with those who will in bringing the work to completion. On account of this the Apostle says: *I am sure that he who produces the good work in you will bring it to completion for the day of Christ Jesus* (Phil 1:6). He, therefore, works without us so that we will, but when we will and will so that we act, he works with us. But without his working so that we will or without his working with us when we will, we can do nothing toward the good works of piety.[20]

And concerning his working so that we will, there is also this passage of Augustine:

> For if faith is simply a matter of free choice and not given by God, why do we pray that those who do not want to believe may believe? We would do this utterly in vain, unless we believed most correctly that almighty God can turn to belief even wills that are perverse and opposed to faith. Man's free choice is addressed when it is said: *Today, if you hear his voice, do not harden your hearts* (Ps 94:8).[21]

---

19 Augustine, *Sermons* (*Sermones*), 26.3, 3 (PL 38:172).

20 Augustine, *On Grace and Free Choice* (*De gratia et libero arbitrio*), 17.33 (PL 44:901).

21 Augustine, *On Grace and Free Choice*, 14.29 (PL 44:898).

Read also the book, *On Rebuke and Grace,*[22] his homilies, *On the Gospel of John,*[23] that most celebrated, beautiful and salutary *Homily on A Verse of the Ninety Fourth Psalm: Come, Let Us Worship and Bow Down*[24] and other works of his, for he speaks about it in nearly all of them, protected by God's grace. If you wish, also read the last book of Bede's *Commentary on the Song of Songs.*[25] Also see what blessed Augustine says in the second part of the *City of God*: "A good man, even if he is a slave, is free, but a bad man, even if he rules, is a slave and not of one or of a man, but—what is far more worse—of as many masters as he has vices."[26] Explaining this, Prosper[27] says among other things:

> Only a sinner is in a wicked servitude. Although he has
> A great kingdom, he is a slave miserable enough,
> Because, when the tyrant of sin rules beyond measure.
> The mind is a slave, given to as many scepters as he has vices.[28]

Read the *Commentary on the Letter to the Romans*[29] of blessed Ambrose, and *On Binding of the She-Ass*[30] by John Chrysostom, and the canons of the two hundred and fourteen bishops, one of whom was Augustine, against the heresy of Pelagius and Celestius,[31] and the three letters of the African bishops to Pope Innocent, and the three letters of him to them,[32] as well as the decrees of the Pope Celestine to all the bishops of Gaul,[33] and *On the Psalms* by Cassiodorus, where he says on the verse: *It is good to hope in the Lord* (Ps 117:8): "The benefit of mortals is never explained by free choice,"[34] and the book by Prosper against

22 Augustine, *On Rebuke and* Grace (*De correptione et gratia*) in PL 44:915-46.

23 Augustine, *Homilies on the Gospel of John* (*In Iohannis evangelium tractatus*) in PL 35:1379-1976.

24 Augustine, *Sermons*, 26 in PL 38:171-8.

25 Bede the Venerable, *On the Song of Songs* (*In Canticum Canticorum*) in PL 91:1223-36. Its last book consists of excerpts from Gregory the Great.

26 Augustine, *On the City of God* (*De civitate Dei*), 4.3 (CSEL 40.1:166).

27 Prosper of Aquitaine (c.390-c.463), a defender of Augustinian theology and author of several poetical works.

28 Prosper, *Excerpts from the Statements of Augustine* (*Epigrammata ex sententiis Augustini*), 53 (PL 51:514B).

29 Ambrosiaster, *Commentary on the Letter to the Romans* (*Commentarium in epistolam ad Romanos*) in PL 17:47-192.

30 John Chrysostom, *Homilies on Matthew* (*Homiliae in Matthaeum*), 66.2 (PG 58:627-8).

31 *The Council of Milevis* (*Concilium Milevitanum*) II, canons 1-8 (CCSL 149:361-9).

32 See Pope Innocent I, *Letters* (*Epistolae*), 26-31 (PL 20:564A-97B).

33 Pope Celestine I, *Letters* (*Epistolae*), 21 (PL 50:528A-37B).

34 Cassiodorus, *Explanation of the Psalms* (*Expositio psalmorum*), On Ps 117:8 (PL 70:828D).

the conference of Cassian, which is entitled *On God's Protection*, and his *Answers to the Gauls, to the Genoese*, and *to the Vincentians*, and his letter which is entitled *To Rufinus*,[35] and the last part of the *Moral Commentary* by holy Gregory, as well as the first part of his *Homilies on Ezekiel*,[36] and you will praise the omnipotent God. It should of course be known that, as Saint Augustine says, free choice, once set free by God's grace, has as much capability and possibility for doing good in a soul, mind, or heart as a healthy eye in a body has for seeing.[37] Nevertheless, just as even a very healthy eye, when placed in darkness, without the assistance of external light cannot see anything, so free choice without God's grace and help also undoubtedly cannot do anything good. But similarly, after his eyes are deservedly lost by God's just judgment, a thief and a highwayman cannot now see as he could formerly, just because he desires to steal others' possessions. The will of course is present, but the capability is lost. In the same way, someone who, having abandoned God, is a servant and a slave to a criminal sin, though he occasionally wills, he cannot be completely free unless he is set free by God. No wonder.

> For someone who uses free choice wrongly destroyed both himself and it. For as someone who kills himself kills himself, of course, when living, but after killing himself, he is not living and cannot restore himself to life when he has died, so, although someone sinned by his own free choice with sin the victor, free choice was also lost. *For one is a slave of him by whom he has been overcome* (2 Pt 2:19). This is certainly the judgment of the apostle Peter. And since it is true, what kind of freedom, I ask, can someone enslaved have, except when it delights him to sin? For, he is freely a slave who does the will of his master gladly. Accordingly, he is free for sinning, who is a slave of sin. Hence he will not be free to act well, until, having been set free from sin, he begins to be a slave of righteousness... And before this begins to take place in a person, how can anyone, who is not yet free for doing good, boast about a good work from free choice?[38]

Read in the *Enchiridion* the whole chapter entitled *On the Loss of the Free Choice*. And as much as I have set forth here about it will be clear and pleasing to you, not—God forbid!—that you should ascribe to me that I set forth such great

35 Prosper of Aquitaine, *On Grace and Free Will against Cassian the Lecturer* (*De gratia et libero arbitrio contra collatorem* in PL 51:213-76), *Answers to the Objections of the Gauls* (*Pro Augustino responsiones ad capitula obiectionum Gallorum calumniantium* in PL 51:155-74); *Answers to the Extracts of the Genoese* (*Pro Augustino repsonsiones ad exerpta Genuensium* in PL 51:187-202); *Answers to the Vincentian Objections* (*Pro Augustino responsiones ad capitula obiectionum Vincentiarum* in PL 51:177-86); and *Letter to Rufinus* (*Epistula ad Rufinum*) in PL 51:77-90).

36 Gregory the Great, *Moral Commentary on Job*, 33 (PL 76:667-718); *Homilies on the Prophet Ezekiel* (*Homiliae in Hiezekielem prophetam*), 1.9 (PL 76:870-86).

37 See Augustine, *On Nature and Grace* (*De natura et gratia*), 36.29 (PL 44:261).

38 Augustine, *Enchiridion on Faith, Hope, and Love* (*Enchiridion de fide, spe, et caritate*), 30 (PL 40:246-7).

things on free choice, especially since I desire that you very speedily be set free by God through God's grace, that is, to become free from the slavery of sin and to become free from the dominion of devil.

On Twofold Predestination

4. In other respects, as it has been most truthfully stated by Saint Isidore:

> Predestination is twofold, either of the elect to rest or of the reprobate to death. Both are done by the divine judgment so that it always makes the elect follow heavenly and interior things and, by abandoning them, always permits the reprobate to take delight in lower and exterior things. Just as a person does not know the limit of light and darkness or what the boundary of each is, so one is more completely ignorant of whom the light of righteousness will anticipate before their end, or who will be blinded by the darkness of sins until their end, or who, having been converted after a lapse into darkness, will rise to the light. All these things lie open for God, but are hidden for human beings. Although the lifestyle of the righteous in this life is good, it is still uncertain for human beings to which end they have been predestined, but everything is kept for future scrutiny.
>
> It is a wonderful arrangement of heavenly distribution by which a righteous person is here made more righteous and an impious person is made more unclean.[39] A bad person is sometimes converted to good; a good person sometimes turns back to evil. Someone wants to be good and is unable; another wants to be bad and is not permitted to perish. To one who wants to be good, it is given; another does not want it, and it is not granted to him to be good. This one is born in error and dies; that one perseveres to the end in the good in which he began. This one stands until he falls; that one, after living badly for a long time, is saved in the end and, having been looked upon, is converted. A righteous person wants to advance in good and does not succeed; an evil person wants to do harm and does succeed. This one wants to devote himself to God, but is prevented by the world; that one desires to be involved in worldly affairs and does not succeed. A bad person rules over a good one; a good person is condemned in the place of an impious one; an impious person is honored in the place of a righteous one. And in this great obscurity, no one is able to search out the divine arrangement or to examine the hidden order of predestination.[40]

Hence, if you want to know more, read the book of Saint Fulgentius, where he discusses this both very plainly and very amply.[41] Nevertheless, lest I should here keep something from you, for whom I want good no less than for myself, know most certainly that the immortal, eternal, and immutable God did not create the angels, whom he nonetheless foreknew were going to be apostates and deserters, or also human beings, whom he likewise foreknew would be perpetu-

39 See Rv 22:11.

40 Isidore of Seville, *Sentences* (*Sententiae*) 2.6, 1-6 (PL 83:606A-C).

41 Fulgentius of Ruspe, *To Moninus* (*Ad Monimum*), 1 (PL 65:153-78). Or *On the Truth of Predestination and Grace* (*De veritate praedestinationis et gratiae*) in PL 65:603-72.

ally reprobate, in order that they would sin against God and abandon him. But those whom he foreknew were going to fall and persevere in evil through their own wrong-doing and outrage, offense and vice, he of course rightly predestined through just judgment, in order that they would suffer and perpetually suffer the punishment of hell, that is, on account of their unjust sins, as is clear, so that they would merit just punishments for them, as is obvious.

On Syllogisms

5. Now I want that the three-part syllogism should be very well known to you, which certainly has been useful, is useful, and will be truly useful both to many others and also to us at the same time. For the most holy apostle Paul had often used it in a single proposition, as was fitting. He of course did that in this way three times in the *Letter to the Galatians*, which is read in the church in the fourteenth week after Pentecost. Nonetheless, pay attention to how you can see the whole of this. For Saint Jerome clarified with a minor proposition and a conclusion what the Apostle brought forth in a single proposition. For example, he says:

> "*If righteousness comes through the law, then Christ died in vain* (Gal 2:21).
> But Christ did not die in vain.
> Therefore, righteousness does not come through the law."[42]

Likewise he says:

> *If the inheritance comes from the law, it no longer comes from the promise* (Gal 3:18).
> But the inheritance comes from the promise.
> Therefore, the inheritance does not come from the law.

Likewise Saint Augustine says:

> *But if Christ has not risen, the dead do not rise either* (1 Cor 15:14-16).
> But Christ has risen.
> Therefore, the dead do rise.[43]

Similarly in the first part of *On the City of God* he uses the three-part syllogism in a wonderful manner: The priests of the idols were worshippers of demons, and they were moreover perpetrators of many other evils. But the Greeks nevertheless said that those priests were to be honored. Still, the Romans denied it, although they said that the gods were to be worshipped. Therefore, on this point he said this as follows in a three-part syllogism:

> The Greeks state: If the gods are to be worshipped, then their priests are to be honored.
> The Romans argue: But their priests are not to be honored.

42 Jerome, *Commentary on the Letter to the Galatians* (*In epistulam ad Galatas*), 1. On Gal 2:21 (PL 26:346C-D).

43 See Augustine, *Unfinished Work in Answer to Julian* (*Opus imperfectum contra Iulianum*), 6.34 (PL 45:1588).

The Christians conclude: Therefore, the gods are not be worshipped.[44]

6. I myself learned this through the grace of God from the book *To the Galatians* many years ago. Therefore, after I was at Quierzy and came here under escort, Bavo and Haldoinus[45] told me that the wretch, barking Aeneas,[46] said that logic brought it about in the books of blessed Augustine that the doctrine of the predestination of the reprobate to death could not be understood by me. And so, on a certain day when Haldoinus[47] asserted this, I stated the example of Saint Jerome in his *Commentary on the Letter to the Galatians* and immediately added: Dialectic distinguishes true things from false ones, but does not—God forbid!—confuse true things with false ones. I tell you, he immediately was silent and did not dare to say anything after that. Therefore, if you want to hear more on this, I beg you, listen joyfully and intelligently, as is necessary:

> If God has not already sent or has not foreordained, that is, has not predestined reprobates to hell, then he will not send or destine them to hell, because, if he does anything that he has not done by predestining it, he will of course immediately change himself.
>
> But God will send the reprobate to hell, for we say with the psalmist: *But you, God, will bring them down into the pit of destruction* (Ps 54:24).
>
> Therefore, God predestined the reprobate to hell, that is, according to what is said in holy scripture: *God has prepared for the sword the one who crosses over from righteousness to sin* (Sir 26:27).

Likewise, the apostle Paul says about the redemption of only the elect:

> *Christ has redeemed us from the curse of the law, having become a curse for us* (Gal 3:13). Therefore, if Christ redeemed the reprobate from the curse of the law, having become a curse for them, then the reprobate will not be cursed, but entirely blessed.
>
> However, the reprobate will not be blessed, but rather accursed, as is clear, for the Son of God is going to say to them: *Depart from me, you accursed ones, into everlasting fire* (Mt 25:41).
>
> Therefore, Christ did not redeem the reprobate from the curse of the law nor did he become a curse for them.

Likewise, the apostle Paul says:

> *If God be for us, who is against us? He who did not spare even his own Son, but handed him over for us all, how has he not also with him given us all things?* (Rom 8:31-32). Therefore, if God handed over his Son also for all of the reprobate, then he has given them all good things with him and through this also eternal life.

---

44 Augustine, *On the City of God* (*De civitate Dei*), 2.13 (PL 41:58).

45 Haldoinus was abbot of the monastery at Hautvillers for part of 840. He was deposed in 853 by the synod of Soissons.

46 Aeneas (d.870) was bishop of Paris in 858.

47 Lambot, 157, has *Hardoino*.

But he has not given them all good things with him.
Therefore, he did not hand him over for them.

Likewise, he says:

But God commends his love for us because while we were yet sinners Christ died for us. Much more now, having been justified in his blood, will we be saved from wrath through him (Rom 5:8-9). Therefore, if Christ died even for the reprobate, then the reprobate too, having been justified in his blood, will be saved from wrath through him.
But the reprobate will not be saved from wrath through him.
Therefore, Christ did not die for the reprobate.

There follows:

For if when we were enemies, we were reconciled to God through the death of his Son, much more, having been reconciled, will we be saved by his life (Rom 5:10). Therefore, if the reprobate were reconciled to God through the death of his Son, they will be saved by his life.
But they will not be saved by his life.
Therefore, the reprobate were not reconciled to God through the death of his Son.

Likewise, the apostle Paul says:

God was in Christ reconciling the world to himself, not imputing to them their sins (2 Cor 5:19). Therefore, if God the Father, who was in Christ hanging on the wood of the cross, reconciled even the reprobate world to himself, then he neither has imputed, nor is imputing, nor will impute to them their sins.
But regarding the reprobate world, God indeed has imputed, is imputing, and will impute their sins to them, namely, those who on account of the enormity and deformity, the magnitude and multitude of their sins have been justly plunged and rightly...[48]

48 The Latin text in Lambot, 158, breaks off abruptly.

ON PREDESTINATION

This text is probably the most representative of Gottschalk's teaching among those discovered by Dom Germain Morin in 1931. It is in fact a collection of testimonies (*schedulae*), gathered under the title *On Predestination* (*De praedestinatione*) in ms. Berne 584 (Bibliothèque de la Ville), fol. 56v-96v. The material is heterogeneous and hardly amenable to exact chronology, even though it is most likely that the units, which comprise it, were written at Hautvillers, after 849. The subdivisions in the present translation are almost the same as in Lambot, but with different numeration: sections VII-XI in Lambot correspond to sections 1-5 here, section XII corresponds to 6 and 7, sections XIII-XVIII to 8-13. Wherever the subtitles occur, they are kept unchanged; those in brackets were added by the translator corresponding to the content of the section. Edition: Lambot, 180-258. Translated by Victor Genke.

1.

GRACE AND NATURE

1. Since the scripture testifies and says: *The souls of the righteous are in the hand of God* (Wis 3:1), it is excellently said, wherever it is found: "May we walk before you by his example."[1] For they walk and run well before him in the hand of him in whose hand they are. *For in him we live and move and have our being* (Acts 17:28). For since he is never distant, but always whole everywhere, we are undoubtedly with him also when we make our way from him, through him, in him, and to him. Therefore, Pope Gregory also says concerning the holy angels: "They run within him,"[2] when they come to him. For when a man who is in a city or a camp runs there in any direction, it is not possible to say correctly that he runs "into the city" or "into the camp." but "in the city" or "in the camp." So with even better reason one cannot find fault when the elect are said to walk before the Lord, who is their place and house.[3]

2. I have never read nor learned from anyone what that step was or rather is concerning which, if I remember correctly, David said to Jonathan: *Death and I*

1 *Collects for the Mass in the Gregorian Sacramentary* (*Collecta ad missam in sacramentario gregoriano*) in HBS 49:23.96.

2 Gregory the Great, *Homilies on the Gospels* (*Homiliae in Evangelia*), 2.34, 13 (PL 76:1255B).

3 See Gregory the Great, *Moral Commentary on Job* (*Moralia in Iob*), 6.33, 67 (PL 75:674C-D).

are separated by only one step (1 Sm 20:3). But, as I think, that step can nonetheless be suitably understood to be the grace of God. For when it gratuitously has set free, is setting free, and will set free the chosen and beloved ones from the law in the members fighting against the law of the mind,[4] from the law of sin,[5] and from the body of death,[6] the elect are also fittingly divided by this one step, when they are divinely set free from their persecutors and from the destruction of bodily death. O step, which is dearer because it is gratuitous, by which we are set free both from carnal concupiscence, that is, from spiritual death, and from bodily death. By it those who *were by nature children of wrath* (Eph 2:3), having become children of mercy, freely come and climb while rejoicing, to the heights, whom their corrupted nature plunged into the depths. Mourning and groaning in those depths, each of the elect still in the flesh daily says to God: *Out of the depths I have cried to you, Lord* (Ps 129:1), with sighs, tears, laments, and loud cries.

3. Let him hear this, who proudly preferred or perhaps still prefers nature to grace.[7] That antiphon that you sing with due reverence concerning the holy cross: "O admirable cross, removal of the wound, restoration of health," overthrows more clearly than daylight and dispels the error that is fabricated as it were concerning the baptized reprobate having been redeemed by it.[8] For since it is certain that this cross neither ever was nor ever is a "removal of the wound" or "restoration of health" for any of them, it is certainly clear that the redemption of none of them was brought about on it, but only of the elect who alone are believed and recognized to be the world redeemed by Christ's passion, that is, as they as suppliants say to their redeemer: "We adore you, O Christ, and bless you, for by your cross you have redeemed the world,"[9] and they alone say: "But we have to boast in the cross of our Lord Jesus Christ by which we have been saved and set free."[10] For *no one can say that Jesus is Lord except in the Holy Spirit* (1 Cor 12:3), that is, as explained by Saint Augustine: "In heart, in mouth, in deed, in spirit, in words, and in action *no one can say that Jesus is Lord except*

4 See Gal 5:17.

5 See Rom 8:2.

6 See Rom 7:23.

7 Gottschalk means either Rabanus Maurus or Hincmar of Reims.

8 Gregory the Great, *Book of Antiphons* (*Antiphonarium*), *Antiphon on the Exaltation of the Holy Cross* (*Antiphona in exaltationem sanctae crucis*) in PL 78:803D.

9 Gregory the Great, *Book of Antiphons*, *Antiphon on the Exaltation of the Holy Cross* in PL 78:804B.

10 Gregory the Great, *Book of Antiphons*, *Antiphon for the Introit of the Thursday of the Lord's Supper* (*Antiphona ad introitum feria quinta de Coena Domini*) in PL 78:675C.

in the Holy Spirit (1 Cor 12:3)."[11] Since *the world cannot receive him* (Jn 14:17), it cannot for this reason say that it has been redeemed by Christ's blood. For whoever says this says nothing, and for this reason he does not say anything even now, because he does not say this in the Holy Spirit, who is *the Spirit of truth* (Jn 14:17; 16:13). For what he says is false and for this reason he does not say anything now because what he says is nothing. For if the baptized reprobate were redeemed by the blood of Christ's cross, they were therefore also saved and set free by him. But those who have been quite rightly already judged, already condemned, already predestined to everlasting death by Christ himself and, as has been said, rightly already hurled down into it, were not saved and set free by him. Therefore, they were not redeemed by the blood of his cross. And so let the mute dog ceasing from barking,[12] for Christ is truly the redeemer, savior, and deliverer not of two worlds, but of one, that is, of elect world alone, namely, his body. Whoever does not see this is blind; whoever denies this is slain.

4. Explaining the passage: *In this was I born* (Jn 18:37) in *On John*, Saint Augustine says: "The syllable of this pronoun is not to be lengthened, but to be shortened, as if it said: 'Into this thing was I born,' that is: 'For this thing.'"[13]

5. Isaiah says: *Lord, you will give us peace, for you have done every work for us* (Is 26:12). For this reason he says: *You have done*, concerning the past, for *he has done what will be* (Is 45:11 LXX). He alone has done all things by predestining them; he also works by inspiring and cooperates by helping those who are already willing because of him.

6. If it is asked where the Son is said to be *the first power*, it is found in Micah: *And you, O cloudy tower of the daughter, Jerusalem, the first power will come to you and will come right to you* (Mi 4:8 VL). And by this sentence the Arian heresy is completely overthrown, for the Son is truly not the second power, but the first, *the first power*, which is naturally one, but personally three.

7. This is the difference between the death that God did not make and death that God has imposed, imposes and, will impose. Concerning the former the scripture says: *God did not make death* (Wis 1:13); concerning the latter it says: *Life and death are from the Lord God* (Sir 11:14), that is, life from God who gives and death from God who vindicates. The former is one, but the latter is double. For upon the death of sin that men have inflicted, inflict, and will inflict on themselves, God has inflicted, inflicts, and will inflict bodily death, that is, the separation of the soul from the body, and the death of hell, that is, on account of the one unjust death the twofold just death. Such is the difference between the unjust evils that every unjust person has committed, commits, and will commit

11 Augustine, *Homilies on the Gospel of John* (*In Iohannis evangelium tractatus*), 74.1 (PL 35:18270.

12 Probably Rabanus or Hincmar.

13 Augustine, *Homilies on the Gospel of John*, 115.4 (PL 35:1940). The accusative form of the pronoun has a short "o," while the ablative has a long "o."

and the just evils that God has paid back, pays back, and will pay back through present adversities and perpetual torments, as the just one sees fit. When the Lord our God and teacher, Jesus Christ, the blessed king and invincible emperor, having already abundantly spoken against the reprobate and speaking in advance, says to the elect: *When these things begin to happen, look and lift up your heads, because your redemption draws near* (Lk 21:28), he sufficiently discloses to those who have ears to hear and eyes to see[14] that, as he was without doubt *was made by God* both *righteousness and sanctification*, so he was also made the *redemption* (1 Cor 1:30) of them alone. For them such consolation is poured out and also conferred by him, and not—God forbid!—on even one of those upon whom, *withering from fear and the expectation of those things that will come over the whole earth* (Lk 21:26), fitting desolation is announced, great tribulation is inflicted, and incomparably greater torment will consequently be imposed, as they deserve.

8. Whoever says that nature is greater than grace, wandering far from *the way of truth* (Ps 118:30), certainly stands forth as highly ungrateful, hostile, and injurious to grace itself, and while, speaking very thoughtlessly, he contradicts the truth with rash garrulousness, he certainly produces not a small, but a huge insult to the Spirit of grace. In order that, with God's help, you may learn all this clearly, it is worth the effort to pay attention prudently to the things that follow. Grace is at times found to be called God the Son or God the Holy Spirit in the sacred scripture. For you read as follows in the Apostle on the Son: *In order that the grace of God might taste death for all* (Heb 2:9), and again: *Let us then come with confidence to the throne of grace* (Heb 4:16). But you read in him about the Holy Spirit: *O wretched man that I am! Who will deliver me from this body of death? The grace of God, through Jesus Christ our Lord* (Rom 7:24-25), and: *But to each one of us grace has been given according to the measure of Christ's gift* (Eph 4:7), and: *Now there are varieties of graces, but the same Spirit* (1 Cor 12:4), and: *That you may revive the grace of God that is in you through* [the laying on of my hands] (2 Tm 1:6). But this is said about the Holy Spirit in Daniel in this way: *God aroused the Holy Spirit of the young lad, whose name was Daniel* (Dn 13:45). For it should not be understood of the created spirit of the lad, but of the creator Spirit. But if it concerns you why the Holy Spirit, although he is the Spirit of God, is called *the Spirit of the lad*, it should be understood to have been given to the lad, as is the statement of the Apostle: *The Spirit of the prophets is subject to the prophets* (1 Cor 14:32) and the words of Elisha to Elijah: *I ask that double your Spirit be in me* (2 Kgs 2:9). If you look at these texts, then you certainly can also see that, just as no one can say that a creature is greater than the creator or something made is greater than its maker, so no one who thinks healthy thoughts can ever say that nature is greater than grace, since grace is of course God and therefore always omnipotent, but nature without grace is

14 See Mt 13:9.

altogether powerless. Is not grace God and omnipotent, which gratuitously sets free and saves whomever it wants? As it is said: *Who will deliver me from this body of death? The grace of God* (Rom 7:24-25), and: *For by grace you have been saved* (Eph 2:8), and: *By whose grace you have been saved* (Eph 2:5), and: *We believe that we are being saved through the grace of Christ, just as they were* (Acts 15:11). Therefore, also Prosper says: "But the grace of Christ is the Savior of all;"[15] and: "Grace restores us; grace justifies us."[16]

Is not grace omnipotent, which is sufficient for the elect against the temptations of devil? As the Lord says to the Apostle: *My grace is sufficient for you* (2 Cor 12:9); he does not say: "Your nature is sufficient for you." For only God is sufficient for a rational and intellectual creature. Therefore, it is seen not obscurely, but clearly that the grace of God undoubtedly is God. For just as the hand of the Lord, the right hand of the Lord, the arm of the Lord, and the mercy of God is God the Son, and just as the finger of God, the gift of God, and the heat of God is the Holy Spirit, so the grace of God is either God the Son or God the Holy Spirit. Both the Son and the Holy Spirit are called grace because each of them is given to us by God the Father gratuitously.

Therefore, let nature that is been vitiated, wounded, debilitated, corrupted countless times, even thousands of times fall silent, because nature that is uncorrupted cannot be truly compared nor corrupted nature—God forbid!—preferred to the creator. But neither can the incorruptible nature of the sort that is in the most blessed angels and that will at some time be gratuitously in us through grace. So let us not be ungrateful to God's grace, since we certainly cannot give adequate thanks for that by which it was been brought about that we, who *were by nature children of wrath just as the others* (Eph 2:3), have not remained guilty, as we were with the others. *Why will dust and ashes be proud?* (Sir 10:9), for he, who was once the first of the angels, overconfident and proud of his nature, fell from heaven conquered, and he who fought against him exists in heaven as victor by God's grace.[17]

If you are waiting for anything greater than these, I ask that you joyfully pay attention to what I will set forth. We believe and confess that two natures are complete and united natures in our Lord Jesus Christ, that is, the divine and the human. Still he who was *beautiful in form beyond the sons of men*, for *grace has been poured out upon* his *lips*, has been blessed by God *for eternity* (Ps 44:3). Look, since in Christ human nature was blessed because grace was poured out upon his lips, he is certainly proud in an excessively dangerous and excessively destructive way who presumes to puff up and hurl down the foulness, infirmity,

---

15 Prosper of Aquitaine, *Excerpts from the Statements of Augustine* (*Epigrammata ex sententiis Augustini*), 16 (PL 51:504A).

16 Prosper, *Excerpts from the Statements of Augustine*, 45 (PL 51:512A).

17 See Rv 12:7.

weakness, destitution, and blindness of our entirely corrupted nature, and for no other reason than that he learned that "nature is greater than teaching" and this because the cat left the wax and caught the mouse.[18] This is the same as if somebody less prudent, who, hearing that a chicken that has a bigger head would have to eat its equal, thinks that he can say fittingly the same thing about a boar of remarkably great size.[19] This comparison is of course quite inappropriate, but, as is clear, more inappropriate than the former. For a chicken's head is incomparably much more like[20] a boar's head than is the nature of the human race in comparison to the grace of Christ. For in the first case a comparison is made of a creature in place to a creature in place, but in the latter a comparison is made of a creature in place to the creator not in place, of something powerless to the omnipotent. I believe these things are sufficient.

As for the rest there is a book of the clearest style by the most holy Augustine, *On Nature and Grace*, in which he most clearly and also most fully discusses this question from both points of view, where this teacher also says most truly among other things: "If justice comes through nature, then Christ has died in vain," in order that by supplying a little, we might add a minor premise and conclude: But Christ did not die in vain; therefore justice does not come through nature.[21] And again: "Why also should I not cry out? Rather, I shall will cry out and rebuke such people with Christian sorrow: *You, who are justified by nature, have been cut off from Christ; you have fallen from grace* (Gal 5:4)."[22] Are they not justified by nature who say that it is greater than grace? We, however, knowing that *we were by nature children of wrath just as the others* (Eph 2:3), and because of this deserving to perish forever, if, by God's gratuitous gift, we did not at some time turn away from evil and do good[23] through the gift of God's grace, let us say together with the Apostle: *By the grace of God I am what I am* (1 Cor 15:10). Augustine also says in the first *Letter to Valentine and the Monks*:

---

18 Lambot pointed to the fact that Gottschalk might have borrowed both the saying and the fable from the tradition which served as a source for *Salomo et Marcolphus* (ed. W. Bernary, Heidelberg, 1914), a medieval parody of the Proverbs, the earliest manuscripts of which date from the fourteenth century. In the twelfth century the fable about the cat is related by Guy de Basoches in his *Apology*.

19 Lambot marked the most part of this sentence as corrupt, perhaps because he connected the word *parem* ("as big as" or "equal in size") with *aper* ("boar"), as is evident from his footnote on p. 187. However the meaning is quite clear if one understands the words *suum debuisset parem comedere* ("would have to eat his equal") to refer to the chicken.

20 I have conjectured *similius* instead of *maius*.

21 Augustine, *On Nature and Grace* (*De natura et gratia*), 2.2 (PL 44:249).

22 Augustine, *On Nature and Grace*, 40.47 (PL 44:270).

23 See Ps 36:27 and 1 Pt 3:11.

> If then there is no grace of God, how does God save the world? And if there is no free choice, how does God judge the world? Understand then in accordance with this faith so that you neither deny God's grace nor defend free choice so that you separate it from the grace of God, as if without it we can in any way either think or do anything according to God, which we absolutely cannot. For, on this account, when the Lord was speaking of the fruit of righteousness, he said to his disciples: *Without me you can do nothing* (Jn 15:5).[24]

And a little later he says:

> Let no one say that the grace of God was given to him because of the merits of his works or because of the merit of his faith, let him not think that what those heretics say is true, namely, that the grace of God is given in accord with our merits, which is utterly false, not because there is no merit, whether the good merit of the pious or the evil merit of the impious ones—for otherwise how will God judge the world?—but God's mercy and grace converts a person. Concerning this the psalm says: *My God, his mercy will come before me* (Ps 58:10) so that the impious may be justified, that is, so that he may become righteous instead of impious, and may begin to possess the good merit that the Lord will crown when the world will be judged.[25]

9. Christ and the church, like bridegroom and bride, like the head, the body, and the members, are one person, as scripture testifies: *They will be two in one flesh* (Gn 2:24), which the Apostle says about *Christ and the church* (Eph 5:32)—which, as he testifies, *is his body and his fullness* (Eph 1:23), *of his flesh and of his bones* (Eph 5:30). Hence we of course correctly believe, rightly hope and trust that the body and blood of Christ were handed over and shed for the church of Christ alone—for the Apostle says: *Christ loved the church and handed himself over for her* (Eph 5:25) and again: *Which he purchased by his own blood* (Acts 20:28)—are united with, cling to, and are joined to the church of Christ, that is, to the adoptive children of God, heirs of God, coheirs of Christ, brothers of Christ, members of Christ, the body of Christ. This certainly should not in any way be believed in that sense about the reprobate, who are the members of the devil and the body of antichrist. For the Lord says to the elect only: *This is my body which will be handed over for you* (1 Cor 11:24), and he says of his blood: "Which will be shed for you and for many for the remission of sins."[26] And the Father says to this Son who is *the power of God and the wisdom of God* (1 Cor 1:24): *Make your dwelling in Jacob, and in Israel receive your inheritance, and in my elect strike your root* (Sir 24:13), and: *Thus I have been established in Zion and sanctified in the city, I have likewise rested, and my power is in Jerusalem, and I took root in an honored people; in the portion of my God is their inheritance, and my possession is in the fullness of the saints* (Sir 24:15-16). See, as is clear, obvious, and manifest,

---

24 Augustine, *Letters* (*Epistulae*), 214.2 (PL 33:969).

25 Augustine, *Letters*, 214.4 (PL 33:970).

26 *Canon of the Roman Mass*. See Lk 22: 20; Mt 26:28; Mk 14:24.

Christ's *possession is in the fullness of the saints*, and for the reason that only the elect church is *his body and his fullness* (Eph 1:23), in it alone, which is the body of Christ, the body and blood of Christ remains unto salvation and prevails as a remedy unto eternal life[27] only in those who are the body of Christ, not in the members of devil and the body of antichrist.

What was briefly also said in the *Canons of Orange*, that is, by Saint Caesarius[28] and his fellow bishops, assembled in the city of Orange, namely, "Let whoever says that God predestined human beings to evil be anathema,"[29] should be understood as "to the evil of sin, trespass, and crime," not as "to the evil of torment, torture, and punishment," as the truth holds. But if anyone says on the contrary that God did not make evil, let him hear the Lord saying to the Lord: *All my enemies have heard of my evil, Lord; they have rejoiced because you have made it* (Lam 1:21), and this: *Will there be in the city evil that the Lord has not made?* (Am 3:6), and this: *If we have received good from the hand of God, why should we not receive evil?* (Jb 2:10), and this: *I, the Lord, form light and create darkness, I make peace and create evil, I am the Lord who does all these things* (Is 45:7). When the psalmist says to God: *O Lord my God, in you I put my trust; save me from all those who persecute me, and set me free lest he seize my soul like a lion, while there is no one to redeem or save me* (Ps 7:2-3), he undoubtedly declares that the reprobate were neither redeemed nor set free by God through the blood of Christ's cross, since the lion seizes their souls. And although they also at times cry out to the Lord, still because *they endure but for a time* (Mk 4:17) and *believe for a time and in time of temptation fall away* (Lk 8:13), he does not hear them in accord with what is said in another psalm: *They cried out, but there was no one to save; they cried out to the Lord, but he did not answer them* (Ps 17:42). But because those temporary believers temporally applaud and flatter themselves over bodily or temporal salvation, let them hear what is rightly said concerning such people elsewhere: *For there is no regard for their death and no strength in their wound; they are not in the labor of human beings, and they will not be scourged with human beings. Therefore, pride has held them fast; they are covered with their iniquity. Their iniquity has come out as from fat; they have passed in the love of their heart. They have thought and spoken wickedness; they have spoken wickedness on high. They have set their mouth against heaven, and their tongue has passed on earth* (Ps 72:4-9). Let all, all the reprobate, know that they will be safe in an incomparably better way after the day of judgment, when they shall have been sent into eternal fire, where they will no longer have any ability to sin, than there was here where they

27 See Jn 6:27.

28 Caesarius of Arles (c. 470-542) convened the second Council of Orange in 529.

29 *The Council of Orange* (*Concilium Arausicum*) II, Conclusion (Mansi, 8:717-8; MGH, Concilia, 1:52; CCSL 148A:63; DS, 397).

misuse their temporal safety so that they are rightly predestined to that place to which, you see, they are even now rightly destined.

11.[30] It is very profitable, my dear son, to consider carefully that just as in the writings of the blessed fathers, catholics seek with very great thirst for the truth by which they may live, so on the contrary heretics seek with very great diligence falsity by which they may kill others. Of this sort is that, for example, which John Chrysostom says: "Nobody who has not been harmed by himself can be harmed by another."[31] The unfortunate Pelagian bishop Julian put this in his books and wanted to strengthen his heresy from it, as much as he could, that is, saying that Adam neither injured nor harmed any of us, and for this reason there is no original sin in little children.[32] Since, of course, none of them was harmed by himself, it is therefore clear, he says, that Adam could not have harmed them. Bede the Venerable admirably responded against this, as you may observe in the first volume of *On the Song of Songs*, when he clearly shows that this statement of John is not true, that is, because simple and foolish people can be unknowingly deceived and therefore also harmed by heretics. From this he showed that all children born from Adam through the union of the two sexes were undoubtedly mortally harmed by Adam.[33] Therefore, if I faithfully tell you what you should beware of in the books of blessed Jerome, you should not by any means—God forbid!—be angry with me. Of this sort is this statement on the sentence of the psalm: *Direct my way before your face* (Ps 5:9): "It is up to me," he says, "to place my foot; it is up to you to direct my step," although no one of course ever has placed, places, or will place a step or foot that the Lord did not make, does not make, or will not make him place.[34] He has of course chosen in Christ all his elect,[35] and Christ has placed all of them in himself, as he himself says: *And I have placed you* (Jn 15:16). Nor does it agree with the truth that *Direct my way before your face* (Ps 5:9), ought not to be said, because he says: "If it is mine, it is not good."[36] What impediment does it cause that it should not be said in that way? Does not the prophet say: *The crooked will become straight* (Is 40:4), and the psalmist himself: *May my ways be made straight* (Ps 118:5)? Therefore, it

30 Section 10 has been omitted. It mainly treats grammatical matters.

31 John Chrysostom, *Book "That Nobody Who Has Not Been Harmed by Himself Can Be Harmed by Another"* (*Liber "Quod qui seipsum non laedit nemo laedere potest"*) in PG 52:459-80.

32 Gottschalk refers to Julian of Eclanum (c. 380-455). Fragments of Julian's *On Love* (*De amore*. CCSL 88:398-401) were preserved in Bede's *Commentary on the Song of Songs* (*Commentarium super canticum canticorum*).

33 See Bede the Venerable, *Commentary on the Song of Songs*, 1, Preface 9 (PL 91:1072-3).

34 Jerome, *Notes on the Psalms* (*Breviculus in psalmos*). On Ps 5:9 (PL 26:831A).

35 See Eph 1:4.

36 The source of this quotation has not been located.

ought to seem surprising to no one that he who often brought forth these and similar things argued that the reprobate are redeemed by Christ, because if this is true, then that is also true—God forbid!—which Origen asserts, namely, that through a cycles of the years the saints will fall from heaven and the unjust will go from hell to heaven and that they will have this alternation of beatitude and misery.[37] But because the latter opinion of Origen is false on account of the words of the Lord: *And they will go into everlasting punishment* (Mt 25:46), the former opinion is also certainly false concerning the redemption of the reprobate, on account of the words of the Apostle: *Through his own blood he entered the holy place once, having obtained eternal redemption* (Heb 9:12).

14.[38] Furthermore, you should know that when that passage in the Gospel was read: *When the king heard, he was angry, and having sent out his armies, he destroyed those murderers and burned up their city* (Mt 22:7), I immediately said: Behold the redeemed, although they were rather the destroyed. I spoke similarly also about the man who was rightly *cast into the outer darkness* (Mt 22:13).

15. What blessed Gregory says was very pleasing: "God the Father prepared the wedding for God the Son,"[39] and these words: "Just as the Father sent me, as God sent God, so I send you, as a man sends men."[40] Therefore, it is clear that, since each person is God essentially, the Holy Spirit is certainly God, who proceeds both from God, who prepared the wedding for God and from God, for whom God prepared the wedding, as well as he who proceeds both from God who sends God and from God who was sent by God, this Holy Spirit by no means has blood—God forbid!—but only the Son, alone God and man, bridegroom and God, according to the passage: *The bridegroom will rejoice over the bride, your God will rejoice over you* (Is 62:5). For he is equally and similarly, naturally and substantially, great God with the Father and the Holy Spirit; and he alone is nevertheless specifically the Lamb, according to what we say to him: "Lord God, Lamb of God,"[41] now and for ever, gratuitously have mercy on me, although on me who am very guilty.

37 Origen, *On First Principles* (*De principiis*), 1.6, 3 (PG 11:168-9). See Jerome, *Letters* (*Epistulae*), 124.1, 4 (PL 22:1062-3).

38 Sections 12 and 13 have been omitted. They treat grammatical matters.

39 Gregory the Great, *Homilies on the Gospels*, 2.38, 3 (PL 76:1283B).

40 Gregory the Great, *Homilies on the Gospels*, 2.26, 2 (PL 76:1198A-B).

41 Words from the "Gloria" of the Roman Mass.

2.

[Testimonies from the Gospels and the Pauline Epistles]

Testimonies from the Gospels concerning Predestination of the Elect or the Reprobate and concerning the Unique Election of the Elect

The Lord says to the disciples: *It has been given to you to know the mysteries of the kingdom of heaven, but to them it has not been given* (Mt 13:11).

Likewise he says: *Every plant that my heavenly Father has not planted will be rooted up* (Mt 15:13).

Likewise he says: *Not all accept this word, but only those to whom it has been given* (Mt 19:11).

Likewise he says: *For many are called, but few chosen* (Mt 20:16).

Likewise he says: *But to sit at my right hand or at my left is not mine to give to you, but to those for whom it has been prepared by my Father* (Mt 20:23).

Likewise he says: *Unless the Lord had shortened those days, no flesh would have been saved, but he shortened those days for the sake of the elect whom he chose* (Mt 24:22).

Likewise he says: *False christs and false prophets will rise and produce great signs and wonders so that even the elect may be led into error, if that is possible* (Mt 24:24).

Likewise he says: *He will send his angels, and they will gather together his elect from the four winds, from one end of heaven to the other* (Mt 24:31).

Likewise he says: *Come, blessed of my Father, inherit the kingdom prepared for you from the foundation of the world* (Mt 25:34).

Likewise he says: *And if a son of peace is there, your peace will rest on him* (Lk 10:6).

Likewise he says: *Rejoice that your names have been written in heaven* (Lk 10:20).

Likewise he says: *He will soon avenge his elect* (Lk 18:7).

Likewise he says: *Today salvation has come to this house, because he is a son of Abraham. For the Son of man has come to seek and to save what was lost* (Lk 19:9-10).

Likewise he says: *Not a hair of your head will be lost* (Lk 21:18).

Likewise he says to Nathanael: *Before Philip called you and when you were under the fig tree, I saw you* (Jn 1:48).

Likewise he says: *I am not speaking of all of you; I know whom I have chosen* (Jn 13:18)

He also said to Jews: *He who is of God hears God's words; therefore, you do not hear because you are not of God* (Jn 8:47).

Likewise he said to the same concerning the good shepherd, that is, himself: *The sheep*, he said, *hear his voice, and he calls his own sheep by name and leads them out. And when he sends out his own sheep he goes before them, and the sheep follow him, because they know his voice. But they do not follow a stranger, but flee from him, because they do not know his voice* (Jn 10:3-5).

Likewise he said concerning the same: *I have come so that they may have life and have it more abundantly* (Jn 10:10).

Likewise he said: *You do not believe because you are not of my sheep. My sheep hear my voice, and I know them, and they follow me, and I give them eternal life, and they will never perish, and no one will snatch them out of my hand. That which my Father has given to me, is greater than all, and no one is able to snatch them out of the hand of my Father* (Jn 10:26-29).

Likewise he says: *When I shall be lifted up from the earth, I shall draw all to myself* (Jn 12:32).

Likewise he says: *This is the will of the Father who sent me, that from all he has given me I should lose nothing, but should raise it up at the last day* (Jn 6:39).

He also said to Pilate: *Everyone who is of the truth hears my voice* (Jn 18:37).

Likewise he says to God the Father: *You have given him authority over all flesh, that he should give eternal life to all that you have given him* (Jn 17:2).

Likewise he says: *I do not pray only for these, but also for those who will believe in me through their word, that they may all be one, even as you, Father, are in me, and I in you, that they also may be one in us, so that the world may believe that you have sent me. I have given them the glory that you have given me that they may be one even as we are one, I in them and you in me, that they may become perfectly one, and that the world may know that you have sent me and have loved them even as you have loved me. Father, I want that they whom you have given me may also be with me where I am that they may see my glory which you gave me because you have loved me before the foundation of the world* (Jn 17:20-24).

Likewise he says: *He will destroy the evil in an evil way* (Mt 21:41).

Likewise he says: *Fear him who can destroy both soul and body in hell* (Mt 10:28).

Likewise he says: *One who defiles the temple of God, God will destroy him* (1 Cor 3:17).

THE TESTIMONIES OF THE APOSTLE PAUL CONCERNING THE AFOREMENTIONED QUESTION

The apostle Paul says in the *Letter to the Romans*: *We know that all things work together for good for those who love God, who have been called to be holy according to his plan, for those whom he foreknew he also predestined to be conformed to the image of his Son, in order that he might be the first-born among many brothers, and whom he predestined he also called, and whom he called he also justified, and whom he justified he also glorified. What then shall we say to these things? If God is for us, who is against us? How will he who did not spare even his own Son but handed him over for us all, not also give us all things with him? Who will bring a charge against God's elect? It is God who justifies; who is it who will condemn? Is it Christ*

Jesus, who died, rather who was also raised from the dead, who is at the right hand of God, who also intercedes for us? Therefore, who will separate us from the love of Christ? Will tribulation, or distress, or persecution, or hunger, or nakedness, or peril, or sword? (Rom 8:28-35).

And a little later he says: *For I am sure that neither death, nor life, nor angels, nor principalities, nor things present, nor things to come, nor strength, nor height, nor depth, nor another creature will be able to separate us from the love of God that is in Christ Jesus our Lord* (Rom 8:38-39).

Likewise he says: *Though they had not yet been born or had done anything good or bad, in order that God's election might remain in accord with his plan, not because of works, but because of God's calling, it was said to her that 'the elder will serve the younger.' As it is written: 'I have loved Jacob, but hated Esau'* (Rom 9:11-13).

Likewise in the *First Letter to the Corinthians* he says: *But we speak in a mystery the hidden wisdom of God, which God predestined before the ages unto our glory* (1 Cor 2:7).

Also he says to the Ephesians: *Blessed be the God and Father of our Lord Jesus Christ, who has blessed us in Christ with every spiritual blessing in the heavenly places, as he chose us in him before the foundation of the world, that we might be holy and blameless in his sight in love. He predestined us to the adoption of the sons of God, through Jesus Christ unto himself, according to the purpose of his will, to the praise of the glory of his grace* (Eph 1:3-6).

And a little later he says: *In whom we have been called by lot, having been predestined according to the plan of him who works all things according to the counsel of his will* (Eph 1:11).

Likewise he says: *For we are his workmanship, created in Christ Jesus for good works, which God prepared beforehand that we might walk in them* (Eph 2:10).

Likewise he says to Timothy: *Work together for the gospel according to the power of God, who set us free and called us by his holy calling, not according to our works, but according to his own plan and the grace, which was given to us in Christ Jesus before all time* (2 Tm 1:8-9).

Likewise he says: *But the firm foundation of God stands, having this seal: The Lord knows who are his* (2 Tm 2:19).

Likewise he says to Titus: *In the hope of eternal life which God, who does not lie, promised before all time* (Ti 1:2).

And what is surprising if he says such things concerning the members, since he fearlessly says these same things about the head himself: *Who was predestined to be the Son of God in power according to the spirit of sanctification* (Rom 1:4)?[42]

---

42 See Augustine, *On the Predestination of the Saints* (*De praedestinatione sanctorum*), 15.30-1 (PL 44:981-3). These chapters have an exposition of Rom. 1:4 and make the point that Christ himself, the head of the church, is the supreme illustration of predestination.

Eye has not seen, nor ear heard, nor has it entered into the heart of man what God has prepared for those who love him (1 Cor 2:9).

3.

[THE BODY OF CHRIST AND THE BODY OF ANTICHRIST]

1. Likewise, God, who does not know how to err nor can err, be deceived or deceive, never had to, has to, or will have to do any thing—God forbid!—except how he once, simultaneously, and eternally has immutably arranged to carry out his foreknown, predestined, already fixed, already prepared, already determined, and already preordained gratuitous benefit of his grace over the elect and the just judgment of his justice over the reprobate, always *according to the counsel of his will* (Eph 1:11), showing mercy to whomever he wills with great goodness, and hardening,[43] abandoning, and consequently condemning whomever he wills with no injustice, but certainly with highest fairness, as befits a just judge, bestowing grace on the elect and rendering justice, judgment and punishment to the reprobate. For as we know that blessed Augustine spoke with great truthfully, so we should believe, know, confess, and assert through a divine gift: "God chooses no one who has deserved it, but by choosing he makes one deserve it; still he punishes no one who does not deserve it."[44]

2. Blessed Augustine, having used this testimony of Jeremiah: *I know, Lord, that the way of a man is not up to him, nor is it in the power of a man to walk and direct his steps* (Jer 10:23) in the Septuagint translation, sets forth and explains it in this way in his *Book for Marcellinus against Pelagius and Caelestius*:

> When Jeremiah said: *I know, O Lord, that the way of a man is not up to him, nor is it in the power of a man to walk and direct his steps,* he added at once: *Chasten me, Lord, but in judgment and not in your wrath* (Jer 10:23-24), as if he would say: I know that it pertains to my rebuke that I am helped by you less in order that my steps might be perfectly directed. I do not, nonetheless, want that you act in this way with me as in your wrath by which you decided to condemn the wicked, but as you do in your judgment, by which you teach your own not to be proud. Therefore it is also said at another place: *Your judgments will help me* (Ps 118:175).[45]

3. The words: "Believe in Christ who suffered for all"[46] have to be understood as "Believe in Christ who suffered for all the elect." For there are two bodies: one Christ's and the other antichrist's, and each one consists of the wholeness or plenitude of its members. It is said of all the members of Christ: *All the ends of*

---

43 See Rom 9:18.

44 Augustine, *Answer to Julian* (*Contra Julianum*), 5.3, 13 (PL 44:791).

45 Augustine, *On the Merits and Forgiveness of Sins and the Baptism of Infants to Marcellinus* (*De peccatorum meritis et remissione et de baptismo parvulorum ad Marcellinum*), 2.17, 26 (PL 44:167).

46 This is probably a quotation from Sedulius' *Easter Hymn* (*Carmen paschale*), which reads: *Credite iam Christum, pro cunctis credite passum* (PL 19:720).

the world will remember and turn to the Lord. And all the families of the nations will worship in his sight, for the kingdom is the Lord's, and he will rule over the nations (Ps 21:28-29). *And all kings of the earth will worship him; all the nations will serve him* (Ps 71:11), and: *All the nations that you have made will come and worship before you, Lord, and will glorify your name* (Ps 85:9), and: *Therefore all died, and he died for all* (2 Cor 5:14-15), and: *He handed him over for us all* (Rom. 8:32), and: *Who wills all men to be saved* (1 Tm 2:4), and: *Who is the Savior of all men, especially of those who believe* (1 Tm 4:10). And on the contrary it is said concerning all the members of antichrist: *They have all gone astray; they have together become useless; there is no one who does good; there is not even one* (Ps 52:4), and: *Let sinners turn away to hell, all the nations that forget God* (Ps 9:18), and: *When the wicked shall have sprouted up like grass and all who work iniquity have appeared in order that they may perish forever* (Ps 91:8), and: *For, behold, your enemies will perish, and all the workers of iniquity will be scattered* (Ps 91:10), and: *You will destroy all those who afflict my soul* (Ps 142:12), and: *You will be hated by all* (Mt 10:22), and: *All seek their own* (Phil 2:21). And the latter are the whole world about which the apostle John says: *The whole world is in the power of the evil one* (1 Jn 5:19). And they are the whole world about which he says in the same letter: *And he himself is the propitiation for our sins, and not only for ours,* he says, *but also for the whole world* (1 Jn 2:2). Therefore, the excellent commentator says: "The whole world is the church and the whole world hates the church. Therefore, the world hates the world; the hostile world hates the reconciled world, the condemned world hates the saved world, and the polluted world hates the cleansed world."[47] Therefore, he who has chosen the world out of the world, made what he chose and did not find it. The Apostle says concerning the elect world: *God was in Christ reconciling the world to himself* (2 Cor 5:19). Likewise concerning the reprobate world he says: *Lest we be condemned with the world* (1 Cor 11:32). Concerning it the Lord also says: *If you were of the world, the world would love its own. But because you are not of the world, but I have chosen you out of the world, the world therefore hates you* (Jn 15:19), and: *Whom you have given me out of the world* (Jn 17:6), and: *They are not of the world as I too am not of the world* (Jn 17:16), and: *I do not pray for the world* (Jn 17:9). From this it is obviously seen brighter than the sun and is more clearly apparent than daylight that the Lord God by no means suffered for the reprobate world, for which he did not deign to pray. He did nonetheless pray in the same discourse for his world, when he said: *So that the world may believe and that the world may know that you have sent me* (Jn 17:21, 23). Of it he says in another place: *For God so loved the world that he gave his only-begotten Son* (Jn 3:16), and: *The Son did not come into the world to judge the world, but that the world might be saved through him* (Jn 3:17), and: *The bread that I will give is my flesh for the life of the world* (Jn 6:52). Therefore, where will

47 Augustine, *Homilies on the Gospel of John*, 87.2 (PL 35:1853).

be the light of our two eyes if we do not notice the most evident redemption of one world, not—God forbid!—of worlds? When the Lord himself says: *The bread that I will give is my flesh for the life of the world*, he does not say: for the life of the worlds. Here there also belong the words of John the Baptist: *Behold, the Lamb of God who takes away the sin of the world* (Jn 1:29), not of the worlds, and many other passages. For he clearly discloses that the Son of God suffered only for the elect when he says: *The Son of man did not come to be served, but to serve, and to give his life as redemption for many* (Mt 20:28), and: "This is the cup of my blood, of the new and everlasting covenant, which will be shed for you and for many for the remission of sins."[48] Glorious Gregory says, following him: "John the Baptist came to preach him who was going to redeem both some from Judea and many from the Gentiles."[49] See which many, see which all Christ redeemed, who certainly did not come—God forbid!—to suffer death for any reprobate.

4. "There" means "in that place," "thither" means "to that place." Still it is said very well: *Thither the tribes will go up, the tribes of the Lord* (Ps 121:4), that is, because the elect of God will go up to that place, and they go up where they already were and are now. Hence, after they said and say: *We shall go into the house of the Lord* (Ps 121:1), they most truly added and add, rejoicing: *Our feet were standing in your courts, Jerusalem* (Ps 121:2). For those who were predestined to that house were already planted there, as the scripture says: *Planted in the house of the Lord, they will flourish in the courts of our God* (Ps 91:14). Therefore, no one could in any way reprehend those who are already by faith and hope in that place where they will be by vision and reality, even if they said: *We shall go into the house of the Lord*, that is, because they are going to that place where they already are, just as rejoicing, they say with the Apostle: *He made us alive together with Christ, by whose grace we have been saved* (Eph 2:5), and: *He raised us up together, and made us sit in the heavenly places in Christ* (Eph 2:6). Therefore, although as those who are in a camp are not regularly said to run into the camp, but in the camp, those who are with their head in the house on high also go up in it by the gratuitous gift of the Lord God. Such are also these words: "May we walk before you by his example."[50] For since the Lord our God is for us a house and place of refuge and since we in turn are his temple through his grace, we certainly run well before him before whom we are. *For in him we live and move and have our being* (Acts 17:28). For the city of God is one; he who is whole everywhere remains in it alone. Therefore, we run in the city in which we are, and we ourselves are that city; and for that reason we walk before the Lord our God, our house, our place, in which *we live and move and have our being*, as the Apostle says. But on the contrary, the reprobate are not the city of God, but the city of devil; and therefore they can

48 *Canon of the Roman Mass*. See Lk 22:20; Mt 26:28; Mk 14:24.

49 Gregory the Great, *Homilies on the Gospels*, 1.20, 1 (PL 76:1160B).

50 *Collects for the Mass in the Gregorian Sacramentary* (HBS 49:23.96).

only falsely say that they walk before God. But know nonetheless that is said in one place: "May we walk before you by his example," and in another one: "To you."[51] For that reason both should be said without rebuke, lest that corrector or rather rebuker should be severely offended.

5. On Syllogisms. A syllogism is an argument and a horned sentence that is wisely and inevitably captious. As syllogisms are formed in many ways, I especially like among other types that three-part kind that consists of a proposition, a minor premise, and a conclusion. The Apostle at times or even often uses a proposition, and his interpreters consequently add a minor and conclude with a regular minor and conclusion, as this one to the Galatians is:

"*If righteousness comes through the law, then Christ died in vain* (Gal 2:21).
But Christ did not die in vain.
Therefore, righteousness does not come through the law."[52]

Likewise the same man writes to the same people:
If the inheritance comes from the law, it no longer comes from the promise (Gal 3:18).
But the inheritance comes from the promise.
Therefore, the inheritance does not come from the law.

Likewise he says:
For if a law had been given that could give life, righteousness absolutely would come from the law (Gal 3:21).
However, righteousness does not come from the law.
Therefore, a law has not been given that can give life.

Likewise in another letter:
If the dead do not rise, Christ too has not risen (1 Cor 15:16).
But Christ has risen.
Therefore, the dead do rise.[53]

Likewise he says:
Christ has redeemed us from the curse of the law, having become a curse for us (Gal 3:13). For that reason, if Christ redeemed even the reprobate from the curse of the law, having become a curse for them, then they who have been redeemed by Christ from the curse of the law certainly are not and will not be cursed, but blessed.

However, they are and will be cursed, as those to whom the Lord is going to say: *Depart from me, you accursed ones, into everlasting fire* (Mt 25:41).

---

51 Gregory says *ad te* or "to you" in other places in the sacramentary, for example in PL 78:44B.

52 Jerome, *Commentary on the Letter to the Galatians* (*In epistolam ad Galatas*), 1. On Gal 2:21 (PL 26:346C).

53 Augustine, *Unfinished Work in Answer to Julian* (*Opus imperfectum contra Iulianum*), 6.34 (PL 45:1588).

Therefore, Christ did not redeem the reprobate from the curse of the law nor did he become a curse for them.

Likewise the Lord says through the prophet:

And those who will have been set free and redeemed by the Lord will walk, and they will return and come to Zion with everlasting praise and joy (Is 35:9-10).

But the reprobate will not come to Zion with everlasting praise and joy.

Therefore, they have not been set free or redeemed by the Lord.

Likewise:

If the reprobate have not been predestined to death, they are not destined for it. However, they are destined for it, for it is written: *But you, God, will bring them down into the pit of destruction* (Ps 54:24).

Therefore, they have already been predestined to it.

6. *Be ashamed, Sidon, the sea has said* (Is 23:4). For, as "Sidon" means "hunting"[54] and "hunting" is used in this passage for "hunters." Similarly "divinity" and "deity" are often used and said instead of "God." In order that you may see this clearly, pay careful attention to what I want to say. All the Venetians, that is, Latin people living in the cities on this side of the sea, never call their lord, that is, the emperor of the Greeks, lord, but lordship. For they say: "Your benign lordship, have mercy on us," and: "We have been before his lordship," and: "His lordship has told us so." But lest their manner of speaking should seem poor to you as rustic, see what is in heaven. For those blessed spirits who are located in sixth ranks among the others are called lordships instead of lords. In that way then "deity" and "divinity" are used instead of "God." Likewise, Dalmatian people, that is, likewise Latin people, but subject to the empire of the Greeks, call the king and emperor by an expression common throughout the whole of Dalmatia, which is a most spacious region, I mean, they call the king and emperor kingdom and empire. For they say: "We were at the kingdom," and: "We stood before the empire," and: "The kingdom has told us so," and: "The empire spoke in that way." But do not think that they say this with no authority, since the holy church in whole world truthfully and favorably as well as quite authoritatively sings joyfully about the Son of God: "I have seen a man sit on a high throne, whom the multitude of the angels adore and sing in one voice: 'Behold him whose name for eternity is empire,'"[55] that is: This is the one whose name is for eternity emperor. Likewise you should also know that all the elect are generally spoken of under the singular number and have been gratuitously made a kingdom, as the words of the Apostle proves: *When he shall have handed over the kingdom to God the*

54 See Jerome, *On the Interpretation of Hebrew Names. From Matthew.* (*De nominibus hebraicis. De Matthaeo*), 92 (PL 23:843).

55 Gregory the Great, *Book of Antiphons, Antiphon for the Introit on the First Sunday after Epiphany* (*Antiphona ad introitum in dominica prima post Epiphaniam*) in PL 78:650A.

Father (1 Cor 15:24), that is, as blessed Augustine says: "When he shall have handed over those whom he redeemed by his blood to contemplate his Father."[56] But the Lord God, our king, will give to this kingdom the kingdom in order that they may reign there with him forever, that is, when the King of Kings himself says to them: "Come, blessed of my Father, receive the kingdom,"[57] as if he would say as he explained it in the sermon of Saint Augustine: "You who were a kingdom, but did not reign, come and reign."[58] Therefore, you should not be surprised if the one king is rightly said to be a kingdom, when so many kings, all the elect, are called a kingdom, which they rightly are. For they are kings by God's gift because they always rule over their bodies under Christ the true king, who rules over their souls.

Be ashamed, Sidon, for the sea has said (Is 23:4). "Sidon" means "hunting," as was said above. But hunting or a hunter is any preacher, as the Lord says through the prophet: *Behold, I will send my hunters and they will hunt them, and my fishermen and they will fish them* (Jer 16:16). But by the sea is signified the common folk and ordinary people. Hence, when the preacher, that is, the hunter, sins openly, and the common folk are the reprimander of him, then these words are fulfilled: *Be ashamed, Sidon, for the sea speaks.*

7. Thus the elect "come to the Son, as he himself says: *All that the Father gives me come to me, and one who comes to me I shall not cast out* (Jn 6:37). And again he says: *This is the will of the Father who sent me, that from all that he has given me I should lose nothing* (Jn 6:39)."[59] "If any one of them perishes, God is mistaken, but none of them perishes, because God is not mistaken. If any one of them perishes, God is defeated by human vice, but none of them perishes, because God is not defeated by anything."[60] Likewise, in the book *On the Rule of the True Faith* it says:

> Hold most firmly and do not by any means doubt that all those whom God makes the vessels of mercy by his gratuitous grace, have been predestined by God before the foundation of the world, and that none of those whom God predestined to the kingdom can perish, and that none of those whom God did not predestine to life can by any means be saved.[61]

Likewise, at the end of the book it says:

---

56 Augustine, *Homilies on the Gospel of John*, 68.2 (PL 35:1814).

57 Gregory the Great, *Book of Antiphons, Antiphon for the Wednesday after Easter* (*Antiphona in feria quarta post Pascha*) in PL 78:679B. See Mt 25:34.

58 Augustine, *Homilies on the Gospel of John*, 68.2 (PL 35:1815).

59 Augustine, *On Rebuke and Grace* (*De correptione et gratia*), 9.23 (PL 44:930).

60 Augustine, *On Rebuke and Grace*, 7.14 (PL 44:924).

61 Fulgentius of Ruspe, *On the Faith for Peter* (*De fide ad Petrum*), 35.77 (CCSL 91A:756; PL 65:703B).

> Meanwhile faithfully believe, firmly hold, truthfully and patiently defend these forty chapters pertaining to the rule of the true faith, and if you know that someone teaches against them, flee him like a pest, and cast him aside like a heretic. For the things that we have set forth agree with the catholic faith so that if somebody wants to contradict not only all, but even individual ones of them, insofar as he contumaciously opposes individual ones of them and does not hesitate to teach things contrary to them, he is seen to be a heretic, an enemy of the Christian faith, and someone who should be anathematized because of this by all catholics.[62]

What else? Nothing more is needed on this.

8. Likewise Saint Ambrose, explaining in *On the Epistle to the Romans* the testimony of the psalm: *They have all turned aside* (Ps 13:3), says:

> The prophet Jeremiah also meant all these, when he said among other things: *Then they all rose against the prophet of the Lord, wanting to kill him* (Jer 26:8) and added: *However, all the people did not permit them* (Jer 26:16). Therefore, he called the former "all" but meant "the evil," and called the latter "all" but meant "the good." And because the psalm says: *They have all turned aside*, it does not mean absolutely the whole people, but this part of the people, as the previously mentioned prophet also reports: *In which all the evil have hidden themselves*.[63] For there are always two peoples in one populace.[64]

9. Likewise Saint Augustine, when explaining the words of the Apostle: *It is not of the one who wills nor of the one who runs, but of God who shows mercy* (Rom 9:16), said: "God did not show mercy because Jacob willed and ran, but Jacob willed and ran because God showed mercy."[65] God also does not now show us mercy because we will and run, but we will and run because God shows us mercy. For he anticipates us so that we will good things and follows us so that we are able and brings it about that we do them. He first works in us, beginning in us without us, who cooperates with us who are already willing from his help, bringing them to completion.[66] Likewise the aforementioned author, when explaining the words of the Lord: *As the branch cannot bear fruit, unless it remains in the vine, so you cannot, unless you remain in me* (Jn 15:4), said: "For whoever thinks that he bears fruit by himself is not in the vine; he who is not in

---

62 Fulgentius, *On the Faith for Peter*, 44.85 (CCSL 91A:760; PL 65:705D-6B).

63 This is probably a quotation from a Vetus Latina translation of Jeremiah, as are most likely the other passages Ambrosiaster cited from Jeremiah that do not match the Vulgate.

64 Ambrosiaster, *Commentary on the Letter to the Romans* (*Commentarius in epistolam ad Romanos*), On Rom 3:17 (PL 17:77C).

65 Augustine, *Unfinished Work in Answer to Julian*, 2.141 (PL 45:1140).

66 See Augustine, *On Grace and Free Choice* (*De gratia et libero arbitrio*), 16.32-17.33 (PL 44:900-01).

the vine is not in Christ; he who is not in Christ is not a Christian."[67] Therefore, let us say with the Apostle: *By the grace of God I am what I am* (1 Cor 15:10), as also Saint Augustine says: "All the merit" of the elect "is grace."[68] Furthermore I want you to hold most firmly and doubt in no way that powerless humanity can do nothing but destroy, be destroyed, perish, ruin and be ruined, unless the omnipotent divinity always gratuitously helps it, which the Lord God declares when he says to his people: *Destruction is your own, Israel; your help is only in me* (Hos 13:9). Therefore, Job also says of himself: *Behold, my help is not in me* (Jb 6:13). Therefore, it is necessary that we beseech the Lord God in order that he may deign to help us thereafter in all things.

4.
[only the elect are redeemed]

After the exposition of the Fifty-fourth Psalm, Cassiodorus said:

> We have heard that he who gives life to creatures gave up his life for the salvation of mortals; we have heard that the impassible God undertook suffering in flesh for sinners; we have heard that he who is coeternal with the Father underwent the punishment of death. O inestimable price that redeemed the human race, holocaust that permitted us to escape eternal flames, death that took away destruction, the end that gave us a good that will remain without end! For when the sting of death came to the innocent one, it came about so that it justly lost those whom it held subject. For in the manner of fish hell swallowed its own destruction, and he who believed that he was catching prey, was rather deceived and admitted his predator. Therefore, Pope Leo, an equal of his see, beautifully said: "Although the death of the many martyrs was precious in the eyes of the Lord, still the slaying of no innocent person was the redemption of sinners. For the righteous received crowns but did not give them, and the fortitude of the faithful produced examples of patience, not gifts of righteousness. There were of course individual deaths in the individuals, and no one pays the debt of another by his own end, but among the sons of men only one emerged, Christ, who truly was the immaculate Lamb, in whom all have been crucified, all have died, all have been buried, and also all have been raised up."[69] Grant, most loving God, that you, who deigned to suffer in the flesh assumed for us, bestow upon us the fellowship of your kingdom.[70]

If all these things have been carefully inspected, it will not thereafter be possible to doubt concerning the truth of the redemption that has of course been given to the elect alone through the blood of Christ's cross. For what the words, "O inestimable price that redeemed the human race," mean is that it has absolutely

67 Augustine, *Homilies on the Gospel of John*, 81.2 (PL 35:1841).

68 Augustine, *On Rebuke and Grace*, 8.13 (PL 44:924).

69 Pope Leo I, *Letters (Epistolae)*, 165.5, 9 (PL 54:1161C-3A).

70 Cassiodorus, *Explanation of the Psalms (Expositio psalmorum)*, On Ps 54, Conclusion (PL 70:393C-D). Cassiodorus most likely borrowed this final formula from some sacramentary.

redeemed that human race, as it said there, which it "permitted to escape eternal flames," for which it "took away destruction," and to which "it gave a good that will remain without end." This is in accord with what blessed Augustine says in the books *On the City of God*:

> We have divided the human race—understand here: the kinds of human beings—into two parts, the one consisting of those who live according to God, the other of those who live according to the world, whom we also mystically call the two cities, of which the one was predestined to reign for eternity with Christ the Lord, the other to undergo eternal punishment with the devil.[71]

For just as "there are two peoples in one populace,"[72] there are in the same way two kinds of human beings in the one human race. Both groups are mentioned in one verse of a psalm: *They have called blessed the people to whom these things belong; blessed is the people whose God is the Lord* (Ps 143:15). The former is the people of perdition and the latter is *the people of acquisition* (1 Pt 2:9), about whom are the words of the Lord: *The people whom I did not know have served me* (Ps 17:45), and: *The people whom the Lord has chosen as his own inheritance* (Ps 32:12), and: *He will save his people from their sins* (Mt 1:21), and: *I announce to you a great joy that will come to all the people* (Lk 2:10); in the Seventieth Psalm[73] the Lord God says as if to oil: *Hear, my people, and I will speak to Israel* (Ps 80:9), and a little later he says of the dregs of oil: *But my people did not hear my voice, and Israel did not pay attention to me*, and so on up to the words: *The enemies of the Lord lied to him* (Ps 80:12-16).

The words of the aforementioned Pope Leo that he says in *The Homily on the Nativity of the Lord*: "As our Savior himself found no one free from guilt, so he came to set free all people,"[74] he said concerning all the elect alone, as the opinion set forth above by Cassiodorus, most clearly reveals, namely, where he says about Christ, the immaculate Lamb: "In whom all have been crucified, all have died, all have been buried, and also all have been raised up."[75]

Therefore, as all these things are so, and they are of no avail among all those who love falsehood and deny the truth, let them see how *hard it is to kick against the goad* (Acts 9:5), let them be terrified, be afraid, and fall silent. For he who considers, as he should, the benevolence of God the Father towards human beings and the obedience, humility, and patience of God the Son, that is, how for the elect he fasted, hungered, thirsted, grew weary, underwent blasphemies, slanders, insults, ignominies, curses, reproaches, taunts, abuses, derision, fetters, slaps, blows, spittle, and whips, how he willingly allowed a crown of thorns to

71 Augustine, *On the City of God* (*De civitate dei*), 15.1, 1 (PL 41:437).

72 Ambrosiaster, *Commentary on the Letter to the Romans*, On Rom 3:17 (PL 17:77C).

73 In fact this is the Eightieth Psalm in the Vulgate.

74 Pope Leo I, *Sermons* (*Sermones*), 21.1 (PL 54:191A).

75 Cassiodorus, *Explanation of the Psalms*. On Ps 54, Conclusion (PL 70:393D).

be put on his head, carried the cross for himself, and suffered it willingly, was hanged upon it at that time and slain by a most shameful death, will undoubtedly admit without hesitation and joyfully state that the loving redeemer redeemed absolutely all whom he redeemed from eternal death at such a price and that he gave them all eternal life. Let them deny this, if they want, who love the dregs more than the oil, the grape skins or seeds more than wine, chaff and weeds more than wheat, kids and goats more than sheep and lambs, because they perhaps come from them. But those who love God, who know that he is omnipotent and believe, know, and sing that he *has done whatever he willed in heaven and on earth, in the sea and in all the deeps* (Ps 134:6), most firmly hold, state, and assert that no one among those who have been redeemed by the blood of Christ perishes eternally, as the Lord himself says: *Father, I have guarded those whom you gave me, and none of them has perished except the son of perdition* (Jn 17:12), and: *I have lost none of those whom you gave me* (Jn 18:9), and: *They will never perish, and no one will snatch them out of my hand* (Jn 10:28), and: *No one is able to snatch them out of the hand of my Father* (Jn 10:29), and: *Not a hair from your head will be lost* (Lk 21:18), that is, none of the elect stolen from Christ will perish eternally, and: *This is the will of the Father who sent me, that from all he has given me I should lose nothing* (Jn 6:39), and: *All that the Father gives me come to me, and one who comes to me I shall not cast out* (Jn 6:37), and: *As you have given him authority over all flesh, that he should give eternal life to all that you have given him* (Jn 17:2), and: *You did not choose me, but I chose you and appointed you that you go and bear fruit, and that your fruit remain* (Jn 15:16). Hence, he speaks in a general way about his church: *On this rock I will build my church, and the gates of hell will not prevail against it* (Mt 16:18). Again he says about the same church, his house, which he, the wise man and the omnipotent Lord God, built on the rock: *The floods came, and the winds blew and beat on that house, and it did not fall, for it was founded on the solid rock* (Mt 7:25). The psalmist also says of this church: *The earth is the Lord's and the fullness thereof; the world, and all who dwell on it, for he has founded it upon the seas and prepared it upon the rivers* (Ps 23:1-2). Likewise he says: *He has established the world, which will not be moved* (Ps 92:1). Likewise he says: *You who established it on its sure foundation; it will not be moved for ever* (Ps 103:5). Thus the apostle Paul also says: *But the firm foundation of God stands, having this seal: The Lord knows who are his* (2 Tm 2:19), and again he says: *Who will bring a charge against God's elect? It is God who justifies; who is it who will condemn? Is it Christ Jesus, who died, rather who was also raised, who is at the right hand of God, who also intercedes for us?* (Rom 8:33-34). All these questions must be answered in the negative. Likewise he says: *If God be for us, who is against us? He who did not spare his own Son, but handed him over for us all, how has he not also with him given us all things?* (Rom 8:31-32).

But we must now see how those *blind men and leaders of the blind* (Mt 15:14) want to obscure such evident, such clear, and such obvious testimonies through the testimonies that are completely hidden for the blind. For they say that those who were redeemed by Christ's blood perish, according to the words of the Apostle: *And through your knowledge will the weak brother perish, for whom Christ died?* (1 Cor 8:11). But God forbid that this one sentence should be contrary to so many testimonies given above. For though the brother for whom Christ died may perish in your knowledge, he still does not perish in his foreknowledge, that is, he who by Christ's blood was redeemed for eternal salvation by God's gratuitous mercy. It is of course true that whoever commits a criminal sin immediately both perishes and destroys one or more who agree with him, as the psalmist testified, who says: *I have gone astray like a sheep that perished* (Ps 118:176). On this there are also the words of the Apostle: *Do not destroy with your food him for whom Christ has died* (Rom 14:15), and these: *Through one man sin entered the world, and death through sin, so that it passed to all human beings, in whom all have sinned* (Rom 5:12). For at that time, as Saint Augustine explains, "All sinned in Adam, when all were that one."[76] On this blessed Ambrose also says: "Adam existed, and we all were in him; Adam perished and all perished in him."[77] On this Isaiah also says: *All of us like sheep have gone astray; each of us has turned to his own way* (Is 53:6). But the elect do not of course perish for God on this account, as Isaiah says in what follows: *The Lord has placed on him,* that is, upon the Son, *the iniquities of us all* (Is 53:6), and: *He bore the sins of many and made intercession for the transgressors* (Is 53:12) in order that they might not perish. *For the Son of man,* as he himself says, *has come to seek and to save what was lost* (Lk 19:10), and as he says again: *Rejoice with me, for I have found my sheep that was lost and my coin that I had lost* (Lk 15:6.9). Behold, the Lord God, the good shepherd, sought, found, redeemed and carried home his lost sheep. And the same Wisdom of God has brought home the coin that had been lost, but was sought and found. And for this reason he certainly has never perished, never perishes and will never perish for the Lord God, as Pope Gregory testifies, who says: "So that the number of the elect should be completed, the tenth man was created, who did not perish for his creator even after sin, because the eternal wisdom, shining forth through the flesh with the miracles, repaired him from the light of the clay."[78]

2. The Apostle says of the Son: *When he shall have handed over the kingdom to God the Father* (1 Cor 15:24). This Saint Augustine explains in this manner: "That is, has handed over those whom he redeemed by his blood to contemplate his Father."[79] Therefore, if Christ redeemed by his blood the baptized repro-

---

76 Augustine, *On the Merits and Forgiveness of Sins,* 1.10, 11 (PL 44:115).

77 Ambrose, *Explanation of the Gospel of Luke* (*Expositio evangelii secundum Lucam*), 7.234 (PL 15:17620.

78 Gregory the Great, *Homilies on the Gospels,* 2.34, 6 (PL 76:1249).

79 Augustine, *Homilies on the Gospel of John,* 68.2 (PL 35:1814).

bate, then he undoubtedly will hand them over to contemplate his Father. But he will not hand them over to contemplate his Father. Therefore, he did not redeem them by his blood. Hence, the Father says to the Son: *Ask of me, and I will give you the nations for your inheritance, and the ends of the earth for your possession* (Ps 2:8). Explaining this, Cassiodorus says: "The nations signify the peoples scattered throughout the whole world, which the distinct and separate blood of the Lamb embraced."[80] The psalmist also asserts of this inheritance: *The Lord will not reject his people, nor will he forsake his inheritance* (Ps 93:14). The aforementioned author explains this as follows: "A human inheritance is transferred to a successor through the passing of the prior owner; however, the heritage of Christ, although it was acquired by his blood, never loses its author, but is nonetheless possessed along with him."[81]

5.
AGAINST THOSE WHO SAY THAT THE REPROBATE WERE REDEEMED

As someone faithful to God, readily pay attention to what I say. The Apostle says of the Holy Spirit: *The Spirit himself pleads for us with inexpressible groanings. But he who searches hearts knows what the Spirit desires, because he pleads according to God for the saints* (Rom 8:26-27), that is, for the elect, about whom, that is, he adds in what follows: *For we know that all things work together for good for those who love God, who have been called to be holy according to his plan* (Rom 8:28). And at times Paul says about the Son: *Who also intercedes for us* (Rom 8:34), that is, for the elect. For he of course in no way intercedes for the reprobate, since he said to his Father: *I do not pray for the world* (Jn 17:9). Therefore, since the Holy Spirit pleads and the Son prays and intercedes for the saints, who but someone most wicked would dare say that one of them can perish perpetually, since the will of the Father and Son and the Holy Spirit is always one and since the Apostle says in the middle of the same chapter about the Father: *If God be for us, who is against us?* (Rom 8:31). For that God did not suffer for the baptized reprobate is clearly seen from the fact that the devil conquers them and subjects them to himself. And for this reason "there follow the words of those chosen for the kingdom"[82] concerning God the Father: *He did not spare even his own Son, but handed him over for us all* (Rom 8:32). The Apostle says elsewhere about them: *For God did not appoint us for wrath, but for obtaining salvation through our Lord Jesus Christ, who died for us, in order that, whether we are awake or asleep, we may live together with him* (1 Thes 5:9-10). This is the fruit of Christ's cross. Let the enemies of Christ's cross blush for shame and fall silent. The Apostle, "a vessel of election, a preacher of the truth and a teacher of the Gentiles in faith

80 Cassiodorus, *Explanation of the Psalms*. On Ps 2:8 (PL 70:39D-40A).

81 Cassiodorus, *Explanation of the Psalms*. On Ps 93:14 (PL 70:668C).

82 Augustine, *On Rebuke and Grace*, 8.15 (PL 44:925).

and truth"[83] says: *I fill up in my flesh what is lacking in the sufferings of Christ, for the sake of his body, which is the church* (Col 1:24), and again he says: *Therefore, I endure all things for the elect in order that they too may obtain the salvation that is in Christ Jesus with celestial glory* (2 Tm 2:10). And *the reprobate with regard to the faith* (2 Tm 3:8) and *irreligious* (2 Tm 3:2) knowingly speak against the Lord Jesus Christ, lying that he was crucified for the baptized reprobate, although the Apostle himself certainly neither prays nor commands us to pray for the reprobate at all, but for all the saints? For he says: *Pray always in the Spirit and in him keep watch with all prayer and supplication for all the saints and for me* (Eph 6:18-19). Since it is clear, let no one of sound mind doubt that all the reprobate, that is, not only the heathens but also all baptized Christians, are children of perdition, for the Lord says about the baptized Judas: *None of them has perished except the son of perdition* (Jn 17:12), and all the elect are children of the promise, for the Apostle says: *The children of the promise are counted in the seed* (Rom 9:8), but the same seed is surely Christ, since the Apostle says: *And to your seed, which is Christ* (Gal 3:16). Moreover, Christ and the church, like bridegroom and bride, are undoubtedly one and the same person; and for this reason not only Christ is the head of the church, but also the church itself as the body and members of its head is said to be and is Christ, as the Apostle says: *For as the body is one and has many members, but all the members of that one body, although they are many, are one body, so also is Christ* (1 Cor 12:12). And again he says: *And if you belong to Christ, then you are Abraham's seed* (Gal 3:29), that is, *you are Christ*. Since this is so, it ought of course to be most certain for all catholics that what blessed Augustine says is absolutely true: "For the children of the promise do not perish, but the children of perdition, for if the body of Christ," that is, the Christian people, "would perish, then Christ would also truly perish. Let these false brethren and false Christians perish, as they deserve. The members and the body of Christ certainly will not perish."[84] On this our Augustine says securely on the psalm: "The mercies of the Lord": "Let those without hope sin as much as they want; let the members of Christ answer: *If God be for us, who is against us?* (Rom 8:31)."[85] And again of this the most sincere lover of truth says there: "This body cannot be beheaded;"[86] and other things of that kind. If, when you can, you carefully and intelligently read these things out of a love for the truth, as is fitting for a son of truth, you will surely obtain and acquire a great advantage for your mind, with God's gratuitous help. For since God the Father says in the same psalm: *But I will not take from him my mercy, nor will I harm him in my*

83 Gregory the Great, *Book of Antiphons. Antiphon for the Feast of Saint Paul* (*Liber Responsalis. Antiphona in festo sancti Pauli*) in PL 78:791A-B.

84 The source of this quotation has not been located.

85 Augustine, *Homilies on the Psalms* (*Enarrationes in psalmos*), 88.2, 4 (PL 37:1133).

86 Augustine, *Homilies on the Psalms*, 88.1, 5 (PL 37:1122).

truth. I will not profane my covenant, nor will I render void the words that proceed from my lips. Once I have sworn by my holiness; I will not lie to David. His seed shall endure forever, and his throne like the sun before me and like the moon perfect forever and a faithful witness in the sky (Ps 88:34-38), who would dare bark in any way against these words except a stubborn unbeliever? But let those enemies of the truth hear blessed Job say to them: *Does God need your lie, so that you should speak deceitfully for him?* (Jb 13:7). Explaining this, blessed Gregory says: "God does not need a lie, because the truth does not seek to be supported by words of falsity."[87]

Speaking about both reprobate and also the elect Jews, the Apostle says: *In terms of the gospel, they are enemies because of you, but in terms of the election, they are beloved because of the patriarchs, for the gifts and the calling of God are irrevocable* (Rom 11:28-29), that is, as Saint Augustine explains: "They are established firmly without change," for he designated the reprobate by "enemies" and the elect by "beloved."[88] If you wish, first read the book of the previously mentioned teacher *For Prosper and Hilary*[89] and the *Letter to Paulinus*.[90] The Apostle likewise says of both in what follows: *For just as you too at one time did not believe in God, but now you have obtained mercy on account of their unbelief, so they too have now not believed for your mercy so that they may also obtain mercy* (Rom 11:30-31). The former and the latter are divided far from each other, that is, as enemies and beloved. Such is that which is said in the psalm: *Behold, your enemies have made an uproar, and those who hated you have lifted up their head* (Ps 82:3), and the other things that follow are said about the reprobate up to where it says: *As the fire that burns the forest and as the flame that sets the mountains on fire, so will you trouble them in your tempest and frighten them in your wrath* (Ps 82:15-16). There follows a prayer for the elect: *Fill their faces with ignominy, and they will seek your name, Lord* (Ps 82:17). And again there follows about the reprobate: *Let them blush and be confounded forever, and let them be dismayed forever and perish* (Ps 82:18). There follows concerning both: *Let them know that the Lord is your name; you alone are the most high in all the earth* (Ps 82:19), that is, over all the earth.

The Apostle says: *For the word of the cross is folly for those who are perishing, but for those who are being saved, that is, for us, it is the power of God* (1 Cor 1:18). And a little later he says: *But because of him you are in Christ Jesus, who by God was made unto us wisdom and righteousness and sanctification and redemption, so that, as it is written, he who glories, should glory in the Lord* (1 Cor 1:30-31). Therefore, this redemption does not pertain to those who are perishing, but to those who are being saved. But that redemption that is brought about by the

87 Gregory the Great, *Moral Commentary on Job*, 11.26, 37 (PL 75:970C).

88 Augustine, *On the Predestination of the Saints*, 16.33 (PL 44:985).

89 Augustine, *On the Predestination of the Saints* (PL 44:959-92).

90 Augustine, *Letters (Epistolae)*, 149 (CSEL 44:348-80; PL 33:630-45).

grace of baptism, which is signified by the hand of Moses, who certainly acted as a figure of Christ, as it is written: *God sent this Moses to be a redeemer by the hand of an angel who appeared to him* (Acts 7:35)—I mean, that redemption that is common to the elect and the reprobate, as it also was then in that people, as the Apostle says: *All our fathers were under the cloud; all passed through the sea; all were baptized into Moses in the cloud and in the sea* (1 Cor 10:1-2), washes away past sins, but does not redeem from future sins, as the Apostle also says about the same people in the following: *But with most of them God was not well pleased, for they were laid low in the desert* (1 Cor 10:5). The Lord God also says of these in the psalm: I *swore to them in my wrath: They will never enter my rest* (Ps 94:11). But that redemption by which the good shepherd laid down his life for his sheep alone,[91] rescued his redeemed *from this present evil age*, according to the sentence of the Apostle: *He gave himself for our sins in order that he might rescue us from this present evil age, according to the will of God and our Father* (Gal 1:4). On this the Father also says: *My word that will go forth from my mouth will not return to me empty, but it will do whatever I have willed, and it will prosper in the things for which I sent it* (Is 55:11). On this David also says: *And whatever he will do will prosper* (Ps 1:3). But, if somebody wants to hear how this word of God has prospered in these things for which the Father sent it, let him hear what the Apostle says on this: *Christ loved the church and handed himself over for her in order that he might sanctify and cleanse her, washing her in the bath of water with the word, in order that he might present to himself a glorious church, not having spot or wrinkle or any such thing, but that she might be holy and spotless* (Eph 5:25-27). Likewise he says: *Christ nourishes and cherishes the church, for we are members of his body of his flesh and of his bones. 'For this reason a man will leave his father and mother and cling to his wife, and they will be two in one flesh.' This is a great mystery, I mean, in Christ and the church* (Eph 5:29-32). Likewise he says:

> *We have redemption and remission of sins in him, who is the image of the invisible God, and he is the head of the body, the Church, who is the beginning, the firstborn from the dead, that he may have the preeminence in all things. For it pleased the Father that all the fullness should dwell in him and by him to reconcile all things to himself, bringing peace by him through the blood of his cross, whether to things on earth or to things in heaven* (Col 1:14-15, 18-20).

But he of course most obviously says all these things only about the elect, as he clearly shows in the *Letter to the Romans*: *If when we were still sinners, Christ died for us, much more now, having been justified in his blood, will we be saved from wrath through him. For if when we were enemies, we were reconciled to God through the death of his Son, much more, having been reconciled, will we be saved by his life* (Rom 5:8-10). Likewise he says: *The house of God is the church of the living God, the pillar and ground of the truth* (1 Tm 3:15).

---

91 See Jn 10:11.

These words of the Apostle: *Here now it is looked for in stewards that one be found faithful* (1 Cor 4:2), should be read ironically as a question, as that which he says somewhat further on: *Have you now become full? Have you now become rich? Have you reigned without us?* (1 Cor 4:8), and these words in the *Second Letter to the Corinthians: You put up with fools gladly, since you yourselves are wise. For you put up with it if someone reduces you into slavery* (2 Cor 11:19-20), and so on.

In *On the Gospel according to John*, blessed Augustine begins a certain homily better, more beautifully, more wisely, and more eloquently than all the others I have seen, when he says:

> The Lord Jesus raises up his people to a great hope, than which there absolutely could not be a greater. Listen and *rejoice in hope* (Rom 12:12). On this account this life is not to be loved, but to be tolerated, so that you may be *patient in tribulation* (Rom 12:12). The Lord Jesus says; the Son of God, the Only-Begotten, who is equal to the Father, says; he who became a man for our sake, but did not, like every man, become a liar,[92] says; the Way, the Truth[93] says; he who overcame the world, says about those for whom he overcame it. Hear, believe, hope for, desire what he says: *Father, I want those whom you have given to me to be with me where I am, and that they may be with me* (Jn 17:24). Who are those whom he says were given to him by the Father,[94]

if not those about whom he says above: "*That he may give eternal life to all that you have given him? Power over all flesh* (Jn 17:2) was of course given to the Son, that is, power over every human being, in order that he who will judge the living and the dead may set free those he wills and condemn those he wills."[95] But those were especially given to him, to all of whom he will give eternal life, "nor can that not happen which the omnipotent Son said to the omnipotent Father that he wanted"[96]—the Son, *the Way, the Truth, and the Life* (Jn 14:6), through whom we come, to whom we arrive, in whom we remain, through whom we run, to whom we run, and in whom we rest.

6.

TESTIMONIES CONCERNING THE AFOREMENTIONED QUESTION

Every plant that Christ's *Father has planted will not be rooted up* (Mt 15:13). The Apostle says this in this way only about the elect, as well as this: *He handed him over for us all* (Rom 8:32), and this: *Therefore all died, and he died for all* (2 Cor 5:14-15). For he undoubtedly gave his Son *for all* those for whom God the Father *did not spare his own Son, but handed him over* (Rom 8:32). And through this he at the same time gave them eternal life and everlasting beatitude with his Son,

92 See Ps 116:2 and Rom 3:4.

93 See Jn 14:6.

94 Augustine, *Homilies on the Gospel of John*, 111.1 (PL 35:1925).

95 Augustine, *Homilies on the Gospel of John*, 111.1 (PL 35:1925).

96 Augustine, *Homilies on the Gospel of John*, 111.1 (PL 35:1925).

that is, as the Apostle says there a little later: *How has he not also with him given us all things?* (Rom 8:32). Therefore, those who have been redeemed by Christ's death do not perish, but only the reprobate, slain by deadly outrages and crimes. He himself says that the Son of God suffered only for the elect: *I lay down my life for my sheep* (Jn 10:15), that is, not—God forbid!—for another's goats and kids. But we should believe Christ, not—God forbid!—heretics, that the sheep of Christ, redeemed by Christ's blood, do not perish. For Christ says: *My sheep hear my voice, and I know them, and they follow me, and I give them eternal life, and they will never perish, and no one will snatch them out of my hand. That which my Father has given me, is greater than all, and no one is able to snatch them out of the hand of my Father* (Jn 10:27-29). Explaining this, our Augustine *is bold and says* (Rom 10:20) openly:

> What can the wolf do? What can the thief and the robber do? They destroy none except those predestined to destruction. But of those sheep about which the Apostle says: *The Lord knows who are his* (2 Tm 2:19) and: *Whom he foreknew, he also predestined to be conformed to the image of his Son, that he might be the firstborn among many brothers, but whom he predestined he also called, and whom he called he also justified, and whom he justified he also glorified* (Rom 8:29-30)—the wolf seizes, or the thief steals, or the robber slays none of these sheep. He who knows what he gave for them is sure of their number. And this is what he says: *No one will snatch them out of my hand* (Jn 10:28).[97]

And: *No one is able to snatch them out of the hand of my Father* (Jn 10:29). In the *Enchiridion* the same teacher also says on this: "*For Christ died and rose in order that he might be Lord of both the dead and the living* (Rom 14:29), and the kingdom of death will not hold him for whom he has died, who is *free among the dead* (Ps 87:6)."[98] Finally, the Lord suffered only for the elect, as he says: *The Son of man did not come to be served but to serve, and to give his life as redemption for many* (Mt 20:28), and again: "This is the cup of my blood, which will be shed for you and for many for the remission of sins."[99] Hence, blessed Gregory also says: "John the Baptist came to preach him who was going to redeem some from Judea and many from the Gentiles."[100] Gregory likewise says: "The author of life handed himself over even to death only for the multitude of the elect."[101] Nevertheless, if those are not enough, let us take the *Exposition of Saint Augustine on the Letter of the Apostle Paul* and read what is said there: *God commends his love for us* (Rom

97 Augustine, *Homilies on the Gospel of John*, 48.6 (PL 35:1743).

98 Augustine, *Enchiridion on Faith, Hope, and Love* (*Enchiridion de fide, spe, et caritate*), 120.31 (PL 40:288).

99 *Canon of the Roman Mass*. See Lk 22:20; Mt 26:28; Mk 14:24.

100 Gregory the Great, *Homilies on the Gospels*, 1.20, 1 (PL 76:1160B).

101 Gregory the Great, *Homilies on the Prophet Ezekiel* (*Homiliae in Hiezechielem prophetam*), 1.2 (PL 76:804).

5:8) and the other two sentences that follow, and their explanation.[102] At the same time know and also say to yourself joyfully that the redemption that takes place in baptism from past sins is common to the elect and the reprobate. The blessed apostle Peter says about it: *Denying the Lord who bought them, bringing upon themselves swift destruction* (2 Pt 2:1). After this redemption all the reprobate, the members of antichrist, *vessels of wrath* (Rom 9:22), children of hell,[103] *children of disobedience* (Eph 2:2), *false brothers* (2 Cor 11:26), *ravenous wolves* (Mt 7:15), perish, that is, as Judas perished, since the Lord says: *None of them has perished except the son of perdition* (Jn 17:12). But that redemption that has been produced by the blood of Christ's cross is proper to and special for the elect only. It is not temporal like the other, but undoubtedly everlasting, since the Apostle says: *Through his own blood he entered the holy place once, having obtained eternal redemption* (Heb 9:12). Only the elect were redeemed by this redemption, that is, only those foreknown and predestined to eternal life, those called, justified, and glorified.[104] And for this reason these *children of the promise* (Rom 9:8) can by no means perish for God, because God the Father, as the Apostle asserts, *made* them *alive together with Christ*, and *raised* them *up together*, and *made* them *sit in the heavenly places in Christ* (Eph 2:6). Saint Augustine says about them:

> Whosoever have been foreknown, predestined, called, justified, and glorified in God's most providential ordering, are foreknown, predestined, called, justified, glorified—I do not mean just those not yet reborn, but also those not yet born—are already children of God and absolutely cannot perish. Thus these come to the Son as he himself says: *All that the Father gives me come to me, and one who comes to me I shall not cast out* (Jn 6:37). And again he says: *This is the will of the Father who sent me, that from all that he has given me I should lose nothing* (Jn 6:39).[105]

---

102 It is uncertain which work exactly Gottschalk has in mind. Rom 5:8-10 is not explained in Augustine's *Exposition of Certain Passages from the Letter to the Romans* (*Expositio quarundam propositionum ex epistola ad Romanos*) nor in his *Incomplete Exposition of the Letter to the Romans* (*Epistolae ad Romanos inchoata expositio*). Perhaps Gottschalk is referring to an explanation of that biblical passage by Augustine in a compilation such as the *Excerpts from the Works of Saint Augustine on the Letters of the Blessed Apostle Paul* (*Collectio Bedae presbiteri ex opusculis sancti Augustini in epistulas Pauli Apostoli*) by Bede or the *Exposition on the Letters of Blessed Paul Collected from the Works of Saint Augustine* (*Expositio in epistolas beati Pauli ex operibus sancti Augustini collecta*) by Florus of Lyons.

103 See Mt 23:15.

104 See Rom 8:29-30.

105 Augustine, *On Rebuke and Grace*, 9.23 (PL 44:930).

"If any one of them perishes, God is mistaken, but none of them perishes, because God is not mistaken. If any one of them perishes, God is defeated by human vice, but none of them perishes, because God is not defeated by anything."[106]

The opinion of Origen, who said that the Lord our God, the Son of God, was going to redeem the devil in the same way that he redeemed the man who had perished and that he was likewise going to die for him, is obviously defeated by the statement of the Lord by which he said of the devil: *The prince of this world has been judged* (Jn 16:11), that is, as Saint Augustine explains, "has been irrevocably destined to the judgment of eternal fire."[107] In the same way those who say that Christ suffered in general for all human beings, that is, in the same way for both the elect and the reprobate, are clearly refuted by the statement of the Lord in which he said of the multitude of unbelievers: *The one who does not believe has already been judged* (Jn 3:18), that is, as our Augustine explains: "Has already been condemned."[108] For "the judgment has not yet appeared, but judgment has already taken place."[109] David also says about them: *Therefore, the ungodly will not rise up in the judgment* (Ps 1:5), "because," as the aforementioned author explains, "they have already been destined to most certain punishments."[110] But those who say that, as Christ redeemed the elect, although he did not redeem pagan reprobates, he nevertheless redeemed all the reprobate who have been baptized or will be baptized, are very easily refuted by the statement of the Lord by which he said of the multitude of the baptized reprobate, although under one name: *But when the king came in to see the guests, he saw a man there who was not clothed in a wedding garment, and he said to him: 'Friend, how did you come in here without a wedding garment?' Then the king said to the servants: 'Bind his hands and feet, and cast him into the outer darkness; there they will weep and gnash their teeth'* (Mt 22:11-13). Therefore, since all the baptized reprobate are signified by this one man, as is soon explained when the Lord says: *Many are called* (Mt 22:14), those who most falsely presume to say that all of these have been redeemed by Christ must be asked from what he redeemed them when he suffered death on the cross. He redeemed them only from either original or actual sins, which they contracted or committed before baptism and from which he redeemed them in baptism, those of course, from which he redeemed them in baptism and redeems them every day ....[111] He did not also redeem them from the death of eternal damnation ....,[112] because it was of course said in a general

106 Augustine, *On Rebuke and Grace*, 7.14 (PL 44:924).

107 Augustine, *Homilies on the Gospel of John*, 95.4 (PL 35:1873).

108 Augustine, *On the Christian Struggle* (*De agone christiano*), 27.29 (PL 40:305).

109 Augustine, *Homilies on the Gospel of John*, 12.12 (PL 35:1490).

110 Augustine, *Homilies on the Psalms*, 1.5 (PL 36:69).

111 A few words are missing in the text.

112 A few words are missing in the text.

way of all the reprobate: *And whoever was not found written in the book of life was cast into the lake of fire* (Rv 20:15). Therefore, it remains that we most certainly believe, understand, and most firmly confess and assert unto death that the Lord suffered for the elect alone and redeemed them through the blood of his cross from absolutely all sins, that is, from past, present and future ones.

He who says that the Lord our God, the Son of God, died for all of the baptized reprobate, must be asked what good this death of Christ did for them, since it did not save them with eternal salvation. For the redeemer and savior of the world saved only his people, according to the words of the angel: *For he will save his people from their sins* (Mt 1:21). Did he will to redeem them by dying, but did not save them, although to redeem by dying is more burdensome than to save by rising? Or did he will to save them, but they refused? Where then is that omnipotence of God, by which, as the psalmist says: *He has done everything that he has willed?* (Ps 113:3). Does he not make willing people out of unwilling ones, as the Apostle says: *For it is God who works in you both the willing and the acting for [his] good pleasure?* (Phil 2:13) Here there also belong these words: *The steps of a man will be directed by the Lord, and he will choose his way* (Ps 36:23), and these words: *The will is prepared by the Lord* (Prv 8:35 LXX). He must also be asked whether God loved the baptized reprobate whom he redeemed but hated the pagans whom he did not redeem. If he answers that it is true, he must be asked next why he loved and redeemed the baptized reprobate, since he certainly foreknew that they were going to be much worse afterward and were going to suffer much greater and much harsher torments, and hated only the pagans, since he certainly foreknew that they were going to be far less evil and were going to suffer lesser torments, that is, according to the words of the Lord: *The servant who did not know the will of his master and did not act worthily, will be beaten with few strokes. But the one who knew his master's will and did not act worthily, will be beaten with many strokes* (Lk 12: 47-48). If you shall have wisely aroused him about these, you will soon be amazed at his ignorance or inability to reasonably reply to these things.

However, I want also prudently to add this, asking that most wicked scoundrel to which of the two worlds he thinks the baptized reprobate belong according to the just judgment of God, that is, to the reconciled and cleansed world[113] or to the hostile, condemned, and polluted world?[114] If he says that they belong to the reconciled, saved, and cleansed world, you will tell him: Therefore, they have been reconciled, saved, and cleansed by the death of the Son of God and for that reason they *will be saved from wrath through him?* (Rom 5:9) If, whether he likes it or not, he sees and says that this is not true and for this reason answers

113 See Jn 1:29 and 2 Cor 5:19.

114 See 1 Cor 11:32 and 1 Jn 2:15-17. This entire paragraph has as its basis the distinction of these two worlds in Augustine's *Homilies on the Gospel of John*, 87.2 (PL 35:1853), quoted by Gottschalk above in Chapter 3.3.

that they rather belong to the hostile, condemned, and polluted world, consequently draw a conclusion and refute him by cornering him, saying cheerfully and confidently: Therefore, whether you like it or not, you finally are forced to believe, understand, and confess that Christ, the Son of God, by no means redeemed by the blood of his cross the baptized reprobate, whom he does not have as reconciled, saved perpetually, and cleansed.

He also has to be asked how he suffered for those for whom he did not even pray, those of course about whom he said to the Father: *I do not pray for the world* (Jn 17:9). Of that world the Apostle says: *Lest we be condemned with this world* (1 Cor 11:32), which is explained by Saint Augustine in this way: "For that world the Lord does not pray, for he is not unaware of that for which it has been predestined."[115] Therefore, it is seen brighter than the sun that he surely did not suffer—which is much more—for those for whom he did not pray—which is much less.

7. THAT THE REPROBATE ARE NOT REDEEMED HAS BEEN AVOIDED

Someone who considers these things faithfully and out of charity, as is right, will never state that the baptized reprobate have been redeemed by the death of Christ. "For he is the true Lamb who destroyed death by dying and restored life by rising,"[116] and, as Cassiodorus asserts: "The Savior granted salvation by dying."[117]

Cassiodorus explains what is said in the psalm: *The Lord reigned from the tree* (Ps 95:10 VL) as follows: "Not from the tree of paradise, from which the devil was seen to hold the human race captive, but from this one, namely, the tree of the cross, from which freedom raised our head and life arose. On the former tree the death of transgression hung; on the latter tree the faith of confession shone forth. The former led to hell; the latter sends to heaven,"[118] that is, so that it is understood that the redeemed are sent by it, who it is undoubtedly clear, whether the enemies of the truth like it or not, are only the elect.

8. [NOTES ON VARIOUS TOPICS]

On thinking the Apostle says: *We are not able or sufficient of ourselves to think of anything as from ourselves, but our sufficiency comes from God* (2 Cor 3:5).

Likewise he says on faith: *By grace you have been saved through faith, and this not of yourselves, but it is a gift of God* (Eph 2:8). Likewise he says: *Having the same spirit of faith* (2 Cor 4:13), where, since he certainly does not say: the same merit of faith, but *the same spirit of faith*, he clearly shows that faith is a gift of

115 Augustine, *Homilies on the Gospel of John*, 110.2 (PL 35:1921).

116 *Gregorian Sacramentary, Easter Preface* (*Sacramentarium gregorianum, Praefatio missae in die Paschae*) in HBS 49:59.

117 Cassiodorus, *Explanation of the Psalms*. On Ps 94:1 (PL 70:672B).

118 Cassiodorus, *Explanation of the Psalms*. On Ps 95:10 (PL 70:680C-D).

God. Here also belongs this passage where, after the Jews had said to the Lord: *What shall we do in order that we may carry out the works of God?* he said: *This is the work of God that you believe in him whom he sent* (Jn 6:28-29).

Likewise on willing and doing, the Apostle says: *For it is God who works in you both the willing and the acting,* or completion, *for [his] good pleasure* (Phil 2:13). In accord with what good will if not that which he produces, who *takes away* from us *a heart of stone and gives* us *a heart of flesh* (Ez 11:19 and 36:26), that is, takes away a hard and inflexible will and gives us a ready and good one? For it is written: *The will is prepared by the Lord* (Prv 8:35 LXX). As it is said by Saint Augustine, he "both prepares the will of man that needs to be helped and helps it once it has been prepared."[119]

Likewise on hope scripture says: *You, Lord, are my hope* (Ps 90:9). But on fear the Lord himself says: *I will put my fear in their hearts so that they will not depart from me* (Jer 32:40).

But on love, which is God,[120] it is well known to you that unless God gives it to us, no one can have it, and for this reason God gives it, as the Apostle says: *The love of God has been poured out in our hearts by the Holy Spirit who was given to us* (Rom 5:5).

On continence the sacred scripture speaks in this way: *No one can be continent unless God gives it* (Wis 8:21).

Thus it also says on the race: *The race does not belong to the swift* (Eccl 9:11). For we run in a salutary manner when we are drawn by God, according to these words: *Draw me to you, and we will run after you* (Sg 1:3). It is of course true that, as the Apostle fought a good fight, finished the race, and has kept the faith,[121] so each of the elect, as each is able, fights a good fight, finishes the race, and keeps the faith, but—*Rivers return to the place from which they came in order that they may flow again* (Eccl 1:7)—they claim nothing for their own powers, but they always credit and earnestly assign everything to the fountain, from which they flow, that is, to the grace of God, by which they are what they are. For they know that it is written that the Lord gives the struggle[122] and: *She gave him a mighty struggle in order that he might win* (Wis 10:12), and: *But thanks be to God, who gave us the victory through our Lord Jesus Christ* (1 Cor 15:57).

But on prayer the Apostle says: *We do not know what we should pray for as we ought, but the Spirit himself pleads for us with inexpressible groanings* (Rom 8:26), that is, he makes us plead.

The holy scriptures also bear witness to similar things about patience, or rather about suffering, such as: *Be subject to God, my soul, for my patience comes from*

119 Augustine, *Enchiridion on Faith, Hope, and Love,* 32 (PL 40:248).

120 See 1 Jn 4:8.

121 See 2 Tm 4:7.

122 See 2 Tm 4:18.

him (Ps 61:6), and: *You are my patience, Lord* (Ps 70:5), and: *Lord, the patience of Israel* (Jer 17:13 VL), and: *For it is better, if it is the will of the Lord, to suffer for doing good than for doing evil* (1 Pt 3:17), and: *To you it has been given on the behalf of Christ, not only to believe in him, but also to suffer for him* (Phil 1:29). Here is sufficient testimony of the Apostle concerning both faith and suffering in one statement. He shows that both are God's gift, since he said that both were given. But to persevere in Christ is undoubtedly given us by him by whom it was given to suffer for Christ. For he certainly delivers from every evil work and saves for his heavenly kingdom those whom he causes to persevere to the end.[123] But all these and whatever other goods there are, are most certainly declared to be God's gifts in order that no one might lifted up, but that each may always be humbled and that *he who boasts may boast in the Lord* (2 Cor 10:17).

On grace: Just as a body needs a soul in order to live, and as both the eyes and the air together need light in order the former may see and the latter may be bright, and as the branches need a vine in order that they may be able to bear fruit, so a rational creature—not merely a human, but also an angelic one—is known always to need divine grace in order that it may please God. Hence, as it can be said most correctly: That a body lives is not due to the living body, but to the vivifying spirit, and that an eye sees and the air is bright is not due to the eye that sees and the air that is bright, but to light that shines, and that a branch that remains in a vine bears fruit is not due to the branch that bears fruit, but to the vine that confers vital sap to the branch, so the Apostle also says most rightly: *It is not of the one who wills nor of the one who runs, but of God who shows mercy* (Rom 9:16), because, that is, it is clear that mercy comes from God who shows mercy. Anticipating the unwilling man, it makes him to will in a good way, and it follows the willing man so that he can. Therefore, the most holy and learned teacher Augustine says in his own way, that is, most truthfully: "God did not show mercy because Jacob willed and ran, but Jacob willed and ran because God showed mercy."[124] Again explaining the words of John the Baptist that have been written in the Gospel: *A man can receive nothing unless it has been given to him from heaven* (Jn 3:27), he says: "If you heard something divine from John, it is due to him who illuminates, not to him who receives."[125] If you read and keep these in mind, you will not accept—God forbid!— what Saint Jerome says: "The kingdom of God is not of him who gives, but of him who receives. *For there is no acceptance of persons with God* (Rom 2:11). But whoever presents himself in order to become worthy of the kingdom of heaven, he receives what was prepared not

123 See Mt 10:22.

124 Augustine, *Unfinished Work in Answer to Julian*, 2.141 (PL 45:1140).

125 Augustine, *Homilies on the Gospel of John*, 16.6 (PL 35:1505).

for that person, but for that life,"[126] because Christ himself clearly contradicts him on the same idea and says: *But for those for whom it has been prepared by my Father* (Mt 20:23). For he did not say "for whose life" but "for whom," where the persons of human beings are certainly understood. But the Lord God had mercy upon blessed Jerome as on someone who was in haste, for he wrote in two weeks a work of many years, that is, his *Commentary on Matthew*, as he himself said.[127] But no one should in any way accept what I put above if one does not want to be answerable to truth. There are of course many other things—who would count all of them?—in which the same Saint Jerome spoke as a man. Among these there is the place in *On the Letter to the Galatians* where he said that there are three spirits in the Trinity and that the apostle Peter did not err on that point about which the apostle Paul writes that he was reprehensible,[128] although in the same epistle "the preacher of the truth"[129] and our *teacher of the Gentiles* (1 Tm 2:7) swears in testifying and says: *But the things I write to you, behold, I do not lie before God* (Gal 1:20). Hence, our Augustine, writing to the same holy Jerome, says: "If Paul lied there, where did he tell the truth?"[130] Likewise he says: "Let those who think otherwise pardon me. I believe the Apostle more when he swears in his own writings and on behalf of them than any highly learned person who discusses another's writings."[131] That is also by no means true, which he asserts in *On Isaiah*, that the number of our days to live is not divinely determined or fixed for each of us. Blessed Gregory gave a more than sufficient answer against this in the third part of his *Moral Commentary*.[132] And it also does not square, agree, and harmonize with the truth that the sun and moon will come to the day of judgment and will receive an increase of brightness as a reward for their services. Replying against this in his book, *Against the Origenists for Orosius*, Saint Augustine briefly but sufficiently answers when he says: "Let it be read in the divine books, and we will believe."[133] Therefore, when I read the works of holy Jerome, I often recall what he himself says in the prologue to his *Commentary on the Letter to the Galatians*: "I read all these and, having gathered many things in

---

126 Jerome, *Commentary on Matthew* (*Commentaria in Matthaeum*), 3. On Mt 20:23 (PL 26:144A).

127 Jerome, *Commentary on Matthew*, Prologue (PL 26:20B).

128 Jerome, *Commentary on the Letter to the Galatians*, 1. On Gal 2:11-13 (PL 26:339).

129 Gregory the Great, *Book of Antiphons*, *Antiphon for the Feast of Saint Paul* (*Antiphona in festo sancti Pauli*) in PL 78:791.

130 Augustine, *Letters*, 40.3, 3 (PL 33:155).

131 Augustine, *Letters*, 82.3, 25 (PL 33:287).

132 Gregory the Great, *Moral Commentary on Job*, 12.52.58 (PL 75:1013A-C); 16.10.14 (PL 75:1127B-28A); and 17.5.7 (PL 76:13C).

133 See Augustine, *Answer to the Priscillianists and Origenists* (*Contra Priscillianistas et Origenistas*), 8.11 (PL 42:675).

my mind, I dictated either my own ideas or another's."[134] Thus I of course willingly follow and embrace all the things he said that are true, and, on the contrary, I gladly and permissibly pass over the other things that he dictated as a man.

9.
ON THE BAPTIZED REPROBATE

How much this bodily and temporal salvation, which is common to good and evil men along with cattle and beasts of burden, and that spiritual and eternal salvation, which is of course proved to be special to the elect, differ! Concerning the latter it is of course said: *My help from God is just, for he saves the upright in heart* (Ps 7:11), and: *You will save a people that is humble, Lord* (Ps 17:28), and: *You have saved me from those going down into the pit* (Ps 29:4), and: *Save your people* (Ps 27:9), that is, on account of whom alone Christ, the Son of God, was called Jesus: *For he,* it says, *will save his people from their sins* (Mt 1:21). Concerning them it is also said: *But the salvation of the righteous comes from the Lord* (Ps 36:39), although to the contrary it says concerning the reprobate: *Salvation is far from sinners* (Ps 118:155), and for this reason none of them is of course saved with eternal salvation, but absolutely only the elect people, to whose lot he of course belongs about whom the Lord says: *He who believes and is baptized will be saved* (Mk 16:16), and: *He who perseveres to the end will be saved* (Mt 10:22). You remember that I said, determined, and distinguished somewhere more clearly than daylight, as I think, how much these two kinds of salvation differ, that is, with the Apostle also helping us here and saying: *The Lord will set me free from every evil deed and will save me in his heavenly kingdom* (2 Tm 4:18), in which it is certainly clear that no reprobate is going to be saved. For God saves by this salvation those upon whom he has mercy in his great goodness, not those whom he hardens with no iniquity. He nonetheless does both by his equally pious and just will and by his most omnipotent power. For the Apostle does not say: He has mercy on whom he wills and hardens whom he does not will, but: *He has mercy on whom he wills, and hardens whom he wills* (Rom 9:18). Hence, those who want the words of the Apostle: *God wills all men to be saved,* to be understood in general both for the elect and for the reprobate, but he saves the elect because they themselves will to be saved, and on the contrary he does not save the reprobate because they do not will to be, can most easily be refuted by the one syllable by which is said: *He hardens whom he wills* (Rom 9:18). For God truly by no means willed to save with eternal salvation those whom he on that account, as scripture testifies, justly *hardens* because he *wills,* not because he does not will. Here let them wake up, if they can, who thus far have not been afraid to believe this and also are not afraid even now. And if they do not blush for shame at what the Lord God said to Moses: *I will have mercy on whom I will have mercy, and I will have compassion on whom I will have compassion, and I will be gracious to whom*

134 Jerome, *Commentary on the Letter to the Galatians,* Prologue (PL 26:309A).

I will be pleased (Ex 33:19)—he did not say: "To him who pleases me"—or at what the psalmist said: *Great are works of the Lord, sought out in all his wills* (Ps 110:2), and: *The Lord has done whatever he willed in heaven and on earth, in the sea and in all the deeps* (Ps 134:6), at least let them blush for shame at what the holy woman said to the Lord God[135] and at what the universal church now harmoniously sings to him: "*In your will, Lord, all things have been placed, and there is no one who can resist your will* (Est 13:9)."[136] Let them diligently attend to, wisely consider, and prudently examine these and so many similar testimonies of the sacred scriptures, and if they are ashamed and fear to be more than frogs are or to be called fools, that is, frogs that fall silent when it thunders, let them at last be aroused, wake up and blush for shame, if they can, that is, if they have not died, but are asleep, at the above words of sacred scripture, which is called heaven and is thunder. Let them blush for shame; I repeat, let them blush for shame and fall silent. Let them sleep *between the lots* (Ps 67:14), that is, let them give assent to the testimonies of the two testaments and finally, assent to the truth, as is good for them, let them rest happily. Otherwise let them hear what blessed Augustine said concerning heretics: "Heaven thunders; let the frogs fall silent."[137] But with those obstinate and exceedingly stubborn people, that is, not alive but dead, left aside, it is undoubtedly most necessary for us not to be killed by their deadly venom. For those who say that God, who generally and universally, equally and without distinction *wills all men to be saved* (1 Tm 2:4), saves the elect because they will to be saved and does not save the reprobate because they themselves do not will to be saved, certainly deny God's grace in the elect and deny, although unknowingly, God's omnipotence in the reprobate. For if he saves only those who will to be saved, then he does not of course save them gratuitously, but because of their merit, and now gives them salvation because of what is owed them. But if he equally wills to save the reprobate, then he has the willing, but where is the power of the omnipotent? But if they say: "The omnipotent has the power, just as he has the will, but their own refusal blocks them," then they should know or rather we should know that, as the Apostle said: *God works in us also the willing* (Phil 2:13). And for this reason if the omnipotent willed anything, then as soon as he willed, he would also produce it in them with complete ease, the highest speed, and omnipotent power. But if the above quoted testimony of the Apostle seems contrary to the same Apostle who said in another place: *To will is present for me* (Rom 7:18), then those unwilling to accept this, persisting *in the futility of their mind* (Eph 4:17) and *in the obstinacy of their hearts* (Sir 16:11), still say that God nonetheless *wills all men to be saved* (1 Tm 2:4), but saves only those

135 Esther, although the prayer is actually that of Mordechai.

136 Gregory the Great, *Book of Antiphons, Antiphon for the Introit on the Twenty-First Sunday after Pentecost* (*Antiphona ad introitum, in dominica 21 post Pentecostem*) in PL 78:720A.

137 Augustine, *Sermons* (*Sermones*), 240.5 (PL 38:1133).

who will to be saved, passing over those who do not will to be saved, have to be asked: Then why does he save little babies who cry when being baptized and resist as much as they can and absolutely do not will to be baptized in their own will? Likewise they have to be asked concerning the reprobate babies, and it should be said to them: Why on the other hand does God not save those who are not unwilling, just as they are not willing? Therefore, you make God more benevolent towards the adults who are surely much worse, because he wills to save them, but they do not will it, than towards babies dying without baptism whom he does not will to save. Still it cannot be said of them that they refuse it, who at that age do not know how to refuse to be saved. Therefore, it remains that those who think or rather foolishly suppose such things, either come to their senses after being defeated or be abandoned, as lost people, who barking like that are insane. But that other testimony of the Apostle, *To will is present for me* (Rom 7:18), is in no way contrary to what I had set forth earlier, that is, because the will that God gave to the elect is present for them, but they do not find how to carry out the good,[138] because they desire against their will, and they do good because they do not consent to desire, but they do not carry out the good because they have desire. They are not therefore worthy of damnation—God forbid!—although they are blameworthy because they have desire, since they do not consent to the desires that they experience involuntarily. For they have the grace of God by which they are always helped so that they do not become guilty by consenting.

10.
[Law and Grace]

Among other copious, numerous, luminous, fruitful volumes of his memory, which he left to humankind redeemed by the blood of Christ, as profitable even unto the day of judgment, blessed Augustine wrote a most distinguished book and certainly one most fruitful for all those who love God, *On the Spirit and the Letter*, that is, calling grace the spirit and law the letter, according to the Apostle's saying: *The letter kills, but the Spirit gives life* (2 Cor 3:6). In this book he quite clearly shows that though the law is good, it is still of no benefit without grace and, as the apostolic testimony says above, it kills rather than is of benefit to anybody, "unless the life-giving Spirit is" gratuitously "present."[139] Hence, at another time the Apostle himself testifies again: *The law brings about wrath* (Rom 4:15). This is surely true if grace does not help. On this the same Saint Augustine quite truthfully asserts somewhere: "The law commands in vain, unless grace helps."[140] In the same book he discusses individually the law, faith,

138 See Rom 7:18.

139 Augustine, *On the Spirit and the Letter* (*De spiritu et littera*), 4.6 (PL 44:203).

140 The source of this quotation has not been located.

and grace, the health or healing of the soul, love or delight of righteousness, and free choice. Although I do not recall the words of any of these individual topics, still recalling their meaning in part, I will set forth some things on them, as I am able. First, he testifies that the law is good, as the Apostle says: *The law is good if one uses it lawfully* (1 Tm 1:8), that is, so that, learning good and evil in it, one does not put one's trust in it or in the knowledge of it, because through it one can by no means fulfill the commandments of God. Rather, from this law that commands, but that kills unless the things that it commands are fulfilled, he "flees through faith to grace"[141] that helps and the spirit that gives life, that is, in order that, having been gratuitously helped and brought to life, he might receive from God the health of the soul and then the love of and delight in righteousness. And then he freely receives free choice gratuitously restored, repaired, and given back for turning away from evil and for doing good through the gratuitous gift of God's grace. For from the time he became *a slave of sin* (Jn 8:34), he is of course shown to have had free choice only for doing evil, as completely lost, according to the words of the Lord: *Truly, truly, I say to you, everyone who commits sin is a slave of sin* (Jn 8:34), and for this reason as long as anyone is a slave of sin, he has no other freedom except for sinning and committing evil and for freely doing the will of his lord, that is, of sin. For carnal desire reigns where the love of God is not present. And for this reason there is no freedom to do good where God's love is not present. For as the apostolic authority truly and alone proclaims: *Where the Spirit of the Lord is, there is freedom* (2 Cor 3:17). "Therefore, the law was given so that the grace might be sought, and grace was given so that the law might be carried out."[142] For *the law was our schoolmaster* (Gal 3:24), and it in no way was, is, or will be able to absolve from sins, but rather has terrified and moreover slain. However, by terrifying the elect of God, as if by the office of a schoolmaster, the law leads them through faith to the grace of Christ by healing them. But after the elect are brought to life through the grace of Christ when health has been recovered from the offense of sin and love of or delight in righteousness has been infused into them and poured out in the hearts of the elect, they at last receive free choice and have it for doing good, as, I think, I showed above clearly and sufficiently, although not completely or in every respect in the words, but still in the meaning of the aforementioned doctor. But when this same great teacher in his fashion, that is, wisely and eloquently, had distinguished between separate functions of the law, of faith, of grace, of health, of love for and delight in righteousness, and of free choice, he added and said the following:

> All these that I have put together as if in a chain, have their own voices in the sacred scripture. The law says: *You shall not covet* (Dt 5:21). Faith says: *I*

141 Augustine, *On the Spirit and the Letter*, 10.16 (PL 44:210).

142 Augustine, *On the Spirit and the Letter*, 20.34 (PL 44:221).

> *said: Heal my soul, Lord, for I have sinned against you* (Ps 40:5). Grace says: *Behold, you have been made well. Sin no more, lest something worse thing happen to you* (Jn. 5:14). The healing of the soul from the defect of sin says: *Lord, my God, I cried out to you, and you healed me* (Ps 29:3). The love for or delight in righteousness says: *The wicked told me of their delights, but not like your law, O Lord* (Ps 118:85). And free choice says: *I will freely sacrifice to you* (Ps 53:8).[143]

II.
[CHRIST THE SCALE]

The scale on which the sins of blessed Job, that is, of the holy church, are weighed, is Christ who, as the Apostle says, *loved the church and handed himself over for her* (Eph 5:25); he of course who, as the same Apostle also says, is *head of the church, the savior of his body* (Eph 5:23). Therefore, it is seen, not obscurely but clearly, and not in just any way but much more brightly than the light of the sun, that whether the enemies of the truth and friends of error, lies, and falsehood like it or not, Christ redeemed only his holy church and only the elect, that is, only his body and members, through the blood of his cross; he was certainly crucified only for them, and he undoubtedly suffered the death of the cross, which was the most disgraceful, ignominious, and shameful death of that time, only for them. We prove and approve this because you, the true light, shine for us, and we refute and disprove the teachers of Satan, that is, the teachers of error. Of course only the sins of your elect, by which they merited wrath, are weighed in Christ the scale, because with all their sins forgiven and absolved, they alone went, go, and will go after their head above the stars, because as Augustine truly says, "Where the head is, there also the other members are."[144] But on the contrary, since the sins of the reprobate, whether of the pagans or of the baptized and those going to be baptized, for which they have merited wrath, were in no way weighed on this scale, as it is most falsely discussed, said, written, recited, and preached, they certainly have justly been cast down, are rightly being cast down before their head, and finally all of them will be cast down and submerged in the infernal regions together with their head, that is, because "where the head is, there also the other members are."

Whoever does not see these things is blind; whoever denies them is slain, and to be sure he is not a sheep, not a lamb, but a rapacious wolf or a shameless goat. Hence, as you, our Lord God and teacher Jesus Christ, refused to speak with the fox Herod,[145] whom you truly foretold to be so, it is thus certainly much more fitting, proper, and suitable to your sheep to be thoroughly on their guard against the attacks of the rapacious wolves and to reply to such people nothing more except when necessity compels us on account of the weak and less capable.

---

143 Augustine, *On the Spirit and the Letter*, 30.52 (PL 44:233-4).

144 Augustine, *Homilies on the Psalms*, 29.2, 14. On Ps 29:5 (PL 36:223).

145 See Lk 13:32.

You, O all-powerful and wise, loving and good shepherd, who laid down your life for your sheep, and not—God forbid!—for the he- or she-goats of another, you, who have your throne on high and reside in heaven, never slumbering or falling asleep,[146] you will always take care of your peaceful and feeble sheep as you do it now, will restlessly foresee the ambushes of the shameless, stubborn, obstinate, rapacious wolves, and as soon as *the time to act* (Ps 118:126) comes, as evidently *the time to have mercy* (Ps 101:14) is now coming, some day you will finally remove them far away from your little sheep, as it is expedient, and will command them [to go] to their own place[147] as quickly as possible, as it is indeed proper. O Lord God who has said to your Father, our Lord God: *Zeal for your house consumes me* (Ps 68:10; Jn 2:17), always freely assist, protect and defend your sheep, for whom alone you gave yourself to the death of the cross willingly enough and with gladness. Amen.

12.
WHY THE SON IS SOMETIMES CALLED EQUAL TO THE FATHER, SOMETIMES LESS THAN HIM

Our Lord Jesus Christ is God and man, the Son of God and the Son of Man, one person from two natures and in two natures united and perfected, as it is evident, clear and apparent. And thus:

> From one sentence of the Apostle two natures are understood in the Son of God, the one in which he is equal to the Father in all things, the other in which he is less than him, where he [the Apostle] says: *Who, although being in the form of God, did not consider it robbery to be equal with God, but he emptied himself, taking the form of a servant* (Phil 2:6-7). Some things in the holy scriptures are spoken so that the Son is understood to be less, as he himself says: *The Father is greater than I* (Jn 14:28), but other things are surely spoken so that he is shown to be equal to the Father, as in the place where he himself says: *I and the Father are one* (Jn 10:30), *one* because of the unity of substance, *are* because of the distinction of the persons. This is why the prudent reader ought to most diligently consider what should be said for which form. For since in *the form of a servant* and in *the form of God* the same [person] is the one and the only begotten Son of God the Father, in the form of God [he is] equal to the Father, [but] in the form of a servant [he is] less than the Father. Therefore not undeservedly the scripture says both: that the Son is equal to the Father and that the Father is greater than the Son, the former indeed on account of the form of God, the latter on account of the form of a servant, without any separation of the person being understood. In the form of God: *In the beginning was the Word* (Jn 1:1); in the form of a servant: *The Word became flesh* (Jn 1:14), that is, God became man, in the former eternally equal to, in the latter

146 See Ps 120:4.

147 See Acts 1:25.

> temporally less [than the Father]; in the form which is equal to the Father he created man, in the form which is less [than him] he became man.[148]

Thus through the same Christ we perceive that there has been, is now, and will be in the future two resurrections of men, the one of course from the death of the souls, the other from the death of the bodies, but the resurrection of the souls is accomplished through Christ as God and the resurrection of the bodies through Christ as man, as it is said in the same Gospel: *The hour is coming, and now is, when the dead hear the voice of the Son of God, and those who hear will live* (Jn 5:25), and a little later: *The hour will come when the dead who are in the graves will hear the voice of the Son of Man and come forth—those who have done good, to the resurrection of life, and those who have done evil, to the resurrection of judgment* (Jn 5:28-29), that is, of condemnation. Whoever gives heed as one should to that which he says above: [*The dead*] *hear the voice of the Son of God,* and this which [he says] above: [*The dead who are in the graves*] *will hear the voice of the Son of Man,* surely distinguishes and clearly discerns the difference between both resurrections, and that the resurrection through [his] divinity, in which he is equal to the Father and one with the Father, as he himself says: *I and the Father are one* (Jn 10:30) is better, and that the inferior resurrection will happen through the humanity of Christ, of which the Father is greater, as the Son himself says: *The Father is greater than I* (Jn 14:28). Let us believe, understand, confess not that there are two Sons or two Christs, God and man, as Nestorius barked. He did not create humanity to this end that—God forbid!—a *quaternity* should be introduced into God the Trinity. Rather the Trinity remains as it was, but there are two natures in Christ, not one, as Eutyches dreamed. Therefore catholics who refuted Nestorius' perfidy altogether rightly affirm and say that it is not that there is one Christ who is God and another Christ who is man, but that there is one and the same Christ, God and man, as it is clearly enough declared in the psalm where it is said: *And the man was born in her, and the Most High established her* (Ps 86:5), and in another one: *Your throne was prepared of old: You are from everlasting* (Ps 92:2). Now he does not say: *You are,* but are *of old,* that is, from the time when you became man, and *you are from everlasting,* when you were not as yet a man. Here there also belongs this from another psalm: *Know that the Lord himself is God* (Ps 99:3), that is, the one who is the Lord according to humanity, is also God according to divinity. Now abhorring also Eutyches' madness, we say that in Christ divinity is one thing and humanity another, which is most clearly declared in the psalm where it is said on behalf of the Father: *I have found my servant David; with my holy oil I have anointed him* (Ps 88:21) and: *He will call upon me: 'You are my Father, my God'* (Ps 88:27) and other things that are said there, both above and below in that [passage]. Here

148 Alcuin of York, *On the Faith of the Holy Trinity* (*De fide sanctae Trinitatis*), 3.7 (PL 101:41C-42B).

this also belongs: *Exalt the Lord our God and worship his footstool, for it is holy* (Ps 98:5), that is, humanity of his divinity, and this: *The Lord said to my Lord: 'Sit at my right hand'* (Ps 109:1)—observe the humanity of the one who sits. Likewise: *I have begotten you before the morning star* (Ps 109:3)—behold his divinity that is begotten now and eternally and is always born from the Father.

13.
ON THE ELECT AND THE REPROBATE

If one of them truthfully says about the elect: *All of us like sheep have gone astray; each of us has turned to his own way* (Is 53:6), then certainly another one of them, who had not a common, but a high place among them during his time says rightly concerning the reprobate: *They are all turned aside; they are together become good for nothing, there is none that does good, no not one* (Ps 13:3). This is most truthfully in agreement with the explanation by Saint Augustine: "There was no one who would do this good, which is to seek after God; there was not even one, but in that kind of people which was predestined to destruction," which [passage] perhaps had not been explained clearly after the coming of the Lord by any catholic teacher before him.[149] Wherefore it is possible to conclude that Origen thought that the above quoted witness of Isaiah: *All of us like sheep have gone astray* up to the words: *The Lord has laid on him the iniquity of us all* (Is 53:6) should be understood in a general way, as referring to both the elect and the reprobate, and for that reason he asserted through ignorance that Christ had suffered universally for all people, as if the Apostle also said in the same sense: *Therefore all died; and he died for all* (2 Cor 5:14-15), and this: *God did not spare his own Son, but handed him over for all* (Rom 8:32). Explaining this or rather trying to explain this, Origen called the truth of predestination an error, saying: "Thus the Father handed over his only-begotten Son not for some people, as the error of predestination supposes, but for all who are in the church,"[150] when according to blessed Augustine it is "the words of those chosen for the kingdom"[151] of God, of those who are predestined: *He handed him over for us all* (Rom 8:32). Yet these *all* are never called in the sacred scriptures of the

149 Augustine, *On the Perfection of Human Righteousness* (*De perfectione iustitiae hominis*), 13.31 (CSEL 42:32; PL 44:308).

150 In a homily *On the Feast of the Apostles* (*In natali apostolorum*), Smaragdus, abbot of Saint-Mihiél (fl. 820s), attributes to Origen the same comment verbatim (PL 102:528). However, Origen's comment on Rom 8:32 in his *Commentary on the Epistle to the Romans* (*Commentarii in epistolam ad Romanos*), 7.9 (PG 14:1129), differs slightly. It reads: "The Father handed over his own Son not only for saints, not only for the great, but also for the least, and for absolutely all who are in the church" (*Non solum pro sanctis, non solum pro magnis, sed et pro minimis, et pro omnibus omnino qui sunt in Ecclesia tradidit Filium proprium Pater*). It says nothing about "the error of predestination."

151 Augustine, *On Rebuke and Grace*, 7.15 (PL 44:925).

Old and New Testaments *some* but *few* in comparison with those who perish, as here: *Many are called, few chosen* (Mt 20:16). But within their own group they are *many*, as in this statement: *He bore the sins of many, and by his knowledge this righteous one justified my many servants* (Is 53:11), and: *He will sprinkle many nations* (Is 52:15), and: *I have made you a father of many nations* (Gn 17:5), and: *Many will come from east and west and sit down with Abraham, Isaac, and Jacob in the kingdom of heaven* (Mt 8:11), and: *I will number them, and they will be multiplied beyond the sand* (Ps 138:18). But the aforementioned Origen did not, as he ought to have, expertly consider these *few* as those same *many*, but thought that in these and similar passages *all* meant not the elect particularly, but the reprobate also with them in general. For this very reason, I think, he erred not slightly but madly concerning this revolving of the righteous and unrighteous who go round or turn in a cycles again and again. And perhaps on that account he seems to have as it were prudently judged or rather affirmed this. For he did not dare to annihilate, nullify, or annul the price of Christ's blood by which, he believed, absolutely all people are redeemed. And he saw that the price would be void, useless, and of no effect for the reprobate, whom he confessed to be redeemed, if they remained lost in torments. If Christ had suffered for the reprobate, which is truly by no means so, then it would have been most truthfully known, most certainly held, and intrepidly asserted that none of them—I do not mean: Not all of them—would eternally perish, for whom, as it is known, such a high price has been shed. But as it is wholly evident that this is most false, the Lord God will rightly tell them: *Depart, you accursed ones, into everlasting fire* (Mt 25:41). And so as to evidently reject and refute more clearly than light the most absurd opinion of Origen and the Origenists, later he did not say as above: *And these will go into everlasting fire*, but *into everlasting punishment* (Mt 25:46), that is, in which they will be tormented forever.

But Saint Jerome, who rightly execrated this most false revolving, equally believed, as that one,[152] that Christ suffered for the reprobate, and conjectured that we are called, become, and are holy not according to the purpose of God,[153] but according to that of each of us, and according to our own will. And therefore he argued that "the kingdom of God is not of him who gives, but of him who receives," and that it was "prepared for life"[154] and not for persons, so that whoever wants it would receive it by living well, having been drawn to it by his own will. He also asserted that anyone who wants it, is worthy of it by human will. Concerning this Saint Augustine says in passing in his book to Prosper and Hilary: "If it is asked and discussed from where anyone is worthy, there are not wanting those who say—from human will. But we say: from divine

152 That is, Origen.

153 See Rom 8:28 and Eph 1:11.

154 Jerome, *Commentary of Matthew*, 3. On Mt 20:23 (PL 26:144A).

grace or predestination. But between grace and predestination there is only this difference, that predestination is the preparation for grace, while grace is the gift itself."[155] Whoever perceives and discerns this difference carefully, as is right, and consequently examines, as he ought to, that which blessed John the Baptist says: *Grace for grace* (Jn 1:16), as well as what the apostle Paul says: *But the grace of God is eternal life* (Rom 6:23), will certainly see that both a good life now and eternal life hereafter is not something of which "anyone can be worthy by human will," but as the aforementioned author says truthfully, "by divine grace or predestination." For it is not divine grace that is dependent on human will, but the human will that is dependent on divine grace. The former is given, helped, nurtured, strengthened and governed as well as delivered, perfected and crowned by the latter. For it is written: *The will is prepared by the Lord* (Prv 8:35 LXX), and: *The steps of a man will be directed by the Lord, and he will choose his way* (Ps 36:23), and: *It is God who works in you both the willing and the acting for [his] good pleasure* (Phil 2:13). Therefore, as you may very easily recall, priests ask God devotedly each year that he may graciously summon to himself "our rebellious wills."[156] And if that passage in the Psalms may be applied to us, where the church of God says: *And I shall confess him from my will* (Ps 27:7), we know that the same will is ours in such a way that we say that it is given to us by God, as we certainly affirm: *The Lord will give goodness, and our land will yield its fruit* (Ps 84:13), certainly not all by itself or naturally, but it was sown freely by him who *went out to sow his seed* (Mt 13:3).

As matters stand this way, I beg you to give full attention to that which Saint Augustine says in his *Commentary on the Letter to the Galatians*. For explaining this apostolic saying: *If we or an angel from heaven announce a gospel to you besides that which we have preached to you, let him be anathema* (Gal 1:8), he says among other things: "Truth is to be loved on account of itself, not on account of the apostle or angel who announces it, for if it were to be loved on account of an apostle or an angel, falsehood would also of course be thought something to be loved, if it were announced by an apostle or an angel."[157] For that reason I considered it as something to keep in mind, that you never assent to anyone who speaks against truth, no matter how great may be his character, authority, reputation, holiness, or genius. Do you approve that I should believe with you,[158] God forbid! what blessed Jerome says in his book of *Hebrew Questions*,

155 Augustine, *On the Predestination of the Saints*, 10.19 (PL 44:974).

156 *Gregorian Sacramentary, Prayer over the Sacrifice on the Saturday before the Lord's Day of the Passion* (*Oratio super oblationem, Sabbatum ante dominicam de Passione*) in HBS 49:42.

157 Augustine, *Commentary on the Letter to the Galatians* (*In epistolam ad Galatas*), 4. On Gal 1:6-9 (PL 35:2108).

158 The "you" probably refers to Rabanus Maurus, who cited Jerome on free will in his *Letter to Eberhard* (*Epistola ad Eberhardum*) in PL 112:1555.

namely, that the Lord God had planted the paradise of delight before he created the heavens and the earth?[159] And where were so many trees if not on the earth? Also, that which he says [in his book] that has for its heading: *Give ear, O my people* (Ps 77:1) is in no way sound, namely, that on account of episimon [vau][160] the Latin interpreter erred, having taken the Greek sign Γ, which is used to designate the sixth hour, for a Γ used for the third hour, and therefore in the *Gospel according to Mark* he translated that the Lord was crucified at the third hour,[161] when in fact, as Saint Augustine teaches in his book *On the Harmony of the Gospels*, it was written so by that same Evangelist that it would be known to everyone that the Lord was crucified at the third hour more by the tongues of the Jews than at the sixth hour by the hands of the soldiers, since at the third hour the Jews cried out: *Crucify, crucify him!* (Lk 23:21).[162]

And to this testimony of the Lord: *I am the Lord who sanctifies you* (Ex 31:13), as well as to these words of Saint Augustine: "*He has made us* both human and righteous, *and not we ourselves* (Ps 99:3),"[163] or as he also says at another place: "*He has made us* both human and good *and not we ourselves*,"[164] those wretches who follow the Pelagians may answer with these words of the blessed apostle John: *And everyone who has this hope in him sanctifies himself, just as he is holy* (1 Jn 3:3). But lest any of the faithful—God forbid!—should be ever snared by the adherents of this worst heresy or even have doubts of however small a degree, I thought it suitable to call to mind what Saint Augustine says and teaches on this account in his four books *Against the Pelagians* that he wrote for blessed Boniface. For he says that sometimes the holy scripture implies without express statement that things done by men through God's action are done by men on behalf of God, and consequently that things which God alone accomplishes in men are said to be done by God, as those words full of grace in Solomon according to the Septuagint read: *Opening the mouth belongs to man, but the answer of the tongue is from the Lord* (Prv 16:1). God forbid, he says, that Solomon should have ignored what his father David had said to the Lord: *O Lord, open my lips, and my mouth will declare your praise* (Ps 50:17).[165] Another example is this saying: *I have set a guard before my mouth* (Ps 38:2), which plainly and clearly has to be understood

159 Jerome, *Hebrew Questions on Genesis* (*Quaestiones Hebraicae in Genesim*). On Gen 2:8 (PL 23:940B).

160 A sign used in Greek to designate the numeral six.

161 See Mk 15:25. Jerome, *Notes on the Psalms* (*Breviculus in psalmos*). On Ps 77:2 (PL 26:1046A).

162 See Augustine, *On the Harmony of the Gospels* (*De consensu evangelistarum*), 3.13, 42-3 (PL 34:1184).

163 Augustine, *Sermons*, 22.11, 12 (PL 38:177).

164 See Augustine, *Sermons*, 2.2; 3.3-4 (PL 38:172).

165 See Augustine, *Answer to the Two Letters of the Pelagians* (*Contra duas epistolas Pelagianorum*), 2.9, 20 (PL 44:585-6).

as something done through God's gift and God's action. Likewise: *I was dumb and kept silence from good things* (Ps 38:3), but this is certainly through God's action, as a little later he declares and says: *I was dumb, and did not open my mouth, because you have made* (Ps 38:10), namely, me. Therefore, it is clear that a man by himself, that is, without God's action, can neither set a guard on his mouth nor open it. Though both things have been abundantly made evident above, yet on account of the most impious heresy, which is sprouting forth again, I will say it again: If by free will alone, without the grace of God a person is able to set a guard on his mouth, the psalmist assuredly would not have said, beseeching God: *Set a guard before my mouth* (Ps 140:3), that is, make it so that I may set a guard before my mouth. Had he not set a guard already when he had said: *I have set a guard before my mouth* (Ps 38:2)? To be sure it is a true statement, but it is clear that he had done so by God's action. Likewise, if a person is able to open his mouth by free will alone, the Lord would not have said to the prophet: And it will be that when you open your mouth and *you speak to them* (Ez 3:11), which truly he himself could not do by any means before that. For, earlier the Lord had said to him: *I will make your tongue cling to the roof of your mouth, so that you will be dumb and not be one to rebuke them, for they are an exasperating house* (Ez 3:26). So when God says to a man: *Open your mouth wide, and I will fill it* (Ps 80:11), in order that a man should do what God commands, he needs to ask God to help him, for the psalmist says, supplicating God: *Be my helper, do not forsake me* (Ps 26:9). Thus he demonstrated that if he had been forsaken [by God], he would not have been able to do good by himself. Accordingly, in the same way the following passages must be understood: *He sanctifies himself, just as he is holy* (1 Jn 3:3), and: *He will vivify his own* soul (Ez 18:27), and: *You have freed your soul* (Ez 3:21), and: *He will save his soul from death* (Jas 5:20), and: *Save your soul!* (Gn 19:17), as well as other similar statements that Pelagians use in their writings against the grace of God and in favor of free will. Thus it should be understood not as they very insanely bark, but quite sanely that anyone who has been chosen vivifies his soul and sanctifies himself only when God helps him, when he inspires his will, when he gives him the ability, and when he makes him do so. For unless he always gratuitously helps us, a person can do nothing but become more and more guilty.[166]

166 The treatise ends with a long quotation from Augustine, *On Grace and Free Choice*, 21.43-24.46 (PL 44:909-12), which is here omitted.

ON DIFFERENT WAYS OF SPEAKING ABOUT REDEMPTION

This text is a short but coherent treatise contained in ms. Berne 584, fol. 106v-109r and published by Lambot as section XX of the *Small Theological Works* (*Opuscula Theologica*) of Gottschalk. Although it was untitled in the Berne manuscript, Lambot entitled it *Quibus modis dicatur redemptio*. Its time of composition is uncertain. Edition: Lambot, 279-82. Translated by Victor Genke.

Saint Augustine says in his book, *Hypomnesticon*: "Let us take courage, resisting them in the grace of the Lord, which is our glory redeeming us from those besieging us."[1] Just as in this place *redeeming* means *setting free* and *rescuing*, so it also frequently shows in other places, for instance: *Rise up, Lord, help us and redeem us* (Ps 43:26), and the Son himself says about the Father: *He will redeem my soul in peace* (Ps 54:19). Hence, Saint Augustine says the same thing: "But from where does this freedom to do good come to a man who is enslaved and sold, unless he is redeemed by him who has said: *If the Son will set you free, you will truly be free* (Jn 8:36)?"[2] Therefore, redemption that takes place in baptism is common to the elect and the reprobate, for both[3] are completely redeemed from past sins. On this blessed Peter said about the reprobate and the lost: *Denying the Lord who bought them* (2 Pt 2:1). And in order that what I am saying may be seen more clearly and more fully, it is made brighter than daylight by the apostle Paul: *Do not grieve*, he says, *the Holy Spirit of God, by whom you were sealed for the day of redemption* (Eph 4:30), that is, when you believed and were baptized, and he also disclosed earlier in the same *Letter to the Ephesians*: *And believing in him you were sealed with the Holy Spirit of promise* (Eph 1:13). Nevertheless there is another special redemption for the elect, which was given to them by the Son of God on the tree of the cross, namely, that because of which they humbly say to the Lamb in heaven: *You have redeemed us for God by your blood* (Rv 5:9). For by it only the elect have been completely redeemed not only from past, but also from present and future sins. Both the apostles and all the other saints, who ever have been, and however many elect still are and will be placed

1 Pseudo-Augustine, *Hypomnesticon against the Pelagians and Celestians* (*Hypomnesticon contra Pelagianos et Caelestianos*), Preface (PL 45:1613).

2 Augustine, *Enchiridion on Faith, Hope, and Love* (*Enchiridion de fide, spe, et caritate*), 30 (PL 40:247).

3 I have conjectured the nominative *utrique* for the genitive *utriusque*.

in time, still awaited, await, and will await the redemption of their body. Holy Augustine said concerning this in *To Count Valerius*:

> If our flesh were not to some degree held captive under this law of sin, that is, under its own concupiscence, how could what the same Apostle says be true: *Awaiting the adoption, the redemption of our body?* (Rom 8:23). Insofar, then, as the redemption of our body is still awaited, it is still in some degree captive under the law of sin. Hence, he also exclaims and says, *O wretched man that I am! Who will deliver me from this body of death? The grace of God, through Jesus Christ our Lord* (Rom 7:24-25).[4]

I said these things in order that we may know that redemption is spoken of in multiple ways. For any of the elect says to his own soul concerning this redemption: *Who redeems your life from destruction* (Ps 102:4), and the Lord says: *Lift up your heads, because your redemption draws near* (Lk 21:28). There is also said to be a redemption by which a man redeems himself from his sins through almsgiving: *The redemption of a man's soul is his riches* (Prv 13:8), and: *Redeem your sins through almsgiving* (Dn 4:24), and the Lord says in the law: *You shall redeem the firstborn of a donkey with a lamb* (Ex 34:20), where he means that the uncleanness of the past life is to be changed into the innocence of a good life. There is also said to be a redemption through inner almsgiving, that is, repentance, by which a man is set free lest he be slain by another, as is said: *Others were tortured, not accepting redemption* (Heb 11:35). A man is also said to be a redeemer of the men whom he liberates from captivity or slavery either by money or by some other means, as blessed Stephen says about Moses: *God sent this Moses as ruler and redeemer by the hand of an angel* (Acts 7:35).

Thus I have shown that redemption is spoken of in ten ways. The first and clearly most precious of them all, that is, the one peculiar and proper to the elect alone, was brought about by the Lord's cross, passion, and death; the second by the grace of baptism; the third by repentance; the fourth by almsgiving; the fifth by the deliverance from danger; the sixth by rescue from the yoke of captivity or slavery; the seventh from the destruction of temporal death. In the eighth way it is said to be and is the redemption of time; in the ninth of the body; in the tenth of life. The two last ways are brought about for the elect in the resurrection. All of them have been proved by divine authority. It remains that frequent and fervent glory is rightly given for this to him alone whose gratuitous grace has held sway over it.

Prudent reader, pay attention to what you are reading. Distinguish the one who has been redeemed through baptismal grace, who remains in sins by his own will, and who deservedly perishes, from the other one who was not only already redeemed by the grace of baptism, but was also in the past redeemed by the passion, death, and blood of Christ the Lord and who for this reason

4 Augustine, *On Marriage and Desire* (*De nuptiis et concupiscentia*), 1.31, 35 (PL 44:433).

cannot perish, because his redeemer, by dying, deigned to find this lost one.[5] By the redemption of baptism the infants are also absolved only from original sin. In the same way any adults are redeemed by baptism only from past sins. But the elect are justified gratuitously by the grace of the mediator in the blood of the second Adam.

Blessed reader, pay special attention to what is said: *One Lord, one faith, one baptism, one God* (Eph 4:5-6). For just as baptism is one, although each Christian is baptized three times, that is, dipped by a threefold immersion, so also the Father and Son and the Holy Spirit are one with respect to the nature and three with respect to the persons—God, the Lord, and the Spirit—and yet each person is undoubtedly in himself perfect God, Lord, and Spirit. Likewise, just as the Lord first baptized the apostles with water and then with the Holy Spirit and fire, as he himself had promised,[6] still let them not be known and believed to have received three baptisms—God forbid!—but rather one, that is, on account of the Holy Spirit, whose baptism is wholly perfect and also complete in power. Even more so God the Trinity is believed and altogether truthfully declared to be one God, one Lord, and one Spirit with respect to nature. For we must not, cannot, and dare not call or invoke God the Trinity as—God forbid!—three Spirits, nor pray to them in adoring three Spirits. The matter with which we are dealing is very important, and for this reason may your brotherhood and that of all the others who do not reject me from their brotherhood be warned not once, but often to be very cautious. Amen.

5 See Lk 15:4.

6 See Mt 3:11.

ANOTHER TREATISE ON PREDESTINATION

This text represents fragments contained in ms. Berne 584, fol. 135v-139v, and united into a single section XXIV entitled *On Predestination* (*De praedestinatione*) by Lambot. It has no title in the original manuscript. Its time of composition is uncertain. Edition: Lambot, 338-46. Translated by Victor Genke.

1. But the clearness of the manifest, pleasing, and moving truth glimmers and shines forth for those who are growing accustomed to it, as God grants, teaches, and guides them, as a certain person says: "Life never grants anything to poor mortals without great labor."[1]

Before he preaches, therefore, a preacher ought to ask omnipotent God to give him words and wisdom,[2] to open his lips,[3] and to grant him, although unworthy, to say to people those things that he mercifully predestined before the ages that he was going to bestow by his grace.

Since [predestination] is by no means somehow improper like foreknowledge, but proper, as it has been most fully shown, although God could not—God forbid!—be predestined, just as he could not be made, produced, or created, and he is still alone properly the maker, producer, and creator of all creatures. In like manner God, that is, fear,[4] is properly feared by us, is properly lord over us, and properly has mercy on us. Hence, it is truly said to him quite properly: "God, for whom it is proper to have mercy," although mercy is improper for him, for whom piety and clemency are proved to be altogether proper.[5] For mercy is improper for him because there is no misery in him—God forbid!—nor can there be in any way. Similarly, he who is known properly to know eternally all future things as well as past and present ones is of course in no way said to foreknow them properly, but improperly. But he is certainly not said to predestine in that way, since if he had not predestined all future things to be brought about from the eternity of his disposition and plan, there would of course never have been a

---

1 Quintus Horatius Flaccus [Horace], *Satires*, 1.9, vv. 60-1.

2 See 1 Chr 1:10.

3 See Ps 50:17.

4 See Isidore of Seville, *Etymologies* (*Etymologiae*), 7.1, 5 (PL 82:259-60).

5 *Gregorian Sacramentary* (*Sacramentarium gregorianum*) in PL 78:197A. Mercy (*misericordia*) is literally misery of heart.

creature made by him—God forbid! Hence, Augustine says more truthfully: If God did not remain immutable in his nature, no mutable nature would remain.[6]

Predestination is said to be twofold so that there are not by any means said to be two predestinations, but one, just as they say that charity is twofold, but one.[7] Hence, Saint Fulgentius also said in his book *To Monimus* that there is "another predestination" by which the reprobate have been predestined to hell, although he by no means failed to know that the two predestinations are one.[8] No one wise of course thinks—not to mention says—that God is predestination as he is essence, wisdom, and clemency. For we know that he who is clearly eternal could by no means be predestined. Nevertheless, his predestination can in no way be truly or even probably said to be improper for him, because it does not come to him—God forbid!—from a predestined future creature, which is to be made out of nothing, but his predestination is truly coeternal with God as the disposition of his plan and will. For since the angelic or human creature, though created out of nothing, is not improper—God forbid!— to the Lord God, but altogether proper, as to its artificer or craftsman, creator, producer, and maker, as he says about himself the shepherd: *He calls his own (proprias) sheep by name, and when he sends out his own sheep he goes before them* (Jn 10:3), his predestination should by no means be said to be improper to him. For it is not—God forbid!—out of nothing, but is in every way out of the deep, pious, and just counsel of his wisdom and out of the multiple, most plentiful, richest, most abundant, and most complete storeroom of everything good.

That which I would say not only with pardon, but also with respect and by your leave,[9] has also not been said often enough with knowledge, circumspection, precision, and expertise, that is, that if God were said to have produced all his works in predestination, predestination would as it were be said to be the Son of God. This does not follow, as is thought and Augustine is wrongly quoted in his book, *On Rebuke and Grace*: "They are already his children in predestination and have been given to Christ, his Son."[10] You see, the Son had in the Father's predestination the glory, which he has now sitting at the right hand of the Father, and still the Son is not for this reason predestination itself. For God's disposition or predestination does not—God forbid!—belong to the Father alone, but it is equally and similarly common—not only the Son, but the preparation of the whole Trinity in every respect. And for this reason God's predestination is

---

6 See Augustine, *On the Trinity (De Trinitate)*, 3.3, 5 (PL 42:950); *Unfinished Work in Answer to Julian (Opus imperfectum contra Iulianum)*, 5.60 (PL 45:1494-5).

7 See Augustine, *Homilies on the Gospel of John (In Iohannis evangelium tractatus)*, 17.6 (PL 35:1531).

8 Fulgentius of Ruspe, *To Moninus (Ad Monimum)*, 1.3, 4 (CCSL 91:5; PL 65:155).

9 Gottschalk is probably addressing Hincmar.

10 Augustine, *On Rebuke and Grace (De correptione et gratia)*, 9.21 (PL 44:929).

quite properly ascribed to him because he eternally made all things that will be. For just as God's foreknowledge or knowledge is rightly not ascribed to a creature that is going to be made in the future, because this creature was eternally foreknown to be going to be, so predestination is of course properly ascribed not to the predestined creature, but rather to the creator who predestined it. It is undoubtedly seen both openly and clearly in this that God's predestination is not out of nothing. If, having set aside animosity, you consider these things carefully, as it is useful for your eloquence, it really will be immediately seen not obscurely, but clearly that discussion is at times much more beneficial and fruitful than reading and meditation.

If it still does not suffice concerning the singleness of predestination, if you do not lick, as it were, the skin of an animal, content with the surface, but search out the inner parts, pursue the depths, take delight in their loftiness, eat marrow, and become full of its pure sweetness, I will gladly say some more things. God's will is at times spoken so that the will of God is understood to be God by our holy doctors. But because predestination is the preparation of God's future works,[11] which still were not existing, it is by no means God, but his eternal foreordination of his works to be created and already created. Nevertheless, although God's predestination has been eternally arranged both over the elect and over the reprobate, it ought not be spoken about in the plural; although predestination is twofold, it was surely established once and for all eternally, according to the words: "*God has spoken once* (Ps 61:12), that is, immutably."[12] Yet God's will, which is God, was not predestined, but in his will God predestined everything and made what was going to be. Therefore, God's wills are generally for this reason spoken of in the plural[13] so that we might understand that God's will is not always said in place of God himself. Such is the case where, although the Lord Jesus said that he was the way in terms of humanity,[14] ways are frequently spoken of in the divine writings in the plural so that Christ the way is distinguished from the ways of God. In order therefore that ambiguity might be avoided, the plural was rightly used in both the ways and wills of the Lord. But in God's twofold predestination that contains his ways, about which it is said: *All the ways of the Lord are mercy and truth* (Ps 24:10), the singular has rightly remained and rightly remains. Therefore, since he *has spoken once* (Ps 62:12), that is, as Saint Augustine explained,[15] immutably arranged all his future works, there are by no means two predestinations, but one. But because as

11 See Augustine, *On the Predestination of the Saints* (*De praedestinatione sanctorum*), 19 (PL 44:975); Fulgentius, *To Monimus*, 1.20, 2 (CCSL 91:20; PL 65:168).

12 Augustine, *On the Spirit and the Letter* (*De spiritu et littera*), 23.58 (PL 44:238).

13 See Ps. 110:2 which says that the Lord is *sought out in all his wills.*

14 See Jn 14:6.

15 See Augustine, *On the Spirit and the Letter* (*De spiritu et littera*), 23.58 (PL 44:238).

the psalmist says in what follows: *I have heard these two things that power belongs to God and that mercy belongs to you, Lord, for you will render to each according to his works* (Ps 62:12). On account of these two predestination is known to be twofold, that is, one in a general sense because it was established eternally once and for all time, neither—God forbid!—unjust, but both just, but twofold in the special sense, because one is owed and the other is gratuitous.

Such is the fact that each of us consisting of a body and soul has these two in himself or rather he is these two. Because of their diversity they are a plurality, as the Apostle says: *The flesh lusts against the spirit, and the spirit against the flesh, and these are contrary to one another so that you do not do the things that you wish* (Gal 5:17). But where these two are spoken of under one name, that is, the outer and inner man, there are by no means two men on account of the diversity of natures, but a man is at the same time one on account of the special character of the one person. In that way of course God's predestination is twofold on account of the mercy by which the elect are gratuitously set free and saved and on account of the truth by which the reprobate are justly judged and condemned. But because in neither is it unjust—God forbid!—but just, there are not two predestinations but one.

I did not desire either to be killed like a fool out of anger or to be slain like a child—God forbid!—out of envy.[16] And just as death of the body is common to the elect and the reprobate, so the resurrection will also be common to both, at least as far as it pertains to the reception of bodies. That redemption of baptism is similarly common, by which both are redeemed from their past original and personal sins. But just as that resurrection is proper to the elect, by which they alone will rise to be changed[17] and to be given eternal glory, so that redemption is truly proper to the elect, by which they alone were redeemed by the blood of Christ's cross and through which they have been set free from absolutely all sins past, present and future by the gratuitous grace of God. Hence, the resurrection will be common for all those who have been raised up in a corporal sense, although the future condition of the body is proper to each of us. But the resurrection will certainly be completely unequal because of their different merits, as eternal torments will receive the reprobate who will be tortured and everlasting beatitude will receive the glorified elect who will be glorified. Both are quite clearly revealed in the Old and New Testament. Daniel says, or rather Gabriel says to Daniel: *Many will rise from the dust of the earth, some to everlasting life, some to everlasting shame* (Dn 12:2). And the Apostle says: *We shall all rise,*

16 Probably these words were written when Gottschalk resumed his work after some interruption, as they have no relation with the context. Here he seems to answer to his enemies' threats or just expresses his firm resolution to thwart the plans of his persecutors.

17 See 1 Cor 15:51.

but not all will be changed (1 Cor 15:51). Therefore, as he in no way[18] redeemed in Judas his thefts and robberies, even those that he committed so many times by taking from the money box what was put in it, and still less that crime and outrage that he committed by selling the Lord and by killing himself shortly afterwards, so he clearly did not redeem, while hanging on the cross, any crime of any reprobate, even if baptized, however small and insignificant a crime, that any of them commit after the redemption of baptism, although he certainly redeemed all the sins of all the elect. And the elect also deserved similarly to be *vessels of wrath* (Rom 9:22), just like the reprobate, if the omnipotent God had not gratuitously made them the *vessels of mercy* (Rom 9:23), as the Apostle says: *We also were by nature children of wrath* (Eph 2:3). For there are two worlds, as is said: "The whole world is the church, and the whole world hates the church."[19] Therefore, Prosper also says in that same chapter:[20] "The redeemer of the world gave his blood for the world, and the world did not want to be redeemed, because the darkness did not receive the light, and the darkness did receive it, to which the Apostle says: *You were once darkness, but now you are light in the Lord* (Eph 5:8)."[21]

And those who will have been set free and redeemed by the Lord will walk (Is 35:9-10). In this prophetic statement it is seen not obscurely, but clearly that the baptized reprobate were not redeemed by the Lord with eternal redemption, for they in no way *will they come to Zion with everlasting praise and joy* (Is 35:10). And where will the light of our two eyes be, if we do not see the most manifest redemption of one world, not two?

2. Saint Athanasius and some others understood the sentence: *The Spirit, the water, and the blood, and these three are one* (1 Jn 5:8), rather of the Trinity and left its exposition for posterity.[22]

3. Likewise, the blessed apostle Paul says: *He was predestined to be the Son of God* (Rom. 1:4) not according to the divinity, which was and is eternally, but according to the humanity, which once was not. *By the resurrection from the dead of Jesus Christ, our Lord* (Rom 1:4) means nothing else than "By the resurrection of his dead," for because Christ and the church like head and body, bridegroom and bride, one person, what in reality has already been done in the head is said to have been done in his members in hope, as the Apostle says: *He made us alive together with Christ and raised us up together and made us sit together in the heavenly places in Christ* (Eph 2:5-6). On this account since he elsewhere said

18 A negative seems to have been omitted. Lambot suggested *nullatenus* which I used.

19 Augustine, *Homilies on the Gospel of John*, 87.2 (PL 35:1853).

20 Gottschalk perhaps had at his disposal a topical collection of *sententiae* which included selections from both Augustine and Prosper.

21 Prosper of Aquitaine, *Answers to the Objections of the Gauls* (*Pro Augustino responsiones ad capitula obiectionum Gallorum calumnantium*), 9 (PL 51:165C).

22 This passage is not found in the index to the extant works of Athanasius, genuine as well as spurious.

about Christ, that is, the head: *Even though we have known Christ according to the flesh, yet [now we know him no longer]*, he added something about the members: *Therefore, from now on we know no one according to the flesh,* (2 Cor 5:16), that is, none of the elect. Hence, since his dead have already risen in the most certain hope, long before the dying Lord Christ redeemed the elect by dying, the baptized reprobate were *cast with hands and feet bound into the outer darkness* (Mt 22:13). They are of course signified by that one man, whom the king saw without a wedding garment; otherwise the Lord would not have added: *Many are called, but few are chosen* (Mt 22:14) but: "Many are chosen, but few are cast out," or: "One is cast out." It is frivolous, quite absurd, and altogether false to say that the baptized reprobate were redeemed by Christ's death, for Christ undoubtedly redeemed only his dead, one of whom says with joyous hope: *God will nonetheless redeem my soul from the power of hell when he will receive me* (Ps 48:16). But let the baptized reprobate hear it said by God about them in the same psalm: *A brother does not redeem; will a man redeem?* (Ps 48:8). Since they are certainly not Christ's sheep, but the antichrist's goats, they are therefore not sheep, but *like sheep they have been placed in hell; death will feed on them* (Ps 48:15). The Lord says about them: *Beware of false prophets who come to you in sheep's clothing.* That is why it says *like sheep, but inwardly they are ravenous wolves* (Mt 7:15). That is why *they have been placed in hell.* Hence, he clearly speaks about the future: *will feed on,* not "has fed on" or "feeds on" those neither redeemed nor going to be redeemed by the death of Christ.

PART 2: OTHER WRITINGS

RABANUS MAURUS

LETTER TO NOTING

In May 840, Rabanus Maurus, abbot of the monastery at Fulda, wrote this brief *Letter to Noting* (*Epistola ad Notingum*), who was the bishop of Verona. It served as a cover letter for his treatise *On Predestination* (*De Praedestinatione*), which he had written against the predestinarian views of Gottschalk, and which he had earlier agreed with Noting that he would compose. In a few short statements it summarizes his main objections to Gottschalk's teaching. Editions: MGH, Epist. 5:428; PL 112:1530-1. Excerpts translated by Francis X. Gumerlock.

Rabanus sends greetings in Christ to the chosen bishop Noting, a venerable man and most worthy of every honor.

When in the village of Logana you recently came to the most serene emperor Louis in the passing of an hostile expedition and, having spoken with me there about the heresy that some people are wickedly defending concerning the predestination of God, *erring and leading* others *into error* (2 Tm 3:13), you made a statement. It was agreed upon between us that I would compose a small treatise from the divine scriptures and statements of the orthodox fathers in order to refute the error of those who believe so wickedly concerning the good and just God.

For they say that his predestination brings it about that no person predestined to life is able to fall into death, and no person predestined to death can in any way recover for life. But God, the author of everything and creator of natures, is the cause of the ruin and destruction of no one, but is the origin of the salvation of many.

Accordingly, accept now this small work that you asked to be composed for you by our littleness. And if you find anything in it pleasing and explained in a catholic sense, attribute it to him from whom you know every good comes.[1] And know that I am prepared in every way and in all things to grant to your charity

1 See Jas 1:17.

whatever benefit I can by his grace. Farewell, and love him who loves you, and do not fail to be mindful of our littleness in your holy prayers.

LETTER TO EBERHARD

Eberhard of Frioul was a German count married to Gisela, daughter of Judith and Louis the Pious, and granddaughter of Charlemagne. In the late 830s and early 840s, Gottschalk stayed with Eberhard, taught in his court, and under his patronage spread the doctrine of predestination throughout the March of Frioul and elsewhere. Rabanus, having advanced from abbot of Fulda to bishop of Mainz, was concerned about the effects that Gottschalk's teaching was having in his see. He wrote this *Letter to Eberhard* (*Epistola ad Eberhardum*) about 846 asking Eberhard to stop Gottschalk from teaching immoderately about predestination. Labeling Gottschalk's brand of predestination a "sect," Rabanus claimed that those opinions were destroying the faith of some. Editions: MGH, Epist. 5:481-7; PL 112:1553-62. Excerpts in Lambot, 5-6. Excerpts translated by Francis X. Gumerlock

Also, about the other things that have been reported in these regions, they say that a certain know-it-all[2] named Gottschalk is staying with you, who is teaching that the predestination of God binds all men in such a way that even if someone would want to be saved and would struggle for this by the correct faith and good works in order to come to eternal life by the grace of God, he would labor in vain and for naught, if he has not been predestined to life, as if God, who is the author of our salvation and not of our perdition, forces a human being to perish by his predestination. And from there this sect has led many into despair over themselves so that they say: "Why is it necessary for me to work for my salvation and eternal life? For if I do good but I have not been predestined to life, it profits me nothing. But if I do evil, it is in no way an obstacle to me. For the predestination of God causes me to come to eternal life." This teaching is a scandal to many in these regions. ... For your teacher is said to have excerpted many testimonies from the works of the most blessed and learned father, Augustine, from which he tries to strengthen his sect. However, the previously mentioned father and

2 Lat. *sciolum*. Isidore of Seville (d. 636) defined a *sciolus* as a *simulator scientiae ac peritiae*, a "pretender of knowledge and expertise." See his *On the Differences of Words* (*De differentiis verborum*), 505 (PL 83:60C). Mayke de Jong ("From Scolastici to Scioli. Alcuin and the Formation of an Intellectual Élite" in L.A. J. R. Houwen and A. A. MacDonald, eds., *Alcuin of York: Scholar at the Carolingian Court*. Proceedings of the Third Germania Latina Conference held at the University of Groningen, 1995 [Groningen: Egbert Forsten, 1998], 45-57 at 55) using Gottschalk as an example describes a ninth-century *sciolus* as "a 'know-all' prepared to defy orthodoxy and monastic discipline for the sake of knowledge." Newton Thompson, who translated Fernand Mourret's *A History of the Catholic Church*, Vol. 3 (Saint Louis: Herder, 1936) into English, rendered *sciolum* as "quasi-scholar" (p. 474).

catholic teacher, writing against the Pelagians who were preachers opposed to the grace of God, was a defender of his grace, not a destroyer of the correct faith...

But he who says that predestination should be preached, just as piety, purity, love, and other virtues should be preached so that he who hears these things with obedience may glory not in a human being nor in himself, but in the Lord,[3] says this in a good way if he tempers his preaching with discretion and in accord with the ability of his hearers[4]....

Therefore, I have written these things to you, dearest friend, that you may know the sort of scandal that this opinion coming from those regions has generated in this people and that, if anyone staying with you is impudently teaching things that are contrary to the correct faith, you may forbid him so that he desists from this sect.

LETTER TO HINCMAR ON THE COUNCIL OF MAINZ

Rabanus wrote this letter to Hincmar, archbishop of Reims, shortly after the synod of Mainz in October 848. Rabanus explains what transpired at the synod regarding Gottschalk, summarizes Gottschalk's teaching on predestination of the reprobate, and informs Hincmar that he is sending Gottschalk to him; for Gottschalk had been ordained in the diocese of Reims now under Hincmar's jurisdiction. Also, since Gottschalk is a wandering monk whose teaching Rabanus finds noxious and pernicious, Rabanus requests that Gottschalk be confined to Hincmar's jurisdiction. Edition: PL 112:1574-6 entitled *Synodal Letter 8 to Hincmar, Archbishop of Reims, concerning Gottschalk* (*Epistola VIII Synodalis, ad Hincmar archiepiscopum Rhemensem de Gothescalco*); Mansi, 14:914-5. Excerpts translated by Francis X. Gumerlock.

Rabanus Maurus, servant of Christ and of his servants, sends greetings in the Lord to the very reverend brother and fellow priest, archbishop Hincmar.

Let it be known to your charity that a certain wandering monk, by the name of Gottschalk, who asserts that he is a priest ordained in your diocese, came from Italy to us at Mainz, introducing new superstitions and a harmful doctrine about God's predestination and leading people into error. For he says that the predestination of God is found in a bad person, just as it is in a good person. He also says that certain people are such in this world that, according to the predestination of God, which compels them to go into death, they cannot correct themselves from error and sin, as if God from the beginning had made them to be incorrigible and to go to destruction, subject to punishment. Therefore, hearing from him this opinion at a synod recently held at Mainz where our most pious King Louis was presiding and in command and finding him incorrigible, we decreed to send him condemned with his pernicious doctrine back to you,

3 See 1 Cor 1:31.

4 That is, so that they do not misinterpret or misapply his teaching on predestination as Rabanus claims they are doing.

so that you may confine him in your diocese, from where he first withdrew in a disorderly manner, and so that you may not allow him to teach error any further or to lead Christian people astray. For, as I have heard, he already has led astray and made them less devout toward their own salvation, who say, "How will it profit me to labor in the service of God? For, if I have been predestined to death, I will never escape it. But if I live badly and I have been predestined to life, I will without any doubt go to eternal rest."

Therefore, we have written these things to you, showing what sort we found his teaching to be. You will also be able to hear more fully from his own mouth what he thinks and then justly decide what should be done about it. May the omnipotent Lord deign to preserve Your Holiness in good health and in prayer for us for eternity.

HINCMAR OF REIMS

SENTENCE AGAINST GOTTSCHALK AT THE SYNOD OF QUIERZY

After the synod at Mainz, Rabanus Maurus sent Gottschalk under escort to the diocese of Reims, the archbishopric of Hincmar. In the palace at Quierzy (also called Carisiacum) twelve bishops convened in February-March 849 with Hincmar presiding; and this *Ecclesiastical Sentence against the Most Stubborn Gottschalk* (*Ecclesiastica sententia in pertinacissimum Gotescalcum*) was passed against Gottschalk. Editions: Wilhelm Gundlach, "Zwei Schriften des Erzbischofs Hinkmar von Reims" *Zeitschrift für Kirchengeschichte* 10 (1889):258-309 at 308-9; Ussher, 61; Mansi, 14:921. Excerpts translated by Francis X. Gumerlock

The ecclesiastical sentence pronounced with ecclesiastical force by twelve bishops at the synod held at Quierzy against the most stubborn Gottschalk because of his incorrigible obstinacy:

Brother Gottschalk, know that the sacrosanct office of the sacerdotal mystery, which you irregularly usurped and have thus far not feared to abuse in all evil morals and actions and perverse teachings has been taken from you by the judgment of the Holy Spirit, if you have somehow undertaken it. For the sacerdotal office is a gift of his grace through the power of the blood of our Lord Jesus Christ. And know that it has been perpetually[1] forbidden that you presume to exercise it hereafter. In addition, because, showing contempt for ecclesiastical laws, you have presumed to disturb both ecclesiastical and civil affairs contrary to the life and name of a monk, we decree by episcopal authority that you be punished with the severest beatings and that according to ecclesiastical regulations you be confined to a cell, and lest you presume to usurp for yourself the teaching office, we impose perpetual silence on your mouth by the power of the eternal Word.

LETTER TO THE MONKS AND SIMPLE FOLK OF HIS DIOCESE

Hincmar, archbishop of Reims, wrote this *Letter to the Monks and Simple Folk of his Diocese* (*Epistola ad reclusos et simplices suae dioeceseos*) in 849 warning them of Gottschalk's teaching. Having examined Gottschalk at Quierzy and

1 I have followed Gundlach's edition which reads *perpetuo*. Ussher's edition reads *penitus*, which here could mean "entirely" or "strictly."

having in his possession three of his writings, Hincmar objects to them. He says that Gottschalk confuses foreknowledge and predestination and misinterprets scripture and the catholic fathers, especially Augustine. Like Rabanus, Hincmar is concerned about the implications of Gottschalk's predestinarian views on the possibility of human conversion. Other objections to Gottschalk's teaching contained in this letter are that it advocates grace without free will, preaches negligence, limits Christ's atonement to the elect, and teaches the non-efficacy of baptismal grace in the case of the reprobate. Edition: Wilhelm Gundlach, "Zwei Schriften des Erzbischofs Hinkmar von Reims," *Zeitschrift für Kirchengeschichte* 10 (1889):258-309. Excerpts in Lambot, 8-10. Excerpts translated by Francis X. Gumerlock.

...And about these things there has risen up in our diocese Gottschalk, known to you by name, face, and conduct, but long known to us by the rotten reputation of his wretched way of life and by the abomination of his perverse preaching. But now, at last, he is known by face and by his very stubborn and obstinate speech. As I have heard, before he left this district excommunicated, living wickedly against ecclesiastical laws but commending himself by religious habit and language, as it seemed, to your ears and eyes as a good man, while cloaking the depravity of his heart [by his zeal], he poured the worst venoms into your hearing and also into your hearts. Confusing the foreknowledge and the predestination of God, teaching that there are some predestined to punishment which no one predestined can escape, no matter what good or how much good the person does, and no one predestined to glory, no matter what evil he does, can perish. If he knew how and had wanted to distinguish between foreknowledge and predestination according to the holy scriptures and the teachings of the catholic fathers, he would not have had to err.

This same Gottschalk also teaches grace without free choice so that in the name of piety he preaches negligence from the heart and through a show of pleasing God and placating God through good works, he removes solicitude and introduces a pernicious security.

He also teaches that the death of Christ was not celebrated for the salvation of the whole world and that original sin was not taken away by the grace of baptism for those not predestined, because they have also not been separated from the mass of sin and perdition,[2] and he teaches that there are two peoples, one predestined to punishment, the other predestined to glory, and for this reason whatever the Lord says whether by himself or by the prophets and by the apostles that a person can be saved through a correct faith and good works by the grace of God and free choice, pertains to the predestined people, and does not at all pertain to those not predestined.

I have omitted collecting many examples from the authoritative writings of the Old and New Testaments on this matter, because he always contends that

---

2 See Rom 9:21.

they pertain only to the predestined people, exhorting them to repentance. And I decided to accept the judgments of the binding authorities, which mock him and suffice for you.

About these perversities, that is, of his, I have received his writings: One, a certain tome given to me by our brothers, which he wrote for a certain monk, Gislemar of the monastery at Corbie, writing under the pretence of a prayer and thanksgiving, in which he speaks great blasphemies instead of praise.[3] And following it, he wrote a letter in which he spoke very obstinate things, and took care to compile them from the Scriptures, which he interpreted in a false manner.

And the second, which he wrote against the venerable archbishop Rabanus.... compiled and filled with flowers of learning from the meadow of the sacred authors, and he either mutilated or corrupted those flowers spoken by catholics and in a catholic manner.[4]

I have also received a third tome, small in quantity, but very great in impiety, given to me by Gottschalk himself[5]....

...It has also come to the attention of our small person that the same brother along with his accomplices has searched and investigated many subtle things about seeing God and has presumed to teach them otherwise than he ought, caring more about how one ought to see God than how one might merit to see him[6]...

...Hence, the unbelieving Gottschalk wrongly understood what he said in his accursed writing to Gislemar, saying, "And so when we hear: *Have I not chosen you twelve, but one of you is a devil?* (Jn 6:71), we ought to understand that they were chosen through mercy, but that he was chosen through justice. Therefore, he chose them to obtain the kingdom, but him to shed his blood."

...he says...that the Savior was not crucified [for] the redemption of the whole world.

...Gottschalk misunderstood what he says about the Lord's words: "This is the cup of my blood, which will be shed for you and for many for the remission of sins,"[7] namely, that God spoke distinctly so that he said "for many" and not "for all."....

...*And the bread that I will give is my flesh for the life of the world* (Jn 6:52). And Gottschalk does not speak sincerely, who makes a distinction in this passage between world and world, so that there is a world that is redeemed in the elect and a world that is not redeemed in those predestined to death ....

---

3 Gottschalk, *Tome to Gislemar* (*Tomus ad Gislemarum*) in Lambot, 9, 41-4.

4 Gottschalk, *Reply to Rabanus Maurus* (*Responsum ad Rabanum Maurum*) in Lambot, 36-44; PL 121:365-8.

5 Gottschalk, *Confession of Faith at Mainz* (*Chartula suae professionis ad Rabanum episcopum*) in Lambot, 38; PL 121:368.

6 This refers to a controversy over the beatific vision in which Gottschalk was involved.

7 *Canon of the Roman Mass*. See Lk 22:20; Mt 26:28; Mk 14:24.

...But on grace and free choice which Gottschalk confuses in a way similar to the way in which confuses foreknowledge and predestination....

...And Gottschalk incorrectly understood because he wants to make a distinction in this passage as if Augustine had said that God had only foreknown, not predestined sinners "in their own sins," but that he understood that sinners had been predestined to punishment because he said that "punishment" had been "predestined for them"[8]—as if he had as much as said—if he had spoken in that way, it would not be true—that they were predestined to punishment so that they could not to return to life by the grace of God through repentance.... Beware of this commentary of the laggard....

...Let us return...to him who says that there is predestination of the reprobate to death....

About this matter, when the confusor of foreknowledge and predestination reads in certain manuscripts that people were "prepared to suffer punishments,"[9] he does not want to make a distinction between what has been prepared by God, what has been prepared by the devil, and what has been prepared by one's own iniquity.

Where blessed Augustine gave an example about this, Gottschalk badly misused the following statement that the same very wise teacher added, saying: "Such is the cause of all who are going to perish, although sin differs from sin."[10]

LETTER TO AMOLO OF LYONS

In the summer of 850, upon receiving Rabanus Maurus' treatises on predestination and a letter from Rabanus, in which the archbishop of Mainz strongly intimated that he would not participate any more in the discussion, Hincmar sent to the church at Lyons a dossier that contained the present *Letter to Amolo of Lyons* (*Epistola ad Amolonem archiepiscopum Lugdunensem*), a letter to Amolo by Pardulus of Laon, and Rabanus' *To Noting on Predestination* (*Ad Notingum de praedestinatione*). Fragments of this *Letter to Amolo of Lyons* are preserved in Florus of Lyons' *On Three Letters* (*De tribus epistolis*) and summarized by Flodoard in his *History of the Church of Reims* (*Historia Remensis ecclesiae*. PL 135:260C). Editions: Lambot, 15-16; PL 121:987-8. Translated by Victor Genke.

8 Pseudo-Augustine, *Hypomnesticon against the Pelagians and the Celestians* (*Hypomnesticon contra Pelagianos et Caelestianos*), 5.7 (PL 45:1661-2).

9 Fulgentius of Ruspe, *On the Truth of Predestination and Grace* (*De veritate praedestinationis et gratiae*), 3.5, 8 (CCSL 91A :527; PL 65:656A).

10 Pseudo-Augustine, *Hypomnesticon against the Pelagians and Celestians*, 5.7 (PL 45:1661).

Having begun his preaching in another way than John did, who said: *Repent, for the kingdom of heaven is at hand* (Mt 3:2) and than Paul who taught us to know the creator of visible and invisible things through visible things,[11] he began to preach:

1. That before all ages and from the beginning before God made anything, he predestined those whom he willed to the kingdom and predestined those whom he willed to destruction,

2. And that those who have been predestined to destruction cannot be saved and those who are predestined to the kingdom cannot perish.

3. And God does not will that all men be saved, but only those who are saved. And in the words of the Apostle: *Who wills all men to be saved* (1 Tm 2:4), "all" means only all those who are saved.

4. Christ did not come to save all, nor did he suffer for all, but only for those who are saved by the mystery of his passion.

5. And after the first man fell by the free choice, none of us can use free choice to do good, but only to do evil.

LETTER TO RUDOLPH AND FROTARIUS

Hincmar of Reims wrote this *Letter to Rudolph of Bourges and Frotarius of Bordeaux, Metropolitans of Aquitaine* (*Epistola ad Rodulfum Bituricensem et Frotarium Burdigalensem, metropolitanos Aquitaniae*) to his fellow archbishops in November of 860 about the scandalous circumstances surrounding a particular royal marriage. In it he briefly mentions modern predestinarians seeking to resurrect an ancient predestination heresy, which he erroneously attributes to the fifth-century Gallic opponents of Augustine's predestinarian views. Edition: PL 126:132-53 at 150. Excerpt translated by Francis X. Gumerlock.

We felt it necessary to include these matters because we have heard that certain people, even those who call themselves teachers, try with pertinacious contention, as if from the words of blessed Ambrose and Saint Augustine, to which they did not carefully attend, to maintain the following, namely, that a husband who was not fornicating, but leaves his fornicating wife, may marry another while his wife is still living; and that she who on the grounds of fornication leaves her husband cannot be reconciled. But if she leaves him for some other reason, and not because of fornication, she should either be reconciled or remain unmarried. They do not notice that words of the Apostle are interpreted in that way in an adulterous sense, just as those men did against whom blessed Augustine once wrote these books, and which the African council, which we mentioned earlier, defined, when it gutted the Celestians and also shook out the very marrow of the Pelagians. Nor is it surprising, for they were so infected with evil doctrine, just like the modern predestinarians, who are working to resurrect the old predestinarian heresy, as if compiled from the words of Saint Augustine, who shattered

11 See Rom 1:20.

the heads and crushed the hairy crowns of those walking in sins. And blessed Pope Celestine crushed them in his decretal *Letter to Venerius and the Other Bishops of Gaul*,[12] as did the same blessed Augustine in his book, *On Rebuke and Grace*, and in *On the Predestination of the Saints* and *On the Good of Perseverance*.[13] But because of a delegation of the Apostolic See, Saint Prosper destroyed their arguments with a catholic mind and with perfect and eloquent teaching of the clearest reason in his resolutions of the objections of the Gauls, the Vincentians, and the Massilians, and also in the books, *On the Call of All Nations*.[14]

LETTER TO POPE NICHOLAS

In 863 archbishop Hincmar was ordered to appear before the council of Metz together with Gottschalk so that the latter's case might be reconsidered by two papal legates. However, Hincmar ignored the summons and did not present himself at the council. Since his standing at Rome became rather low, the archbishop had to write a lengthy apologetic *Letter to Pope Nicholas* (*Epistola ad Nicolaum papam*) in which he endeavored to explain his absence and present his vision of Gottschalk's teaching and behavior. Editions: PL 126:25-46; Lambot, 44-45 (excerpts). Excerpt translated by Victor Genke.

...Besides, Luido told me that with him you had an account of the condemnation and confinement of Gottschalk. Hence, since I had already heard that words had come to Your Holiness by other people, I sent to your authority by bishop Odo[15] certain things from the words and thoughts of catholic men in a scroll

12 Pope Celestine I, *Letters* (*Epistolae*), 21 (PL 50:528A-37B).

13 The Latin text has the title of Augustine's treatise as *On the Good* (*bono*) *of Perserverance* instead of *On the Gift* (*dono*) *of Perseverance*.

14 Prosper of Aquitaine, *Answers to the Objections of the Gauls* (*Pro Augustino responsiones ad capitula obiectionum Gallorum calumniantium*, PL 51:155-74); *Answers to the Vincentian Objections* (*Pro Augustino responsiones ad capitula obiectionum Vincentiarum*, PL 51:177-86); *On Grace and Free Will against Cassian the Lecturer* (*De gratia et libero arbitrio contra collatorem*, PL 51:213-76); *On the Call of All Nations* (*De vocatione omnium gentium*, PL 51:647-722). According to Gustavsson ("Gottschalk Reconsidered," 54): "By reversing historical evidence Hincmar attributed to the heretical anti-predestination Gallic semi-Pelagians ideas held by Gottschalk so that he, Hincmar, could blame Gottschalk for resuscitating a matter previously judged heretical." And on page 151: "[Hincmar] distorts history and turns the heretical anti-predestination Gallic semi-Pelagians of the fifth century into an allegedly predestinarian sect so that he can blame Gottschalk for renewing a matter long ago condemned." And on page 158: "Freystedt [Der Ausgang des Prädestinationsstreites im 9. Jahrhundert," *ZWT* 41 (1898), 114ff] points out that Hincmar invented the heretical fifth century predestinarian sect for the purpose of his proof and reversed the historical facts making the anti-predestination Gallic semi-Pelagians into a predestinarian sect."

15 Odo of Beauvais (801-880). In 851 elected abbot of Corbie, following Paschasius Ratbertus; in 861 he was consecrated as bishop of his native city. He mediated the

about what I hold in opposition to the mind of this pestilential person, but I merited no answer on this. Nonetheless, in order that I might give an account, certain bishops, who had no interest in the matter, since, as they revealed by perfectly clear proofs, neither charity moved them nor did authority compel them, summoned me by a letter of a certain lay person without any advanced notice to the little council recently held in Metz, which, as I understand, you forbade to be called a synod. They called this small council irregularly on the fourth day before it met, although I was separated from this city by more than eighty and Gottschalk by over one hundred miles.

Therefore, I now briefly inform Your Holiness concerning him that, before I came to the rank of the episcopacy, as his abbot and the monks with whom he lived give testimony, in the monastery of the metropolitan church of Reims in the parish of Soissons, which is called Orbais, this man, a monk in his appearance, but a wild beast in his mind, intolerant of peace, but delighted by the novelty of words,[16] and singular in his harmful mobility[17] among his admirers, chose for himself certain points from all the ideas that he knew were incorrectly thought at that time in these regions, in order that he might be able to become known by the novelty of words, to corrupt the minds of simple and deceived men, to draw disciples after himself by usurping the name of a teacher, and to seek—in a disordered manner, since he could not legitimately—to preside over those who *having itching ears, strive to gather teachers for themselves according to their desires* (2 Tm 4:3), through the pretense of a religious life and learning. Having been ordained a priest against regulations by the auxiliary bishop of Reims at the time, he left the monastery against regulations, traveled in many lands, and sowed destructive seeds as a most evil sower. At last, at a synod held in the city of Mainz, he presented a small book of his error to archbishop Rabanus; he was condemned by all the bishops of Germany and dispatched with a synodal letter back to the archbishopric of Reims, over which I presided by the will of the Lord.

Afterwards, having received a hearing by the bishops of the provinces of Belgium, Reims, and Gaul, he was found to be a heretic. Because he did not want to return to his senses from his perversity, and for fear that he who did not want to do good for himself would not cause harm to others, he was by the judgment of the bishops of the aforementioned provinces transferred to our jurisdiction.

---

differences between Pope Nicholas I and Hincmar over Hincmar's deposition of Rothad of Soissons in 862. When Patriarch Photius charged the Roman church of certain errors in faith and practice, Hincmar commissioned Odo to write an apologetic treatise. The work proved to be rather weak. The same task was accomplished much better by Ratramnus of Corbie in *Answer to the Contradictions of the Greeks* (*Contra Graecorum opposite*, PL 121:223-346).

16 See 1 Tm 6:20.

17 Hincmar alludes to the charge that Gottschalk was wandering against monastic regulations.

For Rothad,[18] to whose jurisdiction he belonged, was unable to resist him, and as he loved novelties, we were afraid that he who had refused to learn how to teach what is correct might learn how to hold what is perverse. And for fear that this same Gottschalk, living a common life with others, would make his error common to them, he was confined in a monastery under guard, as the Apostle teaches: *Avoid a heretic after the first and second admonition, knowing that such a person is perverted and self-condemned* (Ti 3:10-11). As Pope Leo says concerning Eutyches,[19] he should have abandoned his opinion as soon as he saw that his foolish ideas were displeasing to catholic ears and not so upset the leaders of the church that he deserved the sentence of condemnation. And if he chose to remain in his opinion, no one would be able to relax it. If he had chosen to return to the catholic opinion from that condemnation, I was always and am ready, because the venerable bishops so judged, to take him back into the communion of the Catholic Church, just as I give orders to provide everything that is necessary for his body.[20]

But if your catholic wisdom would like to know what he is seen to say against the catholic faith from that old predestinarian heresy, which was refuted in the time of Pope Celestine[21] by the authority and perseverance of Saint Prosper, first in Africa and afterward among the Gauls at the same time as the Nestorian heresy arose, I shall indicate things few in number, but not in weight from many point by point.

He says, as the old predestinarians also said, that as God predestined some to eternal life, so he also predestined some to eternal death.

He says, as the old predestinarians also said, that "God does not *will all men to be saved* (1 Tm 2:4), but only those who are saved; however, all those are saved whom he willed to save and for this reason whoever is not saved absolutely do not belong to that will that they be saved. Since if all those whom God wills to be saved are not saved, he has not done whatever he willed, and if he wills what

---

18 Bishop Rothad II of Soissons was the key figure in one of the greatest ecclesiastical affairs during the pontificate of Pope Nicholas I the Great, in which Hincmar was also directly involved. In 862 the archbishop of Reims deposed Rothad for contesting his authority. The bishop of Soissons appealed to Rome against his metropolitan which led to his restoration by Pope Nicholas in 865 by using the so called *False Decretals*.

19 Eutyches (c. 375-454) was an archimandrite (abbot of an Orthodox monastery) at Constantinople, and presumably the founder of Eutychianism, an extreme form of the Monophysite heresy.

20 For the instruction given by Hincmar to the monks in Hautvillers concerning Gottschalk, see PL 126:92-3.

21 Pope Celestine I. During his pontificate (422-432) a massive attack took place against the teaching of Patriarch Nestorius of Constantinople took place, which stressed the independence of human and divine natures of Christ. Celestine also strongly refuted Pelagianism.

he cannot do, he is not omnipotent, but weak. But he is omnipotent who has done whatever he willed, as the scripture says: *The Lord has done whatever he willed in heaven and on earth, in the sea and in all the deeps* (Ps 134:6); and also: *In your will, Lord, all things have been placed, and there is no one who can resist your will. If you decide to save*[22] *us, we will be immediately set free* (Est 13:9)."[23]

He says, as the old predestinarians also said, that our Lord and Savior Jesus Christ was crucified and died not for the redemption of the whole world, that is, not for the salvation and redemption of all men, but only for those who are saved.

He says in some way by a different tradition, an error similar to what the old predestinarians also said, when he explains the statement of the apostle Peter: *Denying him who bought them* (2 Pt 2:1). "He bought them," he says, "by the sacrament of baptism, but did not suffer the cross, undergo death, or shed his blood for them. However, the teacher of Gentiles clearly says that the reception of baptism is called redemption: *Do not grieve the Holy Spirit of God,* he says, *by whom you were sealed for the day of redemption* (Eph 4:30)."[24]

"But that which is proper and specific only to all of the elect, which their loving crucified redeemer imparted only to them, redeemed, rescued, and cleansed those born and going to be born, the living and the dead, that is, all the elect from both past and present sins. These of course, these[25] are the world for which the Lord suffered, as he himself says: *The bread that I will give is my flesh for the life of the world* (Jn 6:52)."[26]

And in another place that same Gottschalk also writes: "God forbid that I should ever want even to dream or only to whisper that the ancient serpent might be able to carry off with him into eternal perdition any of those for whose redemption such precious blood of our Lord his Son has been poured out to God the Father. Amen."[27]

Likewise, speaking to God, he says: "And so it is seen quite clearly that no one who has been redeemed by the blood of your cross ever perishes for you."[28]

What the old predestinarians did not say, this man says in a bolder and a more pernicious way, namely, that the deity of the Holy Trinity is three.

---

22 The quotation from Est 13:9 stops at the word "save." The rest of the sentence is from the *Antiphon on the Introit on the Twenty-First Sunday after Pentecost* (*Antiphona ad introitum in dominica 21 post Pentecostem*). See Gregory the Great, *Book of Antiphons* (*Antiphonarium*) in PL 78:720.

23 Gottschalk, *Fragments and Testimonies* (*Fragmenta et testimonia*), 27 (Lambot, 44-5).

24 Gottschalk, *Tome to Gislemar* (*Tomus ad Gislemarum*), 3 (Lambot, 43).

25 The Latin *ipsi* is repeated.

26 Gottschalk, *Tome to Gislemar*, 4 (Lambot, 43-4).

27 Gottschalk, *Tome to Gislemar*, 1 (Lambot, 41-2).

28 Gottschalk, *Tome to Gislemar*, 5 (Lambot, 44).

There are also other things that he and many others in those parts say which seem to us to be against the sound faith.

When your authority has learned these things through someone other than through my worthless person, you will perhaps pay more careful attention and strive to learn as quickly as possible what is to be feared from them. For the necessity from this will be upon us, because, even if their hearts are boiling in the insanity of their perverse mind, they do not dare to say the evil things they think in the time of our orthodox king, so that we clearly see the words of scripture fulfilled: *Gathering the waters of the sea as in a skin* (Ps 32:7). For the water of the sea is gathered as in a skin because whatever the bitter knowledge of heretics thinks in this kingdom of your son, Lord Charles, it holds in the heart and does not presume to say it openly. And they secretly gnaw with dog's teeth at my small self. However, with the Lord's help, I will easily be able to endure it. For there is little time left for me, and if among the sons of the church they receive the power to afflict me in a bodily manner, they will, with the help of divine grace, test my patience. But even if they oppose me only by thinking wrongly, they will test my knowledge, and as even enemies are loved according to God's commandment,[29] they will test my benevolence.

Regarding the aforementioned Gottschalk, if your authority writes to me that I should release him from custody or that I should give him permission to go to you so that you may examine his doctrine for yourself or to travel to anyone designated by name—because, as you yourself know better, just as nobody can be ordained without being attached to a church, so a monk or anyone bound under a monastic rule also cannot, according to the sacred rules, be released from his place except to be commended to a certain person with the consent of him to whom he is known to belong—I will in no way hold back from your orders. I ask only to have your authority lest by my presumption I seem to give little weight to the judgment of such great bishops.

For I am not delighted over the confinement that he justly endures, stubbornly contemptuous, with however small an annoyance, but I grieve over the perfidy from which he cannot be called back. If your authority decides that he should be commended to someone, he will also provide in this commendation that the one to whom he will be commended is a catholic, has ecclesiastical gravity and vigor and a knowledge of the scriptures, because he is able to recite from memory all day long without any break not only the scriptures violently twisted to his opinion, but also mutilated statements of catholics. That is why he was in the habit not only of leading lay people to admire him, but also of bringing would-be scholars, the careless, and those who *have a zeal for God, but not according to knowledge* (Rom 10:2) to his own view. And he not only desires to be considered the teacher of his teachers, but also quite carefully endeavors to be able to trap

29 See Mt 5:44.

those speaking with him at least with words. And if he cannot do it according to the truth, he will take care to affirm invincibly with oaths that those speaking with him said things that they perhaps did not say, so that he appears truthful and those who contradict him are proven to be liars.

LETTER TO EGILO

In 866 Guntbert, a monk from Hautvillers, fled from the monastery to Rome in order to bring Gottschalk's appeal to the pope. This news worried Hincmar who tried by all means to avoid new undesirable developments in connection with his prisoner. He wrote a series of letters to Egilo, the archbishop of Sens, who was about to make a trip to Rome. In these letters Hincmar tells Egilo that in the *Annals of St Bertin* he found an entry which said that the Roman pontiff supported the idea of twofold predestination, and asks him to find out whether this is true. This *Letter to Egilo* (*Epistola ad Egilonem*) gives an explanation of Gottschalk's teaching as Hincmar understood it. Editions: PL 126:70-6; Lambot, 45-6 (excerpts). Translated by Victor Genke.

Hincmar, the bishop of Reims in name, not in merit, and the servant of God's people, to the most holy and most reverend archbishop Egilo.

If somebody asks you about the teaching of Gottschalk, concerning which I have already written some things to you, you can answer the one who asks, as both his words and writings show: 1. He says that godhead of the holy Trinity is threefold, as there are three persons in the holy Trinity. 2. He says that the predestination of God is twofold so that, as God has predestined some to eternal life, he has predestined others to eternal death. 3. He says that God does not *will all men to be saved* (1 Tm 2:4), but only those who are saved, but that all are saved whom he willed to save, and for this reason that all those who are not saved did not pertain to that will that they be saved. Scripture says: *The Lord has done whatever he willed in heaven and on earth, in the sea and in all the deeps* (Ps 134:6); *In your will, Lord, all things have been placed, and there is no one who is able to resist your will* (Est 13:9). Therefore, he does not will all to be saved, but only those who are saved, because if he wills what he cannot do, he is not omnipotent. 4. He says that our Lord and Savior, Jesus Christ was not crucified for the redemption of the whole world, that is, not for the salvation and redemption of all men, but only for those who are saved. 5. Explaining the words of the apostle Peter: *Denying the Lord who bought them* (2 Pt 2:1), "He bought them," he says, "by the sacrament of baptism, but did not suffer the cross, undergo death, or shed his blood for them."[30] On this, things stated more extensively are found in his writings. From these deadly chapters any catholic and learned person can see the great destructive things that emerge.

1. For from this by the invention of the devil who said to Adam: *You will be like gods,* (Gn 3:5) a plurality of gods is introduced. For, if the godhead is threefold,

30 Gottschalk, *Tome to Gislemar* (*Tomus ad Gislemarum*), 3 (Lambot, 43).

there will be three gods. For it is not one person, but the same essence, that is, the godhead, which is the unity of the Trinity, that constitutes the unity, as the Lord says in the Law: *Hear, O Israel: The Lord your God is one God* (Dt 6:4), and in the Gospel: *Go and teach all the nations, baptizing them in the name of the Father and of the Son and of the Holy Spirit* (Mt 28:19); as the seraphim chant: *Holy, holy, holy is the Lord God of hosts* (Is 6:3), and David sings: *May God, our God, bless us, and may all the ends of the earth fear him* (Ps 66:7-8). And Paul confesses: *From him and through him and in him are all things; to him be glory* (Rom 11:36). When God is said to be one, and anyone who believes is commanded to be baptized in his name, not in his names, and when "holy" is sung three times by the seraphim, and the Lord God of hosts is confessed to be one, and when he is called God by David three times, and it is prayed that he be feared by all the ends of the earth, and when he is glorified by Paul as the one God after the confession of Trinity, the one godhead of the three persons of the holy Trinity, which is the unity of Trinity, is demonstrated. And through this the faith in which we have been baptized and which *we believe in* our *heart unto righteousness and with* our *mouth confess unto salvation* (Rom 10:9-10), is overthrown by this most pernicious heresy, that is, the mother of idolatry, which had been slain by the sword of God's word in the mystical Council of Nicaea and has recently been revived by this man.

2. This perverse doctrine shows that the works of the free will, whether good or bad, are not productive of any merit, but that the predestination of God does everything, whether for life or for death. The merit of damnation is removed from the reprobate, and the merit of salvation is taken from the just. And for this reason the former are not justly condemned because they cannot be just, and the latter are not justly rewarded because they cannot be anything but just. Therefore, merit acquires nothing for the unjust, and grace does not produce anything in the elect, but on each side both perdition and salvation do not come from the judgment upon one's own action, but from the prejudgment of the Lord's will, and everything is imputed to the work of God. For the pot cannot say to him who formed it: *Why have you made me like this?* (Rom 9:20). Therefore no one will be condemned because of free choice, nor will anyone eternally sing the mercies of God because of grace. But if—what this blind man who gropes at noon[31] does not see—there were no free choice, how would the whole world lost in the mass of Adam's perdition along with its own added sins be justly judged? And again, if there were no grace of God, how would the world chosen from the same mass of perdition, that is, chosen by grace, be saved?[32] The psalm says: *Mercy and truth have met; justice and peace have kissed* (Ps 84:11). It is mercy

31 See Dt 28:29 and Jb 5:14.

32 See Augustine, *Letters* (*Epistolae*), 214.2 (PL 33:969); Alcuin of York, *On Faith in the Holy Trinity* (*De fide sanctae Trinitatis*), 2.8 (PL 101:28C).

by which the elect are saved; it is truth by which the rest are abandoned in the mass of perdition. It is justice because the reprobate are not adopted, but it is peace for these by which they are made good by grace out of one and the same mass of perdition. On this Paul says: *For the wages of sin is death, but the grace of God is eternal life* (Rom 6:23).

3. But by wrongly interpreting the scripture: *The Lord has done whatever he willed in heaven and on earth, in the seas and in all the deeps* (Ps 134:6); *In your will, Lord, all things have been placed, and there is no one who is able to resist your will* (Est 13:9), he asserts that God is unjust, who brings his wrath upon those who cannot be saved against his predestination and will and upon these who were sold by another's sin, that is, by that of the first parent and for whom redemption has not been given. And either not understanding or knowingly interpreting falsely from the scriptures what is said well and truthfully in them, he makes God unjust, while he avoids calling him weak, and using himself as the worst teacher, he disdains to learn from another how he should understand, because there are some things that the omnipotent is said to be unable to do, as Paul teaches us: *God remains faithful; he cannot deny himself* (2 Tm 2:13). He also cannot change, lie, be deceived, sin, become unhappy, be defeated, or die. If he could do these things and others like them or could will them, he would not be omnipotent. But it is too long to write about it now, and if this scoundrel had a sound mind, he would not be mistaken concerning this idea. For since he has disdained to be a disciple of the truth, he would become a teacher of error if he were permitted.

4. God said about himself in the great Peter: *The Lord is not slow, but acts patiently, not wanting that any perish, but that all return to repentance* (2 Pt 3:9), and he said in divine Paul: *He wills that all men be saved, who gave himself as a redemption for all* (1 Tm 2:4, 6), and: *By the grace of God he tasted death for all* (Heb 2:9), and: *If one died for all, therefore all died, and Christ died for all* (2 Cor 5:14-15). And he said in the prophet with an oath on account of unbelievers: *As I live, says the Lord, I do not want the death of the sinner, but that he be converted and live* (Ez 33:11). And in the whole Catholic Church, which, in beseeching him on behalf of all people according to the apostolic tradition, establishes the law of believing on this by the law of supplication,[33] he declares the Truth a liar. And since Christ says of the devil: *He is a liar from the beginning and the father of it* (Jn 8:44.), if the same Christ is according to his teaching a liar, then by his own words—which it is wicked to say!—he is proved to be like him, that is, like the devil. But God is truthful, and Gottschalk is a liar,[34] because the one and only the *Sun of justice* (Mal 4:2), Christ, took up the cause of all in order to

33 See Prosper of Aquitaine, *Official Pronouncements of the Apostolic See on Divine Grace and Free Choice* (*Praeteritorum episcoporum sedis apostolicae auctoritates de gratia Dei et libero voluntatis arbitrio*), 8 (PL 51:209C).

34 See Rom 3:4.

repair the life of all. Therefore, with justice flowing into all, where all of human nature was assumed, but not sin, the sun, who rose for all, came to all, and he suffered for all, and he who suffered for all, *wills that all men be saved* (1 Tm 2:4). But he is not seen by all, and all are not saved: *For the light shines in the darkness, and the darkness did not comprehend it* (Jn 1:5), which does not pertain to the fault of the light, but to that of the darkness. For the light came into the world, saying: *I am the light of the world. Whoever follows me does not walk in darkness, but will have the light of life* (Jn 8:12). But *men loved darkness more than light. For their deeds were evil* (Jn 3:19). And to the darkness that accepted the light, the Light himself says through the Apostle: *For you were once darkness, but now you are light in the Lord* (Eph 5:8). But that some following the light are saved is the gift of the Savior, and that some remaining in the darkness perish is the merit of those who perish. For *all the ways of the Lord are mercy and truth* (Ps 24:10). That someone guilty is condemned is the blameless justice of God, but that someone guilty person is justified is the ineffable grace of God. The redemption of the human race was offered to all, but gives salvation to the faithful. *For God so loved the world that he gave his only-begotten Son in order that he who believes in him may not perish, but have everlasting life* (Jn 3:16). *But the one who does not believe has already been judged* (Jn 3:18). The Lord also showed this when he gave the sacraments of his passion to his disciples and apostles, saying: *This is my body which will be given for you* (Lk 22:19), and: "This is my blood that will be shed for you and for many."[35] Both are found in the Gospel. Judas was also present among those to whom he gave them, having the role of the reprobate, while the other disciples had the role of the elect. For he of course did not say "for all" but "for many" because all were not going to believe. For the shedding of the blood of Christ, of *the just for the unjust* (1 Pt 3:18), was of so rich a price that if the universe of those held captive believed in their redeemer, the chains of the devil would have retained no one. For as the incarnation, preaching, and miracles are, so the death of Christ is the salvation and *honor for* those *who believe, but for those who do not believe* they are *a stone of stumbling and a rock of offense* (1 Pt 2:7-8), as those who read find in the scriptures many times and in different passages, and as it is seen in the nature of creatures, through which the invisible things of God are said by Paul to be known.[36] For one and the same sun both dries mud and melts wax, and our creator, redeemer, and savior does not help the righteous by one thought and condemn the unrighteous by some other, but by one and the same power of a singular nature never unlike to itself, he sets in order things that are unlike by his one predestination, which is always to the good, and which is twofold, as the Holy Spirit is one and his gifts two, charity

35 *Canon of the Roman Mass*. See Mt 26:28; Mk 14:24

36 See Rom 1:20.

is one and its commandments two.[37] The predestination of God is one, either pertaining to the gift of the grace or to the retribution of justice. Let it not be believed that God predestined the reprobate to punishment—God forbid!—as it is believed that he predestined the elect to glory and prepared perpetual glory for them. But by his predestination, as is sung to him by the prophet: *Mercy and truth will go before your face* (Ps 88:15); by mercy are conferred those things that pertain to the gift of grace, and those things that are paid back by the retribution of justice are referred to the truth of just judgment. The Lord is good and just in all things, because "it is good when a debt is paid," and "it is just" when something not owed is given "without cheating anyone."[38] *He has mercy on whom he wills, and he hardens whom he wills* (Rom 9:18). God is of course merciful in gratuitously giving mercy and taking away wickedness, but he hardens not by giving malice, but by justly not giving mercy, as he is said to have *hardened Pharaoh's heart* (Ex 9:12), that is, by not softening it through grace, and to have handed over some to an evil mind,[39] that is, out of the retribution of justice, and by not having freed them from an evil mind. And many other things are found in the scripture that are said in this kind of expression.

5. And he spoke through the prophets, as the Spirit of God says through the apostles and evangelists: *There is one God, one faith, one baptism* (Eph 4:5-6), in which the sanctification of the Spirit is brought about by the sprinkling of Christ's blood by which *we have been redeemed from the vain way of life of our paternal tradition* (1 Pt 1:18). For *the blood of* the same *Jesus Christ, the Son of God, cleanses us from all sin* (1 Jn 1:7). *He who came by water and blood, not only by water, but by water and blood, is Jesus Christ. And it is the Spirit who bears witness that Christ is truth, because there are three that bear witness: the Spirit and the water and the blood, and these three are one* (1 Jn 5:6-8). The Spirit of sanctification and the blood of redemption and the water of baptism are three, but remain undivided, and none of them is separated from its connection. By this faith the Catholic Church lives and grows, having been cleansed *in the bath of water with the word* (Eph 5:26), since the one and salutary baptism, which is celebrated in the same Catholic Church, is not either water without the word or the word without the water, but when the word is added to the element, the sacrament is produced, made holy by the Spirit who in the beginning *hovered over the waters* (Gn 1:2). And when *one of the soldiers opened the side* of Christ on the cross *with a lance*, it *immediately gushed forth* from the mystery of divine humanity and human divinity, that is, *blood and water* (Jn 19:34). From it is watered by the bath and the word[40] the church of believers, whose *hearts are purified by faith* (Acts 15:9)

37 See Mt 22:37-40.

38 Augustine, *On the Gift of Perseverance* (*De dono perseverantiae*), 12.28 (PL 45:1010)

39 See Rom 1:24.

40 I have conjectured *verbo* or "word" instead of *populo* or "people."

which is given to them through the Spirit, and they are saved by faith, *because the love of God has been poured out in our hearts by the Holy Spirit who was given to us* (Rom 5:5), and *believing* in it we *were sealed by the Spirit of the holy promise* (Eph 1:13). The same Apostle says: *By whom you were sealed for the day of redemption* (Eph 4:30), that is, in the same sacrament of baptism, in which there is no distinction among those who have been reborn, as the Apostle says: *As many of us as were baptized into Christ Jesus were baptized into his death* (Rom 6:3), and: *Whoever of you have been baptized in Christ have put on Christ. There is neither Jew nor Greek; there is neither slave nor free; there is neither male nor female, for you are all one in Christ Jesus* (Gal 3:27-28). For from the immaculate womb of that divine fountain our mother gives birth by grace to those whom either sex separates in the body or age separates in time, into one infancy, and someone *born again from water and the Spirit* (Jn 3:5) is invisibly made not only spiritual, but also spirit and a son of God, although he appears to those who see him visibly to be flesh and a son of man. And contrary to all this the truth of the one and same baptism is emptied by this most pestilential teaching that does not leave any hope of salvation to believers, and we who believe cannot hope for salvation from it, since, making God unjust and a liar, it dismisses him as one who shows partiality.[41] You know that this as well as his other blasphemies can be easily refuted by the authority of the scriptures and by the tradition of catholics, who have made *the crooked paths straight and the rough ones smooth* (Is 40:4), since the Lord speaks in them, from whose face comes wisdom and understanding, and who teaches man knowledge.

Therefore, what Celestine wrote for and concerning such people, should not be passed over negligently: "If we are lenient toward an error by our silence, the issue rightly points to us. Therefore, let such people be rebuked; let them not have free speech according to their desire. Let novelty cease to tread upon the old teaching, if such is the case; let restlessness cease to disturb the peace of the churches."[42] Otherwise, as Leo says: "The sins of the lower ranks should be referred to none rather than to lazy and careless rulers, who often foster some unpunished plague when they pretend not to have the necessary medicine."[43]

I could have written many things about these matters, but I would have considered writing to you before about other deadly statements of this most impudent man, if it had been permissible. But because at the very moment of the departure of our messenger, whom I was sending to you, it was reported to me that our monk, one only by his habit and an accomplice of the same Gottschalk, had fled into the lands of Italy where you are going, along with those things that he was able to steal from the monastery, I considered it necessary, having

41 See Acts 10:34.

42 Pope Celestine I, *Letters* (*Epistolae*), 21.1 (PL 50 529A).

43 Pope Leo I, *Letters* (*Epistolae*), 1.5 (PL 45:1763).

summoned a secretary, to convey to your wisdom at least those few things and ones set forth in a disorderly language that my mind suggested to my mouth, in order that if this pestilential person sows some things from the tares of his teacher in those lands, and if you are asked by some people about this, you may have some definite things that you can reply to them concerning his teaching, and lest, if our messenger were detained, he would be forced to delay so long that he would have to follow you farther.

AMOLO OF LYONS

LETTER TO GOTTSCHALK

Gottschalk established a dialogue with the church at Lyons, having sent to Amolo its bishop his *Longer Confession* most likely right after its composition in 849 or 850. In this fatherly reply, written between 850 and Amolo's death in March of 852 and sent to Gottschalk through Hincmar, Amolo tried to bring Gottschalk to reason, setting forth in detail what displeased him in his teaching. It is not known whether Hincmar ever delivered this *Letter to Gottschalk* (*Epistola ad Gothescalcum*) to his prisoner. Editions: MGH, Epist. 5:368-78; PL 116:84-96; Lambot, 16-18 (excerpts). Translated by Victor Genke.

Amolo, the humble bishop of the church of Lyons greets his dearest brother Gottschalk.

In the beginning of this letter I call you a brother, though I am not unaware that you are opposed to brotherly unity. I do this, to the extent God grants, by that charity which scripture prescribes when it says: *Say to those who hate you: You are our brothers* (Is 66:5). For even if fraternity has perished on the part of those who are of that sort, the love of this fraternity ought not also to grow cold or die in ourselves for this reason. As to my calling you not only a brother, but even my dearest, the Lord knows that I love you faithfully, wishing you the same things that I wish for myself. Hence I truthfully wish you salvation, both present and future, through that piety of divine worship, which, as the Apostle testifies, *is profitable for all things, having the promise of the life that now is and of that which is to come* (1 Tm 4:8).

Hearing and recognizing those things that you sent me in your writings and that you very strongly demanded be made known to me by a certain brother of ours, I of course hesitated for a long time whether I should reply to you, a man who has been accused of novel presumptions against the church and of considerable errors and who, as I hear, has been condemned by the authority of an episcopal council because of contempt. For I thought that it could seem importune and impudent if I tried to say anything further and respond concerning a case that has been decided by the investigation, knowledge, and sentence of our prudent and reverend brothers; on the other hand, to scorn and pass over in silence so great a plea and supplication of yours did not seem to comply with Christian piety and charity, through which the law of Christ is especially fulfilled in us, as the Apostle testifies and commends: *Bear one another's burdens, and so you will fulfill the law of Christ* (Gal 6:2). Hence, after he had said about himself: *To the weak I became weak in order that I might win the weak. I have become all things to all men in order that I might save all* (1 Cor 9:22), and said a little later: *Not seeking my own profit, but the profit of many in order that they may be saved* (1 Cor 10:33), he immediately added in order to instruct and inform us by his own example and through it by Christ's example: *Imitate me, just as I also imitate Christ* (1 Cor 11:1). For he is that true and pious Samaritan who mercifully had compassion upon the man who *went down from Jerusalem to Jericho*, was robbed on his way by thieves, and *left* wounded and *half dead* by them (Lk 10:30). He *bandaged his wounds* and cared for them *by pouring on wine and oil* (Lk 10:34). Wanting us to be imitators of his great compassion and piety, he says at the end of this parable to each of us: *Go and do likewise* (Lk 10:37), clearly showing that that man is truly a neighbor to a brother, that that man is a true imitator of him, who goes to the aid of a brother's needs and weaknesses out of piety and compassion.

Therefore, motivated by a consideration of this kind and having confidence in the most sincere charity of our venerable brothers and fellow priests, by which we are one in the Lord and ought to share with each other various burdens and offices of the ministry entrusted to us so that their goods may be ours through the spirit of unanimity and ours be theirs, if there can be any by divine mercy, I considered it better and more salutary to write a few things in answer to you, who are my brother, than by useless silence to appear to be in doubt about these questions and to show no care for you, who are so troubled, afflicted, anxious, and disturbed.

For that reason I ask the most bountiful and abundant grace of the omnipotent Lord and Savior that he may deign to grant us profitable and true words for your consolation and instruction and may prepare and calm your spirit so that you accept what we are going to say with pious meekness and humility, and that having put aside animosity and love for contention you may gladly listen to what is true, that you may willingly accept the words that are not ours, but those of God and the holy fathers, and that you may submit your spirit and mind to them in sincere piety. For as the truthful scripture truthfully says: *There are ways that seem right to a man, but their end leads to death* (Prv 16:25), and also: *He who trusts in his own thoughts acts impiously* (Prv 12:2). Hence, the same scripture also elsewhere warns, saying: *And do not rely on your own prudence* (Prv 3:5).

For blessed Ephrem, a father of admirable holiness and most illustrious learning, showed how much a man should avoid this evil, when at the hour of his departure he said, admonishing one of his disciples, a man of a great, keen, and excessively curious mind: "Beware, Paulinus, lest you subject yourself to your own thoughts."[1] The divine words again teach us what a great good obedience is and what a great evil contention and stubbornness is, when it says through the prophet Samuel: *Obedience is better than sacrifices, and to heed better than to offer*

1 See Gennadius of Marseilles, *On Writers of the Church* (*De scriptoribus ecclesiasticis*), 3 (PL 58:1063A).

the fat of rams. For rebellion is like the sin of witchcraft, and stubbornness is like the crime of idolatry (1 Sm 15:22-23).

Therefore, if you desire to be a good, useful, and peaceful son of the church, do not entrust yourself to your own opinion, but readily yield, gladly acquiesce, and obediently submit to the judgments and sentences of your elders or rather to divine and ecclesiastical authorities, so that the Spirit of God may dwell in you, as the Lord says through the prophet: *Upon whom will my Spirit rest if not upon him who is humble and quiet, and who fears my words.*[2]

We certainly are witnessing the last and most dangerous times, foretold by the Apostle long ago, times full of ignorance and sickness of souls, and in which those terrible words of the Lord should constantly be remembered and feared: *If anyone scandalizes one of these little ones who believe in me, it would be better for him if a millstone were hung around his neck, and he were drowned in the depth of the sea* (Mt 18:6). Again he says: *Woe to the world because of scandals! It is necessary that scandals come, but woe to that man by whom scandal comes* (Mt 18:7). We must avoid both *itching ears* (2 Tm 4:3) and tongues, lest we be prompt and ready for hearing or speaking novelties. Because the Apostle equally condemns both *itching ears* and *profane novelties of words*, admonishing us to *avoid the objections of what is falsely called knowledge* (1 Tm 6:20), he immediately adds concerning this false knowledge: *Some promising it have fallen away from the faith* (1 Tm 6:21).

When you were still in parts of the kingdom of Germany, we first of all heard a deplorable rumor over your name, namely, that you were sowing novelties and spreading about *foolish and ignorant questions* (2 Tm 2:23). Afterwards a certain writing of yours was brought to us by the zeal of men of the church in which you set forth what you thought and were teaching very openly and in a lengthy discussion and, as you thought, with testimonies of the scriptures and holy fathers. We have now also received other long treatises of yours that you seem to have written or published for the bishops or even against the bishops who had been present at the council that condemned you. In those writings you undertook carefully to explain what you hold on one question alone, that is, on divine predestination, with as much diligence as you could. In that way it has come about that from both of your writings whether that which we received through others or that we received from you, we think that we quite fully know the questions on which your mind is tossed about or is being shipwrecked, which is to be deplored much more.

Therefore, we thought that it could be summarily and usefully be brought about that we line up in short and distinct chapters those things from that whole series of your writings that seem to us most to contrary to the catholic faith, annexing or adding for each chapter what the holy scripture teaches to the contrary and what the church of God most firmly holds and faithfully teaches everywhere

---

2 See Is 11:2 and 66:2.

in a salutary way. It is necessary that you unquestioningly obey its teaching and views as a faithful and pious son, if you wish to be found a living and healthy member in the unity of its body and not to merit being cut off with the rotten and dead members by a judgment of just severity.

However, with legitimate order and ecclesiastical authority preserved in every way, we have directed the tenor of our letter not to you, who have received excommunication from the church because of your unhappy and pitiable fall, but principally to our most reverend and dearest metropolitan, your bishop, trusting in the Lord's goodness, that when he reads this and learns of our feeling of compassion toward you, he will be moved not by some indignation against you, but by the compassion of a good father and pious pastor, so that, when this writing is fittingly read and explained to you, if you are willing to acquiesce to the truth under the inspiration of divine grace, you may no longer wander from the fold, but having been carried back on the shoulders of the good and highest Shepherd, you, a sheep who was found and redeemed, may be happily restored to unity with the joy of those in heaven and on earth.[3]

These are the things that we have noted in your writings that are to be reprehended and have been reprehended, as they are inimical to the true catholic faith, and we have briefly gathered together how they should be corrected according to the rule of the truth.

1. In the first place, it displeases us much that you say and assert that no one redeemed by the blood of Christ can perish. For this statement is opposed to the catholic faith in two ways. If you maintain that no one from the number of Christians can perish after he has once been baptized and made a sharer in Christ's redemption, you are opposed to the Apostle, who openly preached and testified that *the wicked will not inherit the kingdom of God* (1 Cor 6:9) and that those who committed such or such crimes, *will not attain the kingdom of God* (Gal 5:21) and *do not have an inheritance in the kingdom of Christ* [*our*] *God* (Eph 5:5). Among them are also those who deny Christ, about whom he terrifyingly testifies: *The one who denies me before men, I also will deny before my Father who is in heaven* (Mt 10:33), and those who have faith without fruit, about whom he says: *Not everyone who says to me, 'Lord, Lord,' will enter the kingdom of heaven* (Mt 7:21). But there are also those foolish virgins who did not take oil in their flasks with the lamps, to whom after the door of the kingdom has been closed he is going to say: *Truly I say to you, I do not know you* (Mt 25:12). Or if you do not believe that all regenerated by true faith and devotion through the grace of baptism have been redeemed by the blood of Christ, or rather were baptized in the death and blood of Christ, although many of them perish later either through heresies or through other different crimes, this is quite clearly contrary to the apostle Paul, who says: *As many of us as were baptized into Christ Jesus were*

3 See Lk 15:4-7.

baptized into his death (Rom 6:3), and similarly to the blessed apostle John, who says, bearing witness about the same Lord: *Who loved us and washed us from our sins in his own blood* (Rv 1:5), and also to blessed Peter who speaks in this way about the worst heretics who withdrew from the church after their baptism of Christ's redemption: *They even deny the Lord who bought them, bringing upon themselves swift destruction* (2 Pt 2:1), and to the Lord himself who says about the same heretics through the prophet: *I redeemed them, and they have spoken lies against me* (Hos 7:13). Therefore, according to the catholic, apostolic, prophetic, and evangelical faith, all those who come to the baptism of Christ with faith have been redeemed, not by another price, but by the blood of Christ. But because many among them make this grace fruitless in themselves and therefore perish eternally, for what reason is it true that no one redeemed by the blood of Christ can perish?

2. In the second it displeases us much that you contend that the truest and most sacred sacraments of the church, that is, exorcisms, baptisms, chrisms, communions, and impositions of hands are given negligently and uselessly to all who perish after the reception of them, because you deny that they were redeemed by the blood of Christ, without which these mysteries should be considered, not mysteries, but certain empty and inane mockeries, since the Apostle on the contrary teaches that both the truth of Christ's redemption and the true effect of the divine mysteries are conferred even on those who irrevocably perish, when he says:

> *For it is impossible for those who have been once enlightened and have tasted the heavenly gift and have become partakers of the Holy Spirit and have tasted the good word of God and the powers of the age to come and have fallen away, to be renewed again for repentance, since they crucify again for themselves the Son of God* (Heb 6:4-6).

Again he says: *How much more do you suppose he will deserve worse punishments, who has trampled the Son of God underfoot, considered the blood of the covenant by which he was sanctified something unclean, and insulted the Spirit of grace?* (Heb 10:29). And in another passage he says: *And through your knowledge will the weak brother perish for whom Christ died?* (1 Cor 8:11). Thus the truth of the mysteries carries out its power, if it is received with faith, even in those who do not remain in the truth of the same mysteries. And in that rule of understanding the scripture about the true and false body of Christ, from which you strive, as it were, to confirm your error, you ought truly to know that the falsity of life and morals is meant, and not—God forbid!—of the divine mysteries and sacraments.

3. In the third place it displeases us much that you so perversely misuse both the testimonies of divine scriptures and the most genuine statements of the holy fathers so that you strive in many ways to support by an incorrect understanding of them all these things that you most obviously argue for against the divine truth and paternal faith. Regarding those who perish among the number

of the faithful, you affirm that they were not incorporated into Christ and into the church, whether they were presented by others at a young age or came in adulthood with faith to receive the mysteries of regeneration and of the Lord's sacrifice, and that they were never made his members, sheep who were sought and rescued, and consequently were never Christians. But how is he a Christian who does not belong to the body of Christ and who is not a member of Christ, since the Apostle says on the contrary that even those who sin grievously and who can perish in this great sin are members of Christ and are the temple of the Holy Spirit, as long as they act faithfully and innocently? He says: *Do you not know that your bodies are members of Christ? Shall I then take the members of Christ and make them members of a harlot? God forbid!* (1 Cor 6:15). He also says: *Do you not know that you are the temple of God and that the Spirit of God dwells in you? But if anyone defiles the temple of God, God will destroy him,* and so on (1 Cor 3:16-17).

4. In the fourth place it displeases us much that you think and say so harshly, disorderly, and brutally about divine predestination in the condemnation of the reprobate, that all those who are going to be put to the left on the judgment day and going to be condemned to eternal fire together with the devil and his angels for their evil merits, were divinely predestined to perdition so that none of them all will ever be able to be saved, that none is able to be saved. What else is it to think and say this but to blaspheme grievously and horribly against God, if his predestination irrevocably has imposed this necessity on them so that they can do nothing at all that might help toward their salvation? But may God keep from us the acceptance of this lest the merit of their damnation be the fault of God, who made them to be such, not of those who could not be anything else. Scripture resists this error or rather this immense impiety, when it says about him: *He has commanded no one to act impiously, and has given to no one a space [of time] for sinning* (Sir 15:21). The judge of the living and the dead destroyed this insane lie, who foretold that he would say to those who on the day of judgment day will stand to the left: *Depart from me, you cursed, into the everlasting fire prepared for the devil and his angels* (Mt 25:41). In order to show most clearly why they deserve to be irreparably separated from him, why they are cursed, why they are joined with the devil and his angels in eternal punishment, that is, not from the judgment of the predestination of Christ, but from the merit of their iniquity, he immediately added, saying: *I was hungry and you did not give me food; I was thirsty and you did not give me drink,* and so on (Mt 25:42). Here it is evidently shown that they are not condemned because they could not do the works of their salvation, but because they refused to do them.

Hence, the psalmist also says about this same just and eternal judge: *For you will render to each one according to his work* (Ps 61:13). And the Apostle likewise says: *In the day of wrath and the revelation of the righteous judgment of God, who will render to each according to his works* (Rom 2:5-6).[4] He did not say, "according to his prejudgments," as this insane and raging doctrine tries to assert for no other purpose than *the destruction of those who listen to it* (2 Tm 2:14). On the contrary, since the catholic faith most firmly holds that the devil himself and his angels were never predestined to be such, but that they willed to be such by their own vice, the punishments of everlasting fire were for this reason prepared for them. For omnipotent God is not the author of evil merits either of evil angels or of evil men, but they themselves are the authors of the evil that they have done by their own will. But God is the just judge and avenger in these things that they are going to suffer because of his justice. He therefore eternally foreknew their future evil merits, but his foreknowledge did not impose necessity on them so that they could not be anything else, but he only foresaw that they would not choose to be anything else. He predestined perpetual punishments for the bad angels and reprobate men, not because he made them bad and reprobate, but because he foresaw that they were going to be bad and reprobate by their own vice. Why is it surprising if by his just judgment he predestined them to eternal punishments and fires so that those who sinned willingly might be punished against their will? Therefore, omnipotent God did not predestine in them the iniquities that they were going to do to themselves by their own will, but that which he was going to ordain concerning them by his most righteous judgment. He did not predestine anything unjust, but only what is just; however, as God he foreknew future unjust actions and as a just judge he predestined them to be condemned. Neither by his foreknowledge nor by his predestination did he impose the necessity of acting wrongly upon any of the evil men or angels, but only of suffering eternal punishment for evil actions. Hence scripture most truly says to him: *Eternal God, you who know hidden things, who know all things before they happen* (Dn 13:42). And it again says about him: *For all things were known to the Lord God before they were created, and he similarly sees all things after their completion* (Sir 23:29). And in another passage it says: *He sees from age to age, and nothing is new in his sight* (Sir 39:25).

Some are of course counted among the evil and those to be condemned, who could not be anything else, such as those newborn babies who died under the guilt of the original sin, who could not be helped by the baptism of Christ. There are also those who, not knowing God, could not *call upon him in whom they did not believe*, or *believe him whom they did not hear*, or *hear without a preacher* (Rom 10:14), or have a preacher, because they did not merit one to be sent to them. But even in the case of these people there is no iniquity in God, because original sin dragged the former to death and both original and actual sins the latter. But the judge was just in every case, who out of the whole mass of the human race that was justly condemned on account of the merit of the first transgression, made

4 This sentence is contained in MGH, Epist. 5:372, but not in PL 116:89.

some to be *vessels of mercy* (Rom 9:23) by his gratuitous grace, and he permitted some others to be the *vessels of wrath* (Rom 9:22) by his just judgment.

But if it is asked where in the scripture there is said to be predestination to the bad side, the word used properly in such a sense will perhaps not be easily found; still the meaning of the word is clearly apparent in many passages. For example, among the first places, the blessed apostle Jude says about the fallen angels: *But he has handed over the angels who did not keep their principality, but abandoned their abode, condemned to dark prisons to be kept to be tortured for judgment* (Jude 6). And the apostle Paul says about the antichrist: *And the man of sin will be revealed, the son of perdition, who is opposed to and is exalted over all that is called God or that is worshiped* (2 Thes 2:3-4). And a little later he says: *Whom the Lord will kill with the breath of his mouth and destroy by the brightness of his coming* (2 Thes 2:8). The Lord himself said about Judas the betrayer when he prayed for the apostles: *And none of them has perished except the son of perdition in order that the scripture might be fulfilled* (Jn 17:12). About him the apostles, while praying over the election of his successor Matthias, also say to the Lord: *Show which of these two you have chosen to take the place of this ministry and apostleship from which Judas fell away to go to his own place* (Acts 1:24-25). Such is what is said through Solomon: *The Lord has made everything for himself, even the wicked for the day of evil* (Prv 16:4). And it is written in the *Book of Job*: *For a wicked person is kept for the day of destruction and is led to the day of wrath* (Jb 21:30). It is also said in the *Book of Wisdom* concerning the Egyptians: *For a fitting necessity brought them to this end* (Wis 19:4). And in *Jeremiah* it is said about certain people: *Gather them like sheep for a sacrifice, and prepare them for the day of slaughter* (Jer 12:3). To such people also the prophet Amos says: *You who were separated for the evil day and draw near to the seat of iniquity* (Am 6:3). Likewise it is said about the wicked and sacrilegious sons of Eli: *They did not heed the voice of their father, because God wanted to kill them* (1 Sm 2:25). And the prophet says to Amaziah, the treacherous and impious king: *I know that God has determined to destroy you, because you have done this evil and have not heeded my advice* (2 Chr 25:16).

But all these things have to be weighed with faith so that both the iniquity of the evil, whether angels or men, and the most inviolable justice of God who takes vengeance are known in them. He foreordained and handed over the bad angels to be kept to be tormented at the judgment,[5] but as their impiety demanded, by which they did not preserve their rank and honor, which they could have had under God and with God. Judas had also been foreknown and foretold to be *the son of perdition* (Jn 17:12), but because of the merit of his impious betrayal he went *to his own place*, that is, the place destined and prepared for him in punishments, but because he fell from *the place of the ministry and apostleship* (Acts

5 See Jude 6.

1:25). Thus it is not surprising if because the antichrist was foreknown to be *the man of sin*, he was also foreknown and foretold to be *the son of perdition* (2 Thes 2:3) and, as wicked and impious, is reserved *for the evil day* (Am 6:3) and *kept for the day of destruction and wrath* (Jb 21:30), but because he was wicked and impious by his own volition. The necessity of divine judgment also led the Egyptians to the death and destruction prepared, but it was fitting because it was just in return for their impieties and contempt. Thus those who wanted to be like cattle doomed to eternal death, seeing that by their words and deeds they summoned it,[6] are also collected like the flock of perdition and are sanctified, that is, somehow *separated for the evil day* (Am 6:3) and *the day of slaughter* (Jer 12:3). But the impious sons of Eli and the impious king Amaziah were by the judgment of God considered unworthy to receive counsel about their salvation, and God prepared them for slaughter and perdition. But they of course justly merited to be blinded and to perish, because of the merits of their impieties, which scripture mentions about them earlier. For scripture says: *God has prepared for the sword the one who crosses over from righteousness to sin* (Sir 26:27). Thus he prepared and foreordained such a transgressor for the sword, that is, for death and destruction, but justly because he went from righteousness to sin by his own will. According to this understanding of the divine authority, omnipotent God by his just judgment predestines punishments for the evil, predestines the evil for punishments, but he does not predestine any one to be evil, for he is not the author of evil, but the good author of good and the just avenger of evil actions, and if those who do evil turn to him, he is a merciful forgiver. It should nonetheless be known that, as the word "predestination" was seldom used in the scripture for the bad part, it was also rather rarely used by the doctors, and for this reason one should by no means quarrel over it greatly.

5. In the fifth place we no less detest and abhor that you so burst out in flames against those who are worthy of eternal death that you said they were irrevocably and immutably predestined to perdition, just as God himself is immutable and unalterable. And you exhort the bishops, to whom you write, as if compassionately, that they should preach to people that since they cannot escape the predetermined condemnation, they should plead with God a little and humble themselves so that he may soften a little and lighten the punishments established for them. I ask, where in the sacred scriptures did you ever read that? Where did you find that in the holy and catholic doctors of the church? Why do you not similarly exhort the devil and his angels that, since they cannot escape the condemnation established, they beg and entreat God that the eternal punishments established for them be made milder and more tolerable? Or what more do you leave for them whom you say have been similarly condemned to an irrevocable sentence?

---

6 See Wis 1:16.

The faith of the church is opposed to such atrocious impiety, for it believes that the devil along with his angels fell beyond remedy, but that the door of forgiveness is undoubtedly open for human beings, even impious ones, if they acknowledge their sins, if they weep over them, if they confess them, and if they implore the divine mercy. The prophet teaches and exhorts in that way, when he says: *Seek the Lord while he may be found; call upon him while he is near. Let the impious man forsake his way, and the wicked man his thoughts, and let him return to the Lord, and he will have mercy on him, and to our God, for he is bountiful to forgive* (Is 55:6-7). Again it says: *Who walks in darkness and has no light? Let him hope in the name of the Lord and rely upon his God* (Is 50:10). And the Lord himself says: *Return to me, and I will return to you, says the Lord of hosts* (Mal 3:7). And in another place it says: *Return, you rebellious children, and I will heal your rebellions* (Jer 3:22). Again it says: *The impiety of the impious man will not harm him on whatever day he will have turned away from his impiety* (Ez 33:12). This is faith and piety of the church; for it knows that the devil will remain in his sins without repentance and receive no forgiveness, but the remedy of repentance will be granted and the door of salvation will not be denied to those human beings who have turned to God through his ineffable goodness.

I ask, how has the human race sinned against you? How has the church sinned against you? How have so many of your neighbors and brothers in this church sinned against you that you try to block and bolt so great and so wide open a door of God's goodness? What believing member of the church has ever preached in such a way that you are not ashamed to impose and to affirm these things so emphatically and stubbornly? This hardness is truly not Christian, but heathen or rather diabolical. If you were able to think of and to understand it well, you would immediately make the sign of the cross over your heart and put your hand upon your mouth.[7]

We read in the Gospel that blessed John the Evangelist said about the Jews: *For this reason they could not believe, because Isaiah said 'He has blinded their eyes and hardened their hearts'* (Jn 12:39-40). But as blessed Augustine explains in the fiftieth tractate on this Evangelist in a believing and catholic manner: "And, 'they could not,' was said in that way where we should understand 'they refused to,'" as it was said of the Lord our God: *If we are faithless, he remains faithful; he cannot deny himself* (2 Tm 2:13). *He cannot* was said of the omnipotent. Just as then it is praise of the divine will that the Lord *cannot deny himself*, so it is a sin of the human will that *they could not believe*,"[8] not because they cannot change for the better, but as long as they think proud thoughts, they cannot believe. God foreknew and the prophet predicted this in his Spirit about the Jews who were

7 See Prv 30:32.

8 Augustine, *Homilies on the Gospel of John* (*In Iohannis euangelium tractatus*), 53.9 (PL 35:1778).

blinded and hardened. They could not therefore believe according to the mind of the most faithful doctor, because God had truly foreseen and the prophet had truly foretold by the Spirit of God their future inability, that is, their proud impiety, by which they held in contempt the humility of the Lord. Therefore, let us shut our ears to that unheard-of hardness and to those words of ruin, and let us listen to the aforementioned doctor, who sweetly prays and sweetly argues against the profane and vacuous words of vanity. He says:

> Excessive trust in their own will has raised some up to pride, and excessive diffidence about their own will has cast some down into negligence. The former say: "Why do we ask God in order that we may not be overcome by temptation, because it is in our own power?" The latter say: "Why do we try to live well, when it is in God's power?" O Lord, O *Father, who art in heaven, lead us not into* any of these temptations, *but deliver us from evil* (Mt 6:9, 13)! Let us listen to the Lord, when he says: *I have prayed for you, Peter, that your faith might not fail* (Lk 22:32), lest we think that our faith lies in free choice so that it does not need divine help. Let us listen to the evangelist, when he says: *He gave them the power to become children of God* (Jn 1:12), lest we think that it is not at all in our power that we believe. Still let us acknowledge his gifts in each of them. For we should give thanks because the power has been given and we should pray lest our weakness succumb.[9]

6. In the sixth place we have similarly detested that you say that God and his saints will rejoice and be glad at the perdition of those whom you constantly repeat have been predestined to eternal damnation, although on the contrary scripture most clearly says: *God did not make death, nor does he delight in the destruction of the living* (Wis 1:13). And in a different passage it says: *'As I live,' says the Lord God, 'I do not want the death of the sinner, but that he be converted and live'* (Ez 33:11). And again it says: *'Does the death of the impious come from my will,' says the Lord God, 'and not rather that he turn from his evil way and live?'* (Ez 18:23). How then does he rejoice at the death and condemnation of the impious, when he himself swears that it does not come from his will? Or how is he glad at anybody's ruin, who does not need the evil of anyone, as he does not need the good of anyone, in order to become as if more powerful or more happy?

You of course brought forth, as if to defend your ideas, some testimonies from scripture, but not in an appropriate way and not in the meaning in which they were put there. For example: *I also will laugh and snear over your destruction* (Prv 1:26), which is not said about the general perdition of the impious, as you supposed, but properly about the misery and misfortune of the unbelieving Jews in Deuteronomy: *As the Lord rejoiced over you, doing good to you and multiplying you, so the Lord will rejoice, destroying and overthrowing you* (Dt 28:63). But it needs great and pious consideration in order that one might somehow or other think of the laughter and snearing of God at the destruction of those who are

9 Augustine, *Homilies on the Gospel of John*, 53.8 (PL 35:1778).

lost and his gladness and joy not only at the progress of the just, but also at the overthrow of the evil, since, as was shown above, he rejoices in the death of no one, in the destruction of no one and swears that he does not want anyone to perish. For he does not, like an enemy of his creature, desire the destruction of anyone, but loves in those who perish only the end of their malice and the order and retribution of justice. Therefore, he will laugh and snear at the destruction of the wicked in that way, when, humbling their pride and contempt by fitting punishment and condemning all the vanity and elation of a creature against the creator, he will show that their pride and contempt are worthy of laughter and snearing. Hence, the same divine words were used not in order to say, "I will laugh and snear 'over' your destruction," but 'in' your destruction, that is, not for it, but in it, that is, not for those who perished by their own sin, but because the praise and glory of the creature is increased in their just destruction in the contemplation of a rational and blessed creature, when every chosen creature exults, not in the torments of the wretched, but in the justice and truth of the divine judgments. This is permitted to the souls of the saints even in the present world, as the psalmist says: *The daughters of Judah rejoiced because of your judgments, Lord* (Ps 96:8). But they rejoiced not on account of the destruction of anyone, but on account of the justice of divine equity. In this sense one can understand the words: *The righteous will rejoice when he sees vengeance* (Ps 57:11), and those in Solomon: *And there will be praise in the destruction of the wicked* (Prv 11:10). But omnipotent God rejoices either in doing good to the just or repaying the bad actions of the evil, not because he is changed or varied because of different dispositions, for his rejoicing, like his existing, is eternal and immutable, in whom *there is neither variation nor shadow of change* (Jas 1:17). But as the Spirit of the Father is said to speak in those whom he causes to speak,[10] whom he instructs and teaches to bear witness to truth, and is also said to intercede for the saints, to groan, and to desire[11] because he inspires those whom he fills with the will to pray, groan, and desire,[12] so too he also rejoices in this way in the saints in whom he deigns to dwell, because he undoubtedly makes them rejoice either in the gifts of grace which he gives to the pious or in his judgments and justices by which he punishes the impious. Although, as human beings, they are sad for them out of human affection, as the Apostle says concerning himself,[13] they still do not cease to praise and glorify the just judgments of God under the guidance and illumination of the divine Spirit. Therefore, since the divine words need great and inexpressibly greater caution in order that they might be understood to a

10 See Mt 10:20.

11 See Rom 8:26-27.

12 See Augustine, *On Rebuke and Grace* (*De correptione et gratia*), 15.47 (CSEL 92:277; PL 44:945).

13 See Rom 9:2.

certain extent, they should not be readily brought forth by anyone as if in favor of himself, lest they be found to be against him when they are interpreted correctly.

7. In the seventh place, of course, two serious evils in your morals have displeased us very much. One is that you slash the priests of God and the rulers of the churches with such injuries, insults, and curses and trod on them with such great insult and contempt, having surely been miserably deceived by the spirit of error and pride so that you are seen to have no Christian patience, no Christian reverence at all. Among other things, you are not afraid to call heretics all those who resist the insanity of your thoughts out of zeal for the faith, and you dare to call them Rabanists after a good and learned man and a catholic bishop. Nor do you fear God because you have fallen into such and such great snares of the devil through vain instability of mind and body and vainer curiosity and arrogance. Nor do you blush for shame because you are caught and refuted everywhere and by everyone in so many errors and lies. Nor are you sorry that you have remained, cut off from the body of the church—see for so many years—by a condemnation of just severity and deprived of the companionship and consolation of all good people, like a useless root or dry branch destined for fire. But up to now your *mouth has been full of cursing and bitterness* (Rom 3:14), and having been turned into a bad bow,[14] you are not shot on behalf of the Lord, as you think, but against the Lord, since you scorn the church, your mother, and its leaders, your fathers, with sacrilegious audacity.

The other evil in your morals is that, as your writing shows, in all that you think and say, you never piously and humbly entreat any human being in the fashion of good men and never submit yourself to their mind and authority, nor do you say what piety is often accustomed to say and should say: "I beg you, good man or good brother, if in any way I err in what I say, bear with my weakness, instruct my ignorance, and you will experience my obedience, for I am ready gladly to accept whatever the truth will deign to explain." But you trust in your thoughts and boast of speculating on and contemplating the truth itself so that you do not in your writings even ask God to reveal to you what is better.

Hence, I exhort and warn you much, my brother, and persuade you with a fatherly kindness and brotherly charity that you come back to yourself, return to your heart, shake off far from yourself this vain error and fruitless and pernicious labor, and return yourself to holy mother church, return yourself to the obedience of the Lord, of your priests and fathers, and return yourself to the brotherly charity of all, so that you, who now lie like a broken vessel,[15] with the help of God's grace may become *in his house a useful vessel* (Bar 6:58) ready for every good work.[16] Do not be terrified at the consideration either of the error

14 See Ps 77:57.

15 See Ps 30:13.

16 See 2 Tm 2:21.

that you have fallen into or of the insults that you inflicted on the priests of God, and do not experience them as irreconcilable. We will all pray for you, and they will be forgotten on account of the love of Christ, and in the mind of all past errors will be forgotten, and the good of your present conversion will turn into joy and exultation. Only do not hesitate, do not delay, but *deliver yourself like a deer from the hand, and like a bird from the snares of the fowler* (Prv 6:5), lest caught in such a condemnation by sudden death—God forbid!—you leave forever your mother, the church, for whom you now cause constant grief.

Believe without a doubt that I say all these things out of true and sincere love for you and only out of love for your salvation. Do not at all think that any of the things that I went after above rather harshly and sternly were brought forth for your confusion or condemnation. But know most certainly that they were said only in order to put them before your eyes, as in a mirror, to be truthfully discerned and, with the help of God's grace, to be corrected zealously and as soon as possible. For as you know well: *The wounds received from a friend are better than fraudulent kisses of an enemy* (Prv 27:6).

In conclusion, I briefly convey to you, my dearest brother, that there was in Gaul almost at the time of the blessed Pope Leo or Pope Agapetus,[17] a venerable and very useful council of the church of God of very many bishops over whom the blessed bishop Caesarius of Arles, a man of admirable sanctity, virtues, and miracles presided. It is clear that in it, it was carefully defined how one was to think, hold, teach with a very moderate and carefully weighed manner about the grace of God and the free choice of man and about divine foreknowledge and predestination. Hence, I add a few words here as a reminder for your prudent self in which they say:

> We also believe this in accord with the catholic faith, namely, that after the reception of the grace of baptism all the baptized can and should, with the help and cooperation of Christ, carry out those things that pertain to the salvation of the soul, if they will to work faithfully. We not only do not believe that some have been predestined to evil by the power of God, but we also say anathema to them with great detestation, if there are some who choose believe so great an evil.[18]

ON GRACE AND FOREKNOWLEDGE

The editor of Amolo's works in PL entitled this treatise *On the Grace and Foreknowledge of God, and on Predestination and Free Will, also on the Hope and Confidence of Salvation, and on the Opinion of Saint Augustine* (*De gratia et praescientia Dei, deque praedestinatione et libero arbitrio, de spe item ac fiducia*

17 The Second Council of Orange took place in 529. The pontificate of Pope Leo I was from 440-461, Pope Agapetus I from 535-536.

18 *The Council of Orange* (*Concilium Arausiacum*), II. Conclusion (Mansi, 8:717-8; MGH, Concilia, 1:52; CCSL 148A:63; DS, 397).

salutis et de sententia sancti Augustini). In an ancient codex at Trier the untitled treatise followed an epistle of Amolo. It appears to be missing its beginning. It was clearly written in the context of the Gottschalk controversy. Predestination, it says, should not be preached in such a way that it leads people to despair. Rather predestination and grace are taught in scripture so that we may humble ourselves and trust in Christ. Augustine did not teach predestination of the impious as if God were compelling them to evil, but exhorted his hearers to faithful diligence.

A date near the time of Amolo's *Letter to Gottschalk* (*Epistola ad Godescalcum*), perhaps in 851 or 852, is likely. It is not unusual that the thoughts of Florus of Lyons, deacon and teacher serving under Amolo, are present in the treatise. For Amolo's writings were transcribed under the direction of Florus, who also served as supervisor of the scriptorium at Lyons. Florus is known to have compiled extracts from Augustine on predestination, grace, and free will; and this treatise draws heavily upon Augustine's writings on predestination.[19] Edition: PL 116:101-6. The subheadings were added by the present translator, Francis X. Gumerlock.

On the Grace of God

1. Therefore, we ought to believe in the grace of God by which the human race is saved without any preceding good merits of its own, but by the gracious goodness and mercy of God alone, through the *one mediator of God and man…Jesus Christ* (1 Tm 2:5). The Lord himself teaches this grace in the Gospel, when he says: *For the Son of man has come to seek and to save what was lost* (Lk 19:10). And the Apostle preaches this, saying: *In order that through the grace of God he might taste death for all* (Heb 2:9). And in another place he says: *But God, who is rich in mercy, made us alive together with Christ on account of his great love with which he loved us, even when we were dead in sins* (Eph 2:4-5). He meant this grace where he says to the faithful: *By grace you have been saved through faith, and this not of yourselves, but it is a gift of God* (Eph 2:8), that is, both that you have been saved and that you have been saved through faith, both your salvation and your faith.

Through this grace, that is, his gratuitous gift, God the Father draws to his Son those whom he wills. But he draws, not by necessity, but by a will that can experience delight and by love, as the Son himself said: *No one can come to me unless the Father, who sent me, draws him* (Jn 6:44). The Son himself also draws those same people to himself, as he himself says: *And if I shall be lifted up from the earth, I shall draw all to myself* (Jn 12:32). Young and old who have been

19 The collection of *sententiae* from Augustine on predestination, grace, and free will, attributed to Amolo in PL 116:105-40 has been restored to Florus. Célestin Charlier, "Les manuscripts personnels de Florus de Lyon de son activité littéraire," in *Mélanges E. Podechard* (Lyon: Facultés Catholiques, 1945), 71-84 at 79-80; Gillian R. Evans, "The Grammar of Predestination in the Ninth Century," *Journal of Theological Studies* 33:1 (1982):134-45 at 144, no. 3.

reborn in baptism receive this regeneration, and the faithful daily receive it as well in every good thought, deed, and word. That is, he encourages by inspiring what is good, but he confirms it by preserving what he inspired. For there is nothing good in a person that is not the gift of God. By this grace sins are also daily forgiven us when we confess humbly and ask, as blessed John the apostle testifies and says: *If we confess our sins, he is faithful and just to forgive us our sins and to cleanse us from all iniquity* (1 Jn 1:9).

On Divine Foreknowledge

2. We ought also to believe the foreknowledge of God, by which he foreknew all things in his eternal knowledge and by which whatever is going to be was foreknown to him, not only the good things that he himself causes and rewards in his own people, but also the evil things that he does not cause, but only judges and condemns in others. Hence, scripture also says: *You, who know all things before they happen* (Dn 13:42). For in that eternal foreknowledge all things were eternally and immutably foreknown to him, just as they are also absolutely going to be. And because he most truly and most certainly foreknew them, they will absolutely be, as he foreknew them.

The Apostle says about this foreknowledge of his: *For whom he foreknew, he also predestined to be conformed to the image of his Son* (Rom 8:29). He foreknew those who were going to believe and those who were not going to believe. He therefore foreknew those who were going to persevere in the faith and those who were not going to persevere. He foreknew those who will be in eternal life and those who will burn in eternal fire. Therefore, he foreknows the exact number of his saints. Hence, it is sung mystically in the psalm: *He numbers the multitude of the stars and calls all of them by their names* (Ps 146:4). And the Apostle writes: *The Lord knows who are his* (2 Tm 2:19).

On the Predestination of the Saints

3. We ought also to believe the predestination and election of the saints because he predestined those *whom he foreknew* would be saved and freed by his grace (Rom 8:29), that is, he preordained and chose them, that is, separated them from the mass of perdition and the society of the reprobate, so that by his grace they would become *vessels of mercy which he prepared beforehand for glory* (Rom 9:23).

He did not, therefore, predestine and choose them because he foreknew that they were going to be righteous by themselves, but rather he foreknew and predestined them in order that he might justify them by his gratuitous grace. Thus the Apostle testifies to the entire matter when he says: *For whom he foreknew, he also predestined*, and so on (Rom 8:29-30).

The foreknowledge and predestination of God therefore granted to them that they might become what they were not, that is, that they might become *conformed to the image of his Son* (Rom 8:29), and that they might be called with a calling not merely of the voice externally, but also of grace that inspires and helps internally. This predestination of God is sometimes called the plan of God, as the Apostle says: *For we know that all things work together for good for those who love God, who have been called to be holy according to his plan* (Rom 8:28). About this plan and grace promised and given to the saints before the foundation of the world, before all time, he says again: *In the hope of eternal life, which God, who does not lie, promised before all time, but in his own times manifested his word* (Ti 1:2-3). And in another place he says: *According to the power of God, who set us free and called us by his holy calling, not according to our works, but according to his own plan and grace, which was given to us in Christ Jesus before all time, but now was manifested through the enlightenment by our savior Jesus Christ* (2 Tim 1:8-10). About this calling it was said: *For the gifts and calling of God are without repentance* (Rom 11:29), that is, without change.[20] And so it is necessary that we believe that this good of the perseverance of the saints is not only a gift, but also a great and highly necessary gift of God.[21] For what is the advantage of having begun in these good things and of having lost them before the end or at the end of life?

On Free Will

4. It is also necessary that we believe that the free and upright choice of the will, which was naturally implanted in humans by God from the beginning, became vitiated, weak, and depraved by the merit of the first transgression, so that it cannot rise to the love of truth and righteousness unless it is raised up, healed, and nourished by the gift of Christ and set free from the vice of its own depravity. For Scripture says on this: *God created man upright, and he has entangled himself in an infinity of questions* (Eccl 7:30). And the same scripture says to what humans were subject after the fall of human depravity as follows: *For the mind and thought of the human heart is prone to evil* (Gn 8:21). Therefore, that doctor alone heals this weakness of the free choice, by which the mind and thought of the human being, because of the sin of his condemned origin, is prone and intent to do evil and free choice itself is held captive. He alone set it free and renders it free, the deliverer who says of himself: *It is not the healthy who need a doctor but those who are sick* (Mt 9:12). And again he says: *If the Son will set you free, you will truly be free* (Jn 8:36). He restores free choice which has been set free by his grace, so that, as it was prone and quick to do evil, it is made prone and quick to do good much more attentively and with much more pleasure. The Apostle says of this freedom: *Where the Spirit of the Lord is, there is freedom* (2 Cor 3:17).

---

20 See Augustine, *On the Predestination of the Saints*, 18.37 (PL 44:988).

21 See Augustine, *On the Gift of Perserverance* (*De dono perseverantiae*), 1-3 (PL 44:993-8).

On Hope and Confidence of Salvation

5. Therefore this grace, foreknowledge, predestination, election, calling, and also the downfall and restoration of free choice, so clearly announced in the scriptures, must be most faithfully and firmly held by us. These things are not announced in order to cast a believing human being down from the hope and confidence of salvation and to break him, but in order that, with all human pride humbled and all presumption in one's own strength laid aside, each person might subject and commend himself faithfully to be ruled by God, to be protected by his power, to be helped by his goodness, and to be preserved and perfected by his grace. This grace is nothing else but the mercy and goodness of the redeemer, by whose death we are made alive, by whose blood we are redeemed, by whose righteousness we are forgiven, and by whose cross we are saved, in order that there should be produced in us, not for despair but for salvation, what the Apostle teaches when he says: *But we ourselves had the sentence of death in ourselves so that we would not trust in ourselves, but in God who raises the dead* (2 Cor 1:9). And in another place he says: *But of him you are in Christ Jesus, who by God was made unto us wisdom and righteousness and sanctification and redemption* (1 Cor 1:30).

As he is everything for us and we are wholly his, not trusting partly in ourselves and partly in him, let each of us also say confidently to him with the psalmist: *I am yours, save me!* (Ps 118:94). For why is it that he thought that he should be rather intimately commended to God so that he said: *I am yours,* except that he wanted it to be understood that by his own sin he wanted to be his own, which is the first and greatest sin of disobedience? For this reason, as if saying, "I wanted to be my own, and I destroyed myself," he says: *I am yours, save me!*

Believe firmly in Christ, each of you believers, and commit yourself wholly to him to the extent you can. Do not want to be as if your own and in your own control, but declare yourself a servant of that most clement and beneficent Lord. For in that way he will not cease to lift you up to himself,[22] and he will permit nothing to happen to you but that which is good for you,[23] even if you do not know it. For this is the wisdom of God that speaks and warns, saying:

> *I am the mother of fair love and of fear, of both knowledge and of holy hope. In me is all grace of the way and of the truth; in me is all hope of life and of virtue. Come over to me, all you who desire me, and be filled from my fruits. For my spirit is sweeter than honey, and my inheritance sweeter than honey and honeycomb.... He who listens to me will not be confounded, and those who work in me will not sin* (Sir 24:24-27, 30).

The wise man prays for this, saying: *Send her from your holy heaven and from the throne of your greatness that she may be with me and work with me, that I may know what is acceptable before you* (Wis 9:10).

---

22 See Jas 4:10.

23 See Rom 8:28.

The Opinion of Augustine

6. What we are accustomed to find at times in the words of Saint Augustine and perhaps of other catholic teachers, namely, that the impious have been predestined to eternal damnation or eternal destruction, should not be thought contrary to this. For omnipotent God did not predestine to evil by his divine power, as if judging them in advance, those whom he foresaw were going to perish in their sin, whether original or actual, and in their impiety, so that he forced them to be evil, as by this predestination, and to come to suffering eternal evils. But as one with foreknowledge of all things, by his just judgment he foreordained, and by foreordaining of course predestined, to eternal destruction those whom he foreknew were going to be deserving of perpetual condemnation, either because of their origin justly condemned in Adam or also because of their own impiety.

But let us now hear how blessed Augustine, the principal preacher of predestination and grace after the Apostle, exhorts the faithful to the pursuits of piety and constancy in prayer in order to merit to receive the gift of calling.[24] He says:

> Oh, would that our heart would in some way long for that ineffable glory! Oh, would that we would experience our pilgrimage in groaning, not love the world, and continually knock with a pious mind for him who has called us! Desire is the bosom of the heart. We shall grasp him if we extend that desire as much as we can. The divine scripture says this with us; the congregation of peoples says this; the celebration of the sacraments says this; holy baptism says this; songs of God's praise say this, and this very debate of ours says this in order that this desire may not only be sown and germinate, but also may increase in the manner of so great a capacity that it may be fit to grasp what *eye has not seen, nor ear heard,* and what has not *entered the heart of man* (1 Cor 2:9). But love it along with me. One who loves God does not love money much. I have also experienced infirmity. I did not dare to say "does not love money" but he "does not love it much," as if money should be loved, but not much.
>
> Oh, would that we would love God worthily! We will not love money at all! Money will be to you an instrument of pilgrimage, not an irritant of desire, something to use for necessity, not something to enjoy for delight. Love God if he has done something in you that you hear and praise. Use the world, but let not the world captivate you. Make the journey you entered upon. You have come to leave, not to remain. You are making a journey; this life is the inn. Use money as a traveler uses the table, the glass, the pitcher, and the cot in an inn, as one who is going to leave, not remain there. If you will be such, lift up your hearts, you who can, and listen to me. If you will be such, you will reach his promises. For this is not much for you, because the hand of him who called you is great. He called; let him be called upon. Let it be said to him: "You have called us; we call upon you. Behold, we have heard you calling; hear us calling upon you. Lead us where you promised; finish what you have begun. Do not abandon your gifts; do nor abandon your field. May your crops enter

24 See *On the Gift of Perseverance,* 3-10 (PL 44:996-1007).

the barn." Temptations abound in the world, but he who made the world is greater.[25] Temptations abound, but he does not fail who places his hope in him, in whom there is no failure.[26]

25 See 1 Jn 4:4.

26 The source of these quotations has not been located.

FLORUS OF LYONS

SERMON ON PREDESTINATION

Florus (c. 800-860) served as deacon and teacher in the church at Lyons under the bishops Agobard, Amolo, and Remigius. He wrote several treatises related to the Gottschalk predestination controversy, some of which have been passed down under the names of Amolo and Remigius. Florus wrote this *Sermon on Predestination* (*Sermo de praedestinatione*) in response to certain persons who asked him about divine foreknowledge, predestination, and free will. In a codex at Trier, it was attached to Amolo's *Letter to Gottschalk* (*Epistola ad Godescalcum*). Its concern that predestination does not mean a person is unable to change his spiritual status, and its comments about Gottschalk in the closing paragraph, suggest that it was written about the same time as Amolo's letter, circa 851-852. Between 853-855, serving under Remigius, Florus concerned himself with responses to Hincmar, Pardulus, Rabanus, and Eriugena, and took a more mediating position with regard to Gottschalk. Edition: PL 119:95-102; PL 125:57-9; PL 116:97-100 (attributed to Amolo).[1] The subheadings were added by the present translator, Francis X. Gumerlock.

On Divine Foreknowledge

1 Because he is most truly the true and only God, the omnipotent God completely foreknew in his eternal and immutable knowledge all things before they happened, as scripture testifies, saying: *Eternal God, you are the one who knows hidden things, who knows all things before they happen* (Dn 13:42). Therefore, he without a doubt foreknew both the good things that good people were going to do and the bad things that bad people were going to do. But he brings it about by his grace in good people that they are good. Yet he does not bring it about in the bad people that they are bad—God forbid!—but he only foreknew that they were going to be such by their own vice. For the foreknowledge of God did not impose on them the necessity that they could not be something else, but only what they were going to be by their own will, as God foresaw this from his own omnipotent majesty. Hence, scripture, making known to us his inviolable justice, says about him: *He has commanded no one to act impiously, and gave to no one a space* [of time] *for sinning* (Sir 15:21).

1 An earlier English translation of this sermon was published in Henry Newland, ed., *A Practical and Exegetical Commentary on the Epistle of St. Paul to the Ephesians* (Oxford and London: J. H. and James Parker, 1860), 15-20.

Therefore, because impious and iniquitous people act impiously, and they turn the space of time in this life, which God gave to them for living well, into a time for doing evil, the blame is not God's, but is their own; and therefore they are rightly condemned by his justice.

The same omnipotent God also foreknew their eternal damnation, but from the merit of those whom he foresaw that they were going to persevere in their own malice, not—God forbid!—from his own iniquity. For he decided nothing unjustly and *will render to each according to his works* (Rom 2:6), that is, either eternal good things for living well or perpetual evils for living badly. Therefore, he completely foreknew both that the good would be good through his grace and that they were going to receive eternal rewards through that same grace, that is, that they were going to live well in the present age and that they were going to be happily rewarded in the future, both from the gift of the mercy of God. Hence, the Apostle calls them *vessels of mercy*, when he says: *That he might show the riches of his grace to vessels of mercy which he prepared beforehand for glory* (Rom 9:23).

But on the contrary, he foreknew that the bad were going to be bad through their own malice, and he foreknew that they would be condemned with eternal retribution through his justice. As he foreknew concerning Judas the betrayer that *he would betray him* (Jn 6:65), as the Gospel says, *although he was one of the twelve* (Jn 6:72), he also foreknew his eternal damnation, since he said: *Woe to that man by whom the Son of man will be betrayed. It would have been better for that man if he had not been born* (Mk 14:21). In the same way he also undoubtedly foreknew concerning the impious Jews their future impiety, about which he foretold in the psalm: *They gave gall for my food, and in my thirst they gave me vinegar to drink* (Ps 68:22). He also foreknew their subsequent damnation, about which he added in the same psalm: *Let them be erased from the book of the living and not be written with the righteous* (Ps 68:29). But in these and all the wicked the former came first from their own depravity; the latter follows from divine equity.

On Divine Predestination

2. In this manner it should also be definitely understood concerning the predestination of God that in the good he predestined both their future goodness from the gift of his grace and their eternal reward for that same goodness so that they became good by his gift and would be rewarded by his gift. Hence, the Apostle says: *He predestined us to the adoption of sons, through Jesus Christ unto himself* (Eph 1:5). And in another passage he says: *Whom he foreknew, he also predestined to be conformed to the image of his Son* (Rom 8:29). Therefore, he predestined his elect so that they would now be taken up into the adoption of the sons of God by the grace of baptism and that in the future they would become conformed to the image of the Son of God, once they have been renewed and glorified ac-

cording to his image by that same grace.[2] He absolutely predestined that they be good here, not from themselves but from him, and that they be blessed there, not through themselves but through him. Therefore, in both he foreknew and predestined that his own good things be in them and concerning them.

But in the evil and impious the omnipotent God did not predestine their malice and impiety, that is, that they would be evil and impious and could not be anything else. But those whom he foreknew and predestined were going to be evil and impious by their own vice, he predestined to eternal damnation by a just judgment, not because they could not be anything else, but because they refused to be anything else. Therefore, they themselves were the cause of perdition for themselves. But God is the just judge and just arranger of their damnation. For he did not predestine unjust, but just things. Nevertheless, he predestined both rewards for the just and punishments for the unjust, since both are just. The Apostle commends this justice of his to us, when he says: *Is God unjust, who executes wrath? God forbid!* (Rom 3:5-6)

For he now shows patience toward all so that they might turn to repentance, and those who perish, perish because of their own contempt and stubbornness, because they showed contempt for such great goodness of God. Again he says in another passage: *Do you show contempt for the riches of his goodness and patience and longsuffering, not knowing that the kindness of God leads you to repentance? But according to your stubbornness and impenitent heart, you store up wrath for yourself on the day of wrath and revelation of the just judgment of God, who will render to each according to his works* (Rom 2:4-6). The other scripture also testifies concerning this, saying: *God did not make death, nor does he delight in the destruction of the living....But with their own hands and words the impious have summoned it, and thinking it a friend, they have fallen away and made a covenant with it, because they are worthy to belong to its party* (Wis 1:13, 16). Therefore, the omnipotent God is not the cause of the death or destruction for any person, but the impious summon to themselves death and destruction by *their own hands and words* (Wis 1:16) when by living wickedly and by persuading others more wickedly, they bring damnation upon themselves and others, when the lovers of the way of iniquity and destruction turn aside from the right path and hasten to perpetual damnation because of their own desire and agreement, allies of death and enemies of eternal life, as if having given their right hands to one another in an equal consent to wickedness. In accord with their stubbornness and impenitent heart they *store up for* themselves *wrath on the day of wrath* (Rom 2:5).

Because on that day of the just judgment of God each receives in accord with his works,[3] no one is condemned by the prejudgment of God, but on the basis of the merit of his own iniquity. For he did not predestine anyone to be evil, but

2 The translation of Newland omitted this sentence.

3 See Rom 2:5-6.

truly predestined every evil person not to go unpunished. Every just law has no wrongdoing lest it be unjust. Nevertheless, it punishes the wrongdoer so that it is truly just. Therefore, one who says[4] that those who perish were predestined to perdition, and for that reason it could not turn out otherwise, and similarly concerning the just that they are saved because they were predestined to salvation and could not be anything else, speaks in a very confused and silly manner and takes away the merit of damnation in the former and the merit of salvation in the latter. What else does he do by this, but impose a necessity of perdition on those who are perishing and a necessity of salvation upon those who are saved? And for this reason the former who could not be just are not justly condemned, and the latter are not justly rewarded because they could not be anything but just. In each case perdition and salvation do not come from the judgment of their own actions, but from a prejudgment of divine foreordination. But then where will those words be: *He will render to each according to his works* (Rom 2:6)? And again: *Is God unjust who executes wrath? God forbid!* (Rom 3:5-6). For the cause of the perdition of those who perish is clearly traced back to God, if he predestined them to destruction so that that they could not be anything else. To believe or say this is horrible blasphemy.

Summary of Catholic Teaching on These Matters

3. But the faith of the Catholic Church, whose children and followers we ought to be, teaches that we should hold most firmly as we have briefly defined above according to the authority of holy scripture, namely, that omnipotent God foreknew in the evil their malice because it comes from them. He did not predestine it because it is not from him. But he both foreknew their punishment because he is God and predestined their punishment because he is just, so that the merit of their damnation lies in them and the power and judgment of him who justly condemns them lies in him. For God only predestines what he is going to bring about, but he foreknows many things that he is not going to bring about, such as all the evils—the evils that evildoers bring about, not God.

The faith also teaches that the evil do not perish because they could not be good, but because they refused to be good, and by their own vice they persevered as *vessels of wrath fitted for destruction* (Rom 9:22) and remained in the mass of damnation by either original or actual merit. But in the good, as was shown sufficiently above, the omnipotent God both foreknew and predestined them so that by his grace they might be good in the present life and are also blessed in the future life. For he is the author and giver of each good, that is, both of the present and of the future, and for this reason he undoubtedly foreknows and predestines both, because of themselves the just not only could have been something else, but also were something else before they were made just from ungodly through *him who justifies the ungodly* (Rom 4:5).

4 Gottschalk.

But whether in those who are saved or in those who perish, their own will is rewarded, and their own will is condemned. But because in the former it was saved by the grace of the Lord the Savior so that it was made good and right from evil and bad, it is undoubtedly crowned most worthily. But because in the latter it did not acquiesce to receive salvation through the Savior, they will most justly experience eternal damnation through that same judge.

On Free Will

4. This is briefly the whole that has to be held concerning free will according to the truth of the catholic faith, namely, that God created all humans with free will. But because *through one man sin entered the world, and death through sin, so that it passed to all human beings, in whom all have sinned* (Rom 5:12), free will was vitiated and corrupted in the whole human race by the merit of his fall, blinded and weakened so that it is sufficient for a human being to act wrongly, that is, to the downfall of iniquity and so that it is free for this alone. But for acting well, that is, for the exercise of virtue and fruit of good work, it is not sufficient in any way for one to rise up or become strong unless it is restored, illuminated, and healed through the faith of the *one mediator of God and man, the man Christ Jesus* (1 Tm 2:5) and through the gift of the Holy Spirit, just as the Savior himself promises in the Gospel, when he says: *If the Son will set you free, you will truly be free* (Jn 8:36). And the Apostle says: *Where the Spirit of the Lord is, there is freedom* (2 Cor 3:17).

As set free, illuminated, and healed by the grace of Christ and the Spirit of Christ, let free choice say the words of the psalmist, rejoicing: *The Lord is my light and my salvation. Whom shall I fear?* (Ps 26:1). Therefore, let him who desires to receive this grace of freedom in order that he may become truly free for living well and piously, not rely on his own strength, but let him hand himself over faithfully to him to be healed and strengthened. The same psalmist says about this: *The steps of a man will be directed by the Lord, and he will choose his way* (Ps 36:23). And let him pray and ask him, saying: *Direct my steps according to your word, and let no iniquity have dominion over me* (Ps 118:133). And again let him say: *Lead me, Lord, in your way, and I shall walk in your truth* (Ps 85:11 and Ps 5:9),[5] and other similar passages.[6]

5 The quotation conflates verses from the two psalms.

6 The versions of this sermon in PL 116:97-100 and in the translation of Newland end here. The versions in PL 119:95-102 and PL 125:57-9 contain the concluding paragraph translated here. It shows that this sermon was a written response to an inquiry about foreknowledge, predestination, and free will. It also illustrates Florus' sentiments at that time about Gottschalk.

Conclusion

5. I have briefly written these things to you about the things that you requested. Now I faithfully exhort you and pray that, founded on the simplicity and sincerity of the true faith, you would close your ears to the wicked tongue of this very vain and very wretched man. For although he is ready to argue and is obstinate against the truth, this unfortunate man, puffed up by a diabolical spirit, preferred to separate himself from the church of Christ and its ministers rather than to abandon his profane and vain speech.

BIBLIOGRAPHY

ABBREVIATIONS OF SERIES

CCSL *Corpus christianorum, series latina.* Turnhout: Brepols, 1953-present.

CCCM *Corpus christianorum, continuatio medievalis.* Turnhout: Brepols, 1953-present.

CSEL *Corpus scriptorium ecclesiasticorum latinorum.* Vienna: Hoelder-Pichler-Tempsky, 1866-present.

DS Heinrich Denziger and Adolph Schoenmetzer, *Enchiridion symbolorum, definitionum et declarationum de rebus fidei et morum.* Freiburg: Herder, 1963, 1965, 1967, 1973, 1976.

FC *Fathers of the Church.* New York: Cima Publishing Co., 1947-1949; New York: Fathers of the Church, Inc., 1949-1960; Washington, D.C.: Catholic University of America Press, 1960-present.

HBS *Publications of the Henry Bradshaw Society.* London: 1891-present. Currently published by Boydell and Brewer in Woodridge, UK and Rochester, NY.

Lambot Cyrille Lambot, ed. *Oeuvres théologiques et grammaticales de Godescalc d'Orbais.* Louvain: "Spicilegium Sacrum Lovaniense" Bureaux, 1945. Bound reprint available upon request from Curt Daniel, c/o Good Books, 2456 Devonshire Rd., Springfield, Illinois 62703.

Mansi Giovanni D. Mansi, ed. *Sacrorum conciliorum nova et amplissima collectio.* 31 vols. to 1439. Florence and Venice, 1758-1798. Reprinted and continued to 1902, 53 vols. Paris, Arnhem, and Leipzig, 1903-1927. Reprinted, Graz, 1960-1961.

Mauguin Gilbert Mauguin. *Veterum auctorum qui IX. saeculo de praedestinatione et gratia scripserunt opera et fragmenta plurima nunc primum in luce edita.* Paris: Ioannis Billaine, 1650.

MGH *Monumenta Germaniae Historica.* Berlin, Germany: Weidmann, 1877-present. Available in compact disk from Brepols.

NPNF Philip Schaff, ed. *A Select Library of the Nicene and Post-Nicene Fathers of the Christian Church.* 2 series of 14 volumes each. New York: Christian Literature, 1887-1894. Peabody, MA: Hendrickson, 1989, 1994. Available on compact disk.

PG Jean P. Migne, ed., *Patrologiae cursus completus, series Graeca,* 161 vols. Paris: Petit-Montrouge, 1857-1866. Available in reprint from Brepols.

PL Jean P. Migne, ed., *Patrologiae cursus completus, series Latina,* 221 vols. Paris: Petit-Montrouge, 1844-1864. Available in reprint from Brepols. *Patrologia Latina Database* available on compact disk from Chadwyck-Healey, Inc., Alexandria, Virginia.

Ussher James Ussher. *Gotteschalci, et praedestinatianae controversiae ab eo motae historia: una cum duplice ejusdem confessione, nunc primum in lucem edita.* Dublin, 1631.

Hannover, 1662. In Volume 4 of Charles Richard Elrington, ed., *The Whole Works of the Most Rev. James Ussher, D.D.*, 16 vols. Dublin: Hodges, Smith, and Co., 1864.

PRIMARY SOURCES

Amolo of Lyons. *De gratia et praescientia Dei.* PL 116:101-6.

______. *Epistola ad Gothescalcum.* MGH, Epist. 5:368-78; PL 116:84-96.

Annales Bertiniani. MGH, Scriptores rerum Germanicorum in usum scholarum separatim editi, 5. George Waitz, ed.; F. Grat, J. Vielliard, and S. Clemencet, eds, *Annales de Saint-Bertin.* Paris, 1964; English: Janet L. Nelson, trans. *The Annals of St-Bertin.* Manchester and New York: Manchester University Press, 1991.

Annales Fuldenses. MGH, Scriptores rerum Germanicorum in usum scholarum separatim editi, 7. Friedrich Kurze, ed.; English: Timothy Reuter, trans., *The Annals of Fulda.* New York: Manchester University Press, 1992.

Annales Xantenses. MGH, Scriptores rerum Germanicorum in usum scholarum separatim editi, 12. Bernard von Simson, ed.

Capitula conventiculi Carisiaci. Mansi, 14:919-22; PL 121:1085-6; 125:63-4; English: Henry Denzinger, *The Sources of Catholic Dogma.* Roy J. Deferrari, trans. Saint Louis: Herder, 1957, 126-7.

Capitula synodi Tullensis. PL 125:60-3.

Concilii Valentini canones. Mansi, 15:1-15; Ussher, 172-84. English: Denzinger, *Sources of Catholic Dogma*, 127-32.

Decreta seu canones synodi Lingonensis. Mansi, 15:537-42.

Erigena, John Scot. *De divina praedestinatione.* CCCM 50. Goulven Madec, ed.; PL 122:347-440. English: John Scottus Eriugena, *Treatise on Divine Predestination.* Mary Brennan, trans. Introduction by Avital Wohlman. Notre Dame, Indiana: University of Notre Dame Press, 1998.

Flodoard of Reims. *Historia Remesis ecclesiae.* PL 135:23-328.

Florus of Lyons. *Adversus Iohannis Scoti Erigenae erroneas definitiones liber.* PL 119:101-250.

______. *B. Augustini sententiae de praedestinatione et gratia, et de libero hominis arbitrio.* PL 116:105-40 (attributed to Amolo).

______. *Liberllus de tendenda immobiliter scripturae veritate.* PL 121:1083-134 (attributed to Remigius).

______. *Liber de tribus epistolis.* PL 121:985-1068 (attributed to Remigius). English: "A Reply to the Three Letters (Selections)" (attributed to Remigius). In George E. McCracken, ed. *Early Medieval Theology.* Library of Christian Classics 9. Philadelphia: Westminster, 1957, 148-75.

______. *Sermo de praedestinatione.* PL 116:97-100 (attributed to Amolo); PL 119:95-102; 125:57-9; *S. ecclesiae Lugdunensis seu S. Remigii archiepiscopi et Flori diaconi ecclesiae Lugdunesis libri quattuor de gratia et praedestinatione : accendunt primi sex canones Concilii Valenrini III., S. Prudentii Ep. Trecensis Recapitulatio operis sui de praedestinatione, Flori Sermo de praedestinatione, & epistola ejusdem, ut videtur, Flori.* Pietro Francesco Foggini, ed. Rome : M. Palearinium, 1771. English: "Sermo Flori De Praedestinatione, Sicut Est De Ebonis Scrinio Sumptus." In Henry Newland, *A Practical and Exegetical Commentary on the Epistle of St. Paul to the Ephesians.* Oxford and London: J. H. and James Parker, 1860, 15-20.

Gottschalk of Orbais. *Carmina.* MGH, Poetae, 1:623-4; 3:707-38; 4:934-6; 6:228-46. English: The poems "Why Are You Demanding?" (Ut quid jubes?) and "O my guardian," in Godman, *Poetry of the Carolingian Renaissance,* 228-46. Italian: In Francesco Stella, *La Poesia carolingia.* Florence, Italy: Casa editrice le lettere, 1995.

______. *Chartula suae professionis ad Rabanum episcopum.* Lambot, 38; PL 121:368. English: Dutton, *Carolingian Civilization,* 50; Hanko, "Gotteschalk's Doctrine of Double Predestination," 63; Roberts, "A Translation and Critical Edition of Ratramnus of Corbie's De Predestinatione Dei," 6; Gardner, *Studies in John the Scot,* 59.

______. *Confessio brevior.* Lambot, 52-4; PL 121:347-50; Mauguin, 7; Ussher, 211-3. English: Hanko, "Gotteschalk's Doctrine of Double Predestination," 42-3.

______. *Confessio prolixior.* Lambot, 55-78; PL 121:349-66; Ussher, 211-33; Mauguin, 9ff. English: Hanko, "Gotteschalk's Doctrine of Double Predestination," 44-61.

______. *De corpore et sanguine domini.* Lambot, 324-37.

______. *De diversis.* Lambot, 294-324.

______. *De praedestinatione.* Lambot, 180-258.

______. *De praedestinatione, alternus liber.* Lambot, 338-46.

______. *Epistola ad Lupum.* MGH, Poetae, 3:723-4.

______. *Epistola ad Ratramnum.* PL 121:367-72.

______. *Epistola inedita.* (to Ebbo) Cyrille Lambot, "Lettre inédite de Godescalc d'Orbais." *Revue Bénédictine* 68 (1958):41-51.

______. *Fragmenta et testimonia.* Lambot, 5-46.

______. *Quaestiones de anima.* Lambot, 283-94.

______. *Quibus modis dicatur redemptio.* Lambot, 279-82.

______. *Responsa de diversis.* Lambot, 130-79.

______. *Responsum ad Rabanum Maurum, fragmenta.* Lambot, 36-44; PL 121:365-8. English: Hanko, "Gotteschalk's Doctrine of Double Predestination," 62-3.

______. *Tomus ad Giselmarum, fragmenta.* Lambot, 9, 41-4.

Hatto of Fulda. *Epistola ad Otgarium.* MGH, Epist. 5:529-30.

Hincmar of Reims. *Annales, sive annalium Bertinianorum pars tertia.* PL 125:1203-1302.

______. *De praedestinatione Dei et libero arbitrio posterior dissertation adversus Gottschalcum et caeteros praedestinatianos.* PL 125:65-474.

______. *De una et non trina deitate.* PL 125:473-618.

_____. *Ecclesiastica sententia in pertinacissimum Gotescalcum.* In Wilhelm Gundlach, "Zwei Schriften des Erzbischofs Hinkmar von Reims," *Zeitschrift für Kirchengeschichte* 10 (1889):258-309 at 308-9; Ussher, 61; Mansi, 14:921.

_____. *Epistola ad Amolonem archiepiscopum Lugdunensem, compendium et excerpta.* Lambot, 15-6; PL 121:987-8.

_____. *Epistola ad ecclesiam Lugdunensem, excerpta.* PL 121:1027.

_____. *Epistola ad Carolum regem priori ejus Praedestinatianos Operi praefixa.* PL 125:49-56.

_____. *Epistola ad Egilonem* (Ep. IX). PL 126:68-71.

_____. *Epistola ad Egilonem* (Ep. X). PL 126:71-6.

_____. *Epistola ad Nicolaum papam.* PL 126:25-46.

_____. *Epistola ad Rodulfum Bituricensem et Frotarium Burdigalensem, metropolitanos Aquitaniae.* PL 126:132-53.

_____. *Epistola ad reclusos et simplices suae dioeceseos.* Wilhelm Gundlach, "Zwei Schriften des Erzbischofs Hinkmar von Reims." *Zeitschrift für Kirchengeschichte,* 10 (1889):258-309; Excerpts in Lambot, 8-10.

_____. *Epistula concilii Tusiacensis ad rerum ecclesiasticarum pervasores et ad pauperum praedatores.* PL 126:122-32.

Lupus of Ferrières. *Collectaneum de tribus quaestionibus.* PL 119:647-66.

_____. *Epistola ad dominum regem.* PL 119:601-5. English: Regenos, *Letters of Lupus of Ferrières,* 86-91.

_____. *Epistola ad Eginhardum.* PL 119:429-36.

_____. *Epistola ad Godescalcum.* MGH, Epist. 5:36-9; PL 119:491-5; *Loup de Ferrières, Correspondance,* Vol. 2. Léon Levillain, ed. Paris: H. Champion, 1935, 42-55. Excerpts in Lambot, 7. English: Regenos, 94-8.

_____. *Epistola ad Hincmarum.* PL 119:606-8. English: Regenos, 91-4.

_____. *Liber de tribus quaestionibus.* PL 119:619-48.

Prudentius of Troyes. *De praedestinatione contra Joannem Scotum.* PL 115:1009-366.

_____. *Epistula ad Hincmarum et Pardulum.* PL 115:971-1010.

_____. *Epistula tractoria ad Venilonem* (cover letter for *De praedestinatione*). PL 115:1265-8; 125:64-6. English: Gumerlock, "The *Tractoria* of Prudentius of Troyes (d. 861).

_____. *Epistula tractoria ad Venilonem.* PL 115:1365-8; 125:64-6.

Rabanus Maurus. *De oblatione puerorum.* PL 107:419-40.

_____. *De praedestinatione.* PL 112:1531-53.

_____. *Epistola ad Notingum.* MGH, Epist. 5:428; PL 112:1530-1; Excerpt in Lambot, 5. English: Dutton, *Carolingian Civilization,* 49-50.

_____. *Epistola ad Eberhardum.* MGH, Epist. 5:481-7; PL 112:1553-62; Excerpts in Lambot, 5-6.

_____. *Epistola ad Hincmarum Remensem.* (VIII) MGH, Epist. 5:487-90; PL 112:1574-6; Excerpts in Lambot, 11-12.

_____. *Epistola ad Hincmarum Remensem.* (IV) MGH, Epist. 5:490-9; PL 112:1518-30; Excerpts in Lambot, 12-13.

_____. *Epistola synodalis, ad Hincmarum archiepiscopum Rhemensem de Gothescalco.* PL 112:1574-6; Mansi, 14:914-5.

Ratramnus of Corbie. *Contra Graecorum opposita.* PL 121:223-346.

_____. *De praedestinatione Dei.* PL 121:11-80. English: Timothy Roland Roberts, "A Translation and Critical Edition of Ratramnus of Corbie's De Predestinatione Dei." Ph.D. diss. University of Missouri-Columbia, 1977.

Remigius of Lyons. *Absolutio cuiusdam quaestionis de generali per Adam damantione omnium et speciali per Christum ex eadem ereptione electorum.* PL 121:1067-84.

Rimbert of Hamburg. *Vita Sancti Anshcarii.* PL 118:961-1012.

Walafrid Strabo. *Versus Gotescalco monacho, qui et Fulgentius.* MGH, Poetae, 2:362; PL 114:1115-7.

SECONDARY SOURCES

Gottschalk and the Predestination Controversy

Aegerter, Emmanuel. "Gottschalk et le problème de la prédestination au IXe siècle," *Revue de l'histoire des religions,* 116 (1937):187-233.

Amann, Émile. "La controverse prédestinatienne." In Augustin Fliche and Victor Martin, eds., *Histoire de l'église depuis les origines jusqu'à nos jours.* Paris: Bloud and Gay, 1947, 320-44.

_____. "Loup Servat" and "Prédestinatianisme." In *Dictionnaire de théologie catholique.* Paris: Letouzey et Ané, 1920, 963-7, 2803-9.

Bischoff, Bernhard. "Gottschalks Lied für den reichenauer Freund." In *Medium Aevum Vivum: Festschrift für Walther Bulst.* Hans Robert Jauss and Dieter Schaller, eds. Heidelberg: C. Winter, 1960, 61-8.

Boller, Bernard. *Gottschalk d'Orbais de Fulda à Hautvillers: une dissidence.* Préface de Michel Wieviorka. Paris: Société des Écrivains, 2004.

Borrasch, Victor. *Der Mönch Gottschalk von Orbais: sein Leben und seine Lehre.* Thorn, [no publisher given], 1868.

Bouhot, Jean-Paul. "Le *De divina praedestinatione* de Jean Scot." *Revue des études augustiniennes* 25 (1979):256-63.

_____. *Ratramnus de Corbie: Histoire littéraire et controverses doctrinales.* Paris: Études Augustiniennes, 1976.

Cappuyns, Maïeul. *Jean Scot Erigène. Sa vie, son oeuvre, sa pensée.* Louvain : Abbaye du Mont César, 1933.

Cellot, Louis. *Historia Gotteschalci praedestinatiani.* Paris: Sêbastien Mabre-Cramoisy, 1655.

Charlier, Célestin. "Les manuscrits personnels de Florus de Lyon et son activité littéraire." In *Mélanges E. Podechard.* Lyon: Facultés Catholiques, 1945, 71-84.

Châtillon, F. Review of Cyrille Lambot's *Oeuvres théologiques et grammaticales de Godescalc d'Orbais. Revue du moyen âge latin* 5 (1949):255-72.

Christiani, Marta. "La notion de loi dans le 'De praedestinatione' de Jean Scot." In *Jean Scot Érigène et l'histoire de la philosophie,* 277-88.

Cross, Frank Leslie and Elizabeth A. Livingstone, eds. "Gottschalk" In *The Oxford Dictionary of the Christian Church.* New York : Oxford University Press, 1997, 696.

Crouse, Robert. "Predestination, Human Freedom and the Augustinian Theology of History in Eriugena's *De Divina Praedestinatione,*" in James McEvoy and Michael Dunne, eds., *History and Eschatology in John Scottus Eriugena and His Time.* Leuven: University Press, 2002, 303-11.

Cruz, A. Etchegaray. "L'*enarratio* Augustinienne sur le Ps. 50 et *O Deus, miseri* de Gottschalk d'Orbais," *Studia Patristica,* 17.3 (1982):1245-50.

Devisse, Jean. *Hincmar archevêque de Reims 845-882.* 3 vols. Geneva: Librairie Droz, 1975-1976.

Diem, Albrecht. "Een Verstoorder Van De 'Ordo': Gottschalk Van Orbais En Zijn Leer Van De Dubble Predestinatie." In Mayke de Jong, Marie-Therese Bos, and Carine van Rijn, eds. *Macht Et Gezag in De IXde Eeuw.* Utrechtse Historische Cahiers 16. Hilversum: Verloren, 1995, 115-31.

Dinkler, Erich. *Gottschalk der Sachse.* Stuttgart: W. Kahlhammer, 1936.

Dörries, Hermann. *Gottschalk, ein christlicher Zeuge der deutschen Frühzeit.* Göttingen: Franz-Seldte, 1939.

Du Bout, Nicholas. *Histoire de l'abbaye d'Orbais.* Paris: A. Picard; Rheims: F. Michaud, 1890.

Estes, Heide. "Gottschalk of Orbais (c. 804-869)." In Jana K. Schulman, ed., *The Rise of the Medieval World 500-1300: A Biographical Dictionary.* Westport, CT: Greenwood, 2002, 171-2.

Evans, Gillian R. "The Grammar of Predestination in the Ninth Century." *Journal of Theological Studies,* N.S., 33.1 (1982):134-45.

Evert, Boyd Harry. "Gottschalk of Orbais and the Debate over Predestination in the Ninth Century." Master's thesis. University of Dallas, 1994.

Fickermann, Norbert. "Wiedererkannte Dichtungen Gottschalks." *Revue Bénédictine* 44 (1932):314-21.

Freystedt, Albert. "Der Ausgang des Prädestinationsstreites im 9 Jahrhundert." *Zeitschrift für wissenschaftliche Theologie* 41 (1898):112-35.

_____. "Gottschalk, der Monch." In *Encyclopädie für protestantische Theologie und Kirche,* Vol. 7. Leipzig: Hinrichs, 1889, 39-41.

_____. "Der Streit über die göttliche Trinität im 9. Jahrhundert." *Zeitschrift für wissenschaftliche Theologie* 41 (1898):392-401.

_____. "Studien zu Gottschalks Leben und Lehre" Parts 1-3. *Zeitschrift für Kirchengeschichte* 18 (1897/1898): 1-22, 161-81, 529-45.

_____. "Der Synodale Kampf im Prädestinationsstreit der 9. Jahrhunderts in den Jahren 853 bis 860." *Zeitschrift für wissenschaftliche Theologie* 36 (1893):447-78.

_____. "Der wissenschaftliche Kampf im Prädestinationsstreit des 9. Jahrhunderts." *Zeitschrift für wissenschaftliche Theologie* 36 (1893):315-68.

Ganz, David. *Corbie in the Carolingian Renaissance*. Sigmaringen, Germany: Jan Thorbecke, 1990.

_____. "The Debate on Predestination." In Gibson and Nelson, *Charles the Bald*, 283-302.

Gardner, Alice. *Studies in John the Scot (Erigena)*. London: Henry Frowde, 1900.

Gaudard, Frédéric J. *Gottschalk moine d'Orbais; ou, le commencement de la controverse sur la prédestination au IXe siècle*. Saint-Quentin: J.Moureau, 1887.

Genke, Victor. "Gotshalk (um. 868 g.) i ego uchenie o predopredelenii." In Makarov, Dmitry, ed. *Problemy teologii. Vypusk 4. Materialy chetvertoy mezhdunarodnoy bogoslovskoy nauchno-prakticheskoy konferentsii 14 fevralya 2007 g.* Ekaterinburg, 2007, 94-114.

_____. "Gotshalk iz Orbe. Molitva Khristu-Vesam." In *Acta eruditorum. Nauchnye doclady i soobshcheniya* 4 (2007):90-1.

_____. "Gotshalk pri dvore Trpimira I." In Pervushkin, V. I., ed. *Istoricheskije zapiski. Mezhvuzovskij sbornik nauchnykh trudov*. Penza, 2007, 3-6.

_____. "Spor o predopredelenii v kontekste tserkovno-politicheskikh protivorechiy v epokhu karolingov." In *Aktual'nye problemy gumanitarnykh i estestvennykh nauk* 4 (2009):50-4.

Gibson, Margaret T. and Janet L. Nelson, eds. *Charles the Bald. Court and Kingdom*, 2nd ed. Brookfield, VT: Variorum, 1990.

Gillis, Matthew Bryan. "Gottschalk of Orbais: A Study of Spirituality and Power in a Ninth-Century Life," diss. University of Virginia, 2009.

Godet, Philippe. "Florus" and "Gotescale ou Gottschalk." In *Dictionnaire de théologie catholique*, Vol. 6. Paris: Letouzey et Ané, 1920, 53-5, 1500-2.

Godman, Peter, ed., *Poetry of the Carolingian Renaissance*. Norman, OK: University of Oklahoma Press, 1985.

Gorman, Michael M. "Harvard's Oldest Latin Manuscript (Houghton Library, fMS Typ 495). A Patristic Miscellany from the Predestinarian Controversy of the Ninth Century." *Scriptorium* 39 (1985):185-96.

Gumerlock, Francis X. "Gottschalk of Orbais: A Medieval Predestinarian." *Kerux* 22:3 (Dec 2007):17-34.

_____. "Predestination in the Century Before Gottschalk, " Parts 1 & 2. *Evangelical Quarterly* 81:3 (July 2009):195-209; 81:4 (Oct 2009):319-37.

_____. "The *Tractoria* of Prudentius of Troyes (d. 861)," *Kerux* 25:1 (May 2010):11-23.

Günther, Max Hermann Rudolf Gerhard. "Der Mönch Gottschalk." *Deutsche Volkstum* (1928): 264-7.

Gustavsson, Louise Reinecke. "Gottschalk Reconsidered: A Study of His Thought as It Bears on His Notion of Predestination." Ph.D. diss. Yale University, 1964.

Hanko, Herman. "Rabanus and the Victory of Semi-Pelagianism." (Part 1) *Standard Bearer* 76 (January 15, 2000):179-81; (Part 2) *Standard Bearer* 76 (February 1, 2000):206-8.

Hanko, Ronald. "Gottschalk's Doctrine of Double Predestination," *Protestant Reformed Theological Journal*, 12.1 (1978):31-64.

Hartmann, Wilfried. "Die Mainzer Synoden des Hrabanus Maurus." In Kottje and Zimmermann, *Hrabanus Maurus*, 130-44.

Herding, Otto. "Über die Dichtungen Gottschalks von Fulda." In *Festschrift Paul Kluckhohn und Hermann Schneider gewidmet zu ihrem 60 Geburtstag*. Tübingen: Mohr, 1948, 46-72.

"Hincmar et le concile de Valence dans l'affaire de Godescalc." [no author listed] *Analecta juris pontificalis* 7e serie, 61 e liv. (1864) :540-63.

Hottinger, Johann Jakob. *Diatribe historico-theologica, qua praedestinatianam et Godescalci pseudohaereses commenta esse demonstratur*. Zurich : Typis Heideggeri et Rahnii, 1718.

Jean Scot Érigène et l'histoire de la philosophie. [editor not listed] Colloques Internationaux du Centre National de la Recherche Scientifique, No. 561. Paris: Éditions du Centre National de la Recherche Scientifique, 1977.

Johnson, Gregory. "A Bibliographical Review of Historiography on Gottschalk." Paper, Saint Louis University, 1999.

Jolivet, Jean. "L'enjeu de la grammaire pour Godescalc," in *Jean Scot Érigène et l'histoire de la philosophie*, 79-87.

_____. *Godescalc d'Orbais et la trinité: la méthode de la théolgie à l'époque carolingienne*. Paris: J. Vrin, 1958.

Kadner, D. "Aus den neuentdeckten Traktaten des Mönches Gottschalk." *Zeitschrift für Kirchengeschichte* 61 (1942) :348-58.

Kagerah, Walter. "Bisher unbekannte Worte des Mönches Gottschalk." *Die Wartburg* 36 (1937) : 80-4.

_____. "Gottschalk der Sachse." *Die Wartburg* 34 (1935) :386-91.

_____. "Gottschalk der Sachse." Diss. Greifswald, 1938.

_____. *Gottschalk der Sachse: ein Gottsucher aus deutscher Frühzeit*. Berlin: Evangel. Bundes, 1936.

Katić, Lovre. "Saksonac Gottschalk na dvoru kneza Trpimira." *Bogoslovska Smotra* 30 (1932), 403-32.

Kottje, Raymund and Harald Zimmerman, eds. *Hrabanus Maurus. Lehrer, Abt und Bischof*. Wiesbaden: Steiner, 1982.

Lambot, Cyrille. "Godescalco d'Orbais." In *Enciclopedia Cattolica*, Vol. 6. Vatican City : Ente per l'Enciclopedia cattolica e per il Libro cattolico, 1951, 888-9.

_____. "Opuscules grammaticaux de Gottschalk." *Revue Bénédictine* 44 (1932) :120-4. Lavaud, Benoît. "Précurseur de Calvin ou témoin de l'augustinisme? Le cas de Godescalc." *Revue thomiste* 15 (1932), 71-101.

_____."Prédestination. IV. La controverse sur la prédestination au IXe siècle," *Dictionnaire de théologie catholique*, Vol. 12. Paris: Letouzey et Ané, 1935, 2901-35.

Manitius, Max."Zu Johannes Scottus und Remigius." *Didaskaleion* 2 (1913):43-88.

Marenbon, John."John Scottus and Carolingian Theology: From the *De Praedestinatione*, Its Background and Its Critics, to the *Periphyseon*." In Gibson and Nelson, *Charles the Bald*, 303-25.

McKeon, Peter R. "The Carolingian Councils of Savonnières (859) and Tusey (860) and Their Background," *Revue Bénédictine*, 84 (1974):75-110.

Monnier, F. "De Gothescalci et Johannis Scoti Erigenae controversia." Diss. Paris, 1853.

Moran, Dermot. *The Philosophy of John Scottus Eriugena*. New York: Cambridge University Press, 1989.

Morin, Germain. "Gottschalk retrouvé," *Revue Bénédictine*, 43 (1931):303-12.

Navarro Giron, Maria-Angeles. *La Carne De Cristo. El Misterio Eucaristico a La Luz De La Controversia Entre Pascasio Radberto, Ratramno, Rabano Mauro Y Godescalco.* Publicaciones De La Universidad Pontificia Comillas. S. I. Estudios 44. Madrid: Universidad Pontificia Comillas ad Madrid, 1989.

Niemeijer, Cornelis Johan. *De strijd over de leer der praedestinatie in de IXde eeuw.* Groningen: Gerbroeders Hoitsema, 1889.

Nineham, Dennis Eric. "Gottschalk of Orbais: Reactionary or Precursor of the Reformation?" *Journal of Ecclesiastical History*, 40.1 (1989):1-18.

Noris, Enrico. *Historiae Gothescalcanae synopsis*. In his *Opera omnia*, Vol. 4. Verona: Tumermaniana, 1729; Venice: Typographia Bassanensi, 1769.

O'Donnell, J. M. "Gottschalk of Orbais." In *New Catholic Encyclopedia*, 2nd ed. Vol. 6. New York: Thomson, 2003, 371-2.

O' Meara, John Joseph. *Eriugena*. Oxford: Clarendon Press, 1988.

Perugi, Giuseppe Ludovico. *Gottschalc*. Rome: Athenaeum, 1911.

Picavet, François. "Les discussions sur la liberté au temps de Gottschalk, de Raban

Maur, d'Hincmar et de Jean Scot." *Séances et travaux de l'Académie des Sciences morales et politiques* 145 (1896):644-69. Reprinted in François Picavet, *Esquisse d'une histoire générale et comparée des philosophies médiévales*. Paris, 1905, 136-50.

Prichard, James Cowles. *The Life and Times of Hincmar, archbishop of Rheims*. Littlemore: A. A. Masson, 1849.

Rädle, Fidel. "Gottschalk der Sachse." In *Die deutsche Literatur des Mittelalters, Verfasserlexikon*, Vol. 3. Berlin and New York, 1981, 189-99.

_____. "Gottschalks Gedicht an seinen letzen Freund." In Sigrid Krämer and Michael Bernhard, eds. *Scire Litteras. Forschungen zum mittelalterishen Geistesleben*. Munich: Bayerische Akademie der Wissenschaften 1988, 315-25.

Regenos, Graydon W., trans. *The Letters of Lupus of Ferrières*. The Hague: Martinus Nijhoff, 1966.

Roberts, Timothy Roland. "Gottschalk of Orbais." In Joseph R. Strayer, ed., *Dictionary of the Middle Ages*, Vol. 5. New York: Charles Scribner's Sons, 1985, 638-9.

______. "A Translation and Critical Edition of Ratramnus of Corbie's De Predestinatione Dei," Ph.D. diss. University of Missouri-Columbia, 1977.

Rosa, E. "Il Monaco Gottescalco e la controversia predestinaziona." *La civiltà cattolica* 62 (1911), 188-201.

Schrimpf, Gangolf. "Der Beitrag des Johannes Scottus zum Prädestinationsstreit." In Heinz Löwe, ed. *Die Iren und Europa im früheren Mittelalter*, Vol. 2. Stuttgart: Klett-Cotta, 1982, 819-65.

______. "Die ethischen Implikationen der Auseinandersetzung zwischen Hraban und Gottschalk um die Prädestinationslehre." In Winfried Böhne, ed. *Hrabanus Maurus und seine Schule*. Fulda: Rabanus Maurus Schule, 1980, 164-74.

______. "Hraban und der Prädestinationsstreit des 9. Jahrhunderts." In Kottje and Zimmermann, *Hrabanus Maurus*, 145-53.

Schrörs, Heinrich. *Hinkmar, Erzbischof von Reims; sein Leben und seine Schriften*. Freiburg: Herder, 1884; Hildesheim: G. Olms, 1967.

______. *Der Streit über die Prädestination im IX. Jahrhundert*. Freiburg: Herder, 1884.

Sirmond, Jacques. *Historia praedestinatiana*. Paris: Sébastien et Gabriel Cramoisy frères, 1648.

Stegmüller, Otto. "Martin von Tours oder Gottschalk von Orbais." *Revue Bénédictine* 76 (1966), 177-230.

Tavard, George H. *Trina Deitas. The Controversy between Hincmar and Gottschalk*. Milwaukee: Marquette University Press, 1996.

Troube, Lüdwig. *Prooemium* to *Godescalci Carmina*. MGH, *Poetae Latini Aevi Carolini*, 3:707-22.

Turmel, Joseph. "La controverse prédestinatienne au IXe siècle." *Revue d'histoire de la littérature religieuse* 10 (1905):47-69.

Veldman, Henry. 'The Doctrine of Sin. The Third Period-730-1517 A.D. Gottschalk.' *The Standard Bearer* 45 (1968-69): 114-6, 138-40, 160-2, 204-6, 233-5.

Vielhaber, Klaus. *Gottschalk der Sachse*. Bonner historische Forschungen, 5. Bonn: L. Röhrscheid, 1956.

Weber, Marie-Luise. *Die Gedichte des Gottschalk von Orbais*. Frankfurt: P. Lang, 1992.

Weizsacker, J. "Das Dogma von der göttlichen Vorherbestimmung im neunten Jahrhundert." *Jahrbücher für Deutsche Theologie* 4 (1859):527-76.

Wiggers, Gustav Friedrich. "Schicksale der augustinischen Anthropologie von der Verdammung des Semipelagionismus auf dem Synoden zu Orange und Valence 529 bis zur Reaction des Mönchs Gottschalk für den Augustinismus. Fünfte Abteilung: Der Mönch Gottschalk." *Zeitschrift für die historische Theologie* 29 (1859):471-594.

Wohlman, Avital. "Introduction to the English translation." In *John Scottus Eriugena, Treatise on Divine Predestination*. Mary Brennan, trans. Notre Dame, Indiana: University of Notre Dame Press, 1998.

Zechiel-Eckes, Klaus. "Die Kontroverse um die göttliche Prädestination." In his *Florus von Lyon als Kirchenpolitiker und Publizist*. Stuttgart: Thorbecke, 1999, 77-177.

RELATED WORKS

Augustine, Saint. *The City of God*. Marcus Dods, trans. New York: Random House, 1950.

______. *The Enchiridion on Faith, Hope, and Love*. Henry Paolucci, ed. Chicago: Regnery Gateway, 1961.

______. *On Christian Teaching*. R.P.H. Green ed. and trans. Oxford: Clarendon, 1995.

______. *The Retractations*. Sr. Mary Inez Bogan, trans. FC 60. Washington, D.C.: Catholic University of America Press, 1968.

Basnage de Beauval, Jacques. *Histoire de l'Eglise*. Rotterdam: Reinier Leers, 1699.

Bede the Venerable. *Excerpts from the Works of Saint Augustine on the Letters of the Blessed Apostle Paul*. David Hurst, trans. Kalamazoo, MI: Cistercian Publications, 1999.

Beeson, Charles Henry. *Lupus of Ferrières as Scribe and Text Critic*. Cambridge, MA: Mediaeval Academy of America, 1930.

Bernino, Domenico. *Historia di tutte l'heresie*. Venice: Stamperia Baglioni, 1724.

Bishop, Jane Carol. "Pope Nicholas I and the First Age of Papal Independence." Ph.D. diss. Columbia University, 1980.

Brennan, Mary. *A Bibliography of Publications in the Field of Eriugenian Studies 1800-1975*. Spoleto: Centro Italiano di Studi sull'Alto Medioevo, 1977.

______. *A Guide to Eriugenian Studies. A Survey of Publications 1930-1987*. Paris: Éditions du Cerf, 1989.

Bright, Pamela. *The Book of Rules of Tyconius : Its Purpose and Inner Logic*. Notre Dame, IN : University of Notre Dame Press, 1988.

Brown, Howard Haines III. "Archbishop Hincmar of Rheims (circa 806-882): His Idea of Ministerium in Theory and Praxis." Ph.D. diss. Michigan State University, 1968.

Bunson, Matthew E. *Encyclopedia of the Middle Ages*. New York: Facts on File, Inc., 1995.

Butler, Cuthbert. *Benedictine Monachism: Studies in Benedictine Life and Rule*. London: Longmans, Green, and Co., 1924.

Cabaniss, Allen. "Florus of Lyons." *Classica et Mediaevalia* 19 (1958):212-32.

Chisholm, John E., ed. *The Pseudo-Augustinian Hypomnesticon Against the Pelagians and Celestians*, 2 vols. Fribourg: University Press, 1980.

Daniel, Curt D. "Hyper-Calvinism and John Gill." Ph.D. diss. University of Edinburgh, 1983; Bound reprint: Springfield, IL: Good Books, 2007.

Denzinger, Henry. *The Sources of Catholic Dogma*. Roy J. Deferrari, trans. Saint Louis: Herder, 1957.

Dods, Marcus, trans. *The Works of Aurelius Augustine*. Edinburgh: T & T Clark, 1872.

Duckett, Eleanor Shipley. *Carolingian Portraits: A Study of the Ninth Century*. Ann Arbor: University of Michigan Press, 1962.

Du Fresne du Cange, Charles. *Glossarium ad Scriptores Mediae et Infimae Latinitatis*. Paris. Librarie des sciences et des arts; Stockholm: G. Rönnell, 1938.

Dutton, Paul Edward. *Carolingian Civilization. A Reader*. Petersborough, Ontario: Broadview, 1993.

Evans, Gillian R. *Fifty Key Medieval Thinkers*. New York: Routledge, 2002.

Fanning, John Edward. "Sacramentality in the Marriage Doctrine of Hincmar of Rheims." Diss. Rome: Pontificia Universitas Gregoriana, 1993.

Farrelly, M. John. *Predestination, Grace, and Free Will*. Westminster, Maryland: Newman Press, 1964.

Fransen, Peter. *Divine Grace and Man*. New York: New American Library, 1965.

Fulgentius. *Selected Works*. Robert B. Eno, trans. FC 95.

Gariépy, Robert J. *Lupus of Ferrières and the Classics*. Darien, CT: Monographic Press, 1967.

Garrigou-Langrange, R. *Predestination*. Saint Louis: Herder, 1953.

Gersh, Stephen. "Per Se Ipsum. The Problem of Immediate and Mediate Causation in Eriugena and his Neoplatonic Predecessors." In *Jean Scot Érigène et l'histoire de la philosophie*, 367-76.

Gumerlock, Francis X. *Fulgentius of Ruspe on the Saving Will of God: TheDevelopment of a Sixth-Century African Bishop's Interpretation of 1 Timothy 2:4 During the Semi-Pelagian Controversy*. Lewiston, NY: Edwin Mellen, 2009.

Hefele, Karl Josef von. *Histoire des conciles d'après les documents originaux*. Paris: Letouzey et Ané, 1911.

Hercigonja, Eduard. *Tropismena i trojezična kultura hrvatskoga srednjovjekovlja*. Zagreb: Matica hrvatska, 1994.

Hottinger, Johann Jakob. *Fata doctrinae de praedestinatione et gratia Dei salutari*. Zurich: Typis Heideggeri et Rahnii, 1727.

Houwen, L. A. J. R. and A. A. MacDonald, eds. *Alcuin of York. Scholar at the Carolingian Court*. Groningen: Egbert Forsten, 1998.

Jong Mayke, de. "From Scolastici to Scioli: Alcuin and the Formation of an Intellectual Élite." In Houwen and MacDonald, *Alcuin of York*, 45-57.

Katičić, Radoslav. *Litterarum studia. Književnost i naobrazba ranoga hrvatskog srednjovjekovlja*. Zagreb: Matica hrvatska, 1998.

Kiš, Antonija Zaradija. *Sveti Martin: Kult sveca i njegova tradicija u Hrvatskoj*. Zagreb: Institut za etnologiju i folkloristiku, 2004.

Kohake, Cletus Paul. "The Life and Educational Writings of Rabanus Maurus." Ph.D. diss. Cornell University, 1948.

Köhler, Ernst. *Hrabanus Maurus und die Schule zu Fulda*. Chemnitz: Druck von J.C.F. Pickenhahn und Sohn, 1870.

Laistner, Max L. W. "Fulgentius in the Carolingian Age." In his *The Intellectual Heritage of the Early Middle Ages: Selected Essays*. 1957. Reprint, New York: Octagon, 1972, 202-15.

Landes, Paula Fredriksen. *Augustine On Romans*. Chico, CA: Scholars Press, 1982.

Lesne, Emile. "Hincmar et l'empereur Lothaire." *Revue des questions historiques* 34 (1905):5-58.

Manceaux, Jean Baptiste. *Histoire de l'abbaye et du village d'Hautvillers*, Vol. 1. Epernay, France: L. Doublat, 1880.

Mathisen, Ralph W. *Ecclesiastical Factionalism and Religious Controversy in Fifth-Century Gaul*. Washington, D.C.: Catholic University of America Press, 1989.

Matter, E. Ann. "Florus of Lyon." In William W. Kibler and Grover A. Zinn, eds. *Medieval France: An Encyclopedia*. New York: Garland, 1995, 354.

Maurer, Konrad von. *Die Bekehrung des Norwegischen Stammes zum Christentume*, Vol. 1. Munich: Kaiser, 1855.

McCracken, George E., ed. and trans. *Early Medieval Theology*. Library of Christian Classics 9. London: SCM, 1957.

McGinn, Bernard and Willemein Otten, eds. *Eriugena: East and West*. Notre Dame, Indiana: University of Notre Dame Press, 1991.

McKeon, Peter R. *Hincmar of Laon and Carolingian Politics*. Urbana, IL: University of Illinois Press, 1978.

McKetterick, Rosamond. *The Frankish Kingdoms under the Carolingians, 751-987*. New York: Longmans, 1983.

Most, William G. *Grace, Predestination, and the Salvific Will of God. New Answers to Old Questions*. Front Royal, VA: Christendom, 1997.

Moxon, Reginald Stewart. *The Doctrine of Sin. A Critical and Historical Investigation into the Views of the Concept of Sin Held in Early Christian, Mediaeval & Modern Times*. London: Allen and Unwin, 1922.

Mozley, James Bowling. *A Treatise on the Augustinian Doctrine of Predestination*. London: J. Murray, 1855.

Nelson, Janet. *Charles the Bald*. London and New York: Longman, 1992.

Nusbaum, Daniel Charles. "Lupus of Ferrières: Scholar, Humanist, Monk." Ph.D. diss. Fordham University, 1977.

O'Keefe, Peter P. "A History of the Metropolitan Office at Rheims from Hincmar (845-882) to the Romana Ecclesia of Innocent IV (1243-1254)." Ph.D. diss. Fordham University, 1971.

O'Meara, John J. and Ludwig Bieler, eds. *The Mind of Eriugena*. Dublin: Irish University Press, 1973.

Origen. *Commentary on the Epistle to the Romans, Books 6-10*. Thomas P. Scheck, trans. FC 104.

Otten, Willemien. *The Anthropology of Johannes Scottus Eriugena*. Leiden: Brill, 1991.

______. "Carolingian Theology." In Gillian R. Evans, ed., *The Medieval Theologians*. Oxford: Blackwell, 2001, 65-82.

Palazzini, Pietro. *Dizionario dei concili*. Rome: Città Nuova Editrice, 1963.

Palmer, "Rimbert's *Vita Anskarii* and Scandinavian Mission in the Ninth Century," *Journal of Ecclesiastical History* 55 (2004):235-56.

Pelikan, Jaroslav. *The Christian Tradition. A History of the Development of Doctrine*. Vol. 3: The Growth of Medieval Theology (600-1300). Chicago and London: University of Chicago Press, 1978.

Peltier, Henri. "Raban Maur" and "Ratramne." In *Dictionnaire de théologie catholique*. Paris: Letouzey et Ané, 1920, 1600-20, 1780-7.

Pierquin, Abbé. *Histoire d'Hautvillers*. Manuscript in the Archives of the Academy of Reims, f. 4, 1853.

Prosper of Aquitaine. *Defense of St. Augustine*. Prudentius De Letter, trans. Ancient Christian Writers 32. New York: Newman, 1963.

Quantin, Jean-Louis. "Combat doctrinal et chasse à l'inédit au XVII siècle. Vignier, Quesnel et les sept livres contre Fauste de Fulgence de Ruspe." *Revue des Études Augustiniennes* 44 (1998):269-97.

Raby, Frederic J. E. *History of Christian-Latin Poetry*. Oxford: Clarendon, 1953.

Rainbow, Jonathan Herbold. "Redemptor Ecclesiae, Redemptor Mundi: An Historical and Theological Study of John Calvin's Doctrine of the Extent of Redemption." Ph.D. diss. University of California, Santa Barbara, 1986.

______. *The Will of God and the Cross: An Historical and Theological Study of John Calvin's Doctrine of Limited Redemption*. Allison Park, PA: Pickwick Publications, 1990.

Reinhart, Jürgen. *Fulda von allen Seiten*. Fulda: Parzeller, 1994.

Reinke, Edgar Carl. "The Latinity of the *Epistolae* of Hrabanus Maurus." Ph.D. diss. University of Chicago, 1936.

Schnitt, Anton. *Führer durch Fulda*. Fulda: Pazeller, 1995.

Šišić, Ferdo. *Povijest Hrvata u vrijeme narodnih vladara*. Zagreb: Nakladni zavod Matice hrvatske, 1925.

Souter, Alexander. *A Glossary of Later Latin*. Oxford: Clarendon, 1949.

Spelsberg, Helmut. *Hrabanus Maurus: Bibliographie*. Fulda: Hessische Landesbibliotek, 1984.

Taeger, Burkhard. *Zahlensymbolik bei Hraban, bei Hincmar und im Heliand?* Münich: Beck, 1970.

Tafel, Siegfried. "The Lyons Scriptorium." *Palaeographia Latina* 2 (1923):66-73; 4 (1925):40-70.

Turmel, Joseph. "Histoire de l'interprétation de I Tim. II,4," *Revue d'histoire et de littérature religieuses*, 5 (1900):385-415.

Van Riel, Gerd. "A Bibliographical Survey of Eriugenian Studies, 1987-1995." In Van Riel, et al. *Iohannes Scottus Eriugena*, 367-400.

Van Riel, Gerd, Carlos Steel, and James McEvoy, eds. *Iohannes Scottus Eriugena. The Bible and Hermeneutics*. Leuven: University Press, 1996.

Wallace-Hadrill, John M. *The Frankish Church*. Oxford: Clarendon, 1983.

Watson, George Ronald. "Theta nigrum." *Journal of Roman Studies* 42 (1952): 56-62.

West, Andrew Fleming. *Alcuin and the Rise of the Christian Schools*. New York: Charles Scribner's Sons, 1892.

RECOMMENDED WEB RESOURCES

http://francisgumerlock.com

Gumerlock, Francis X. Several journal articles on Gottschalk.

http://gottschalk.inrebus.com

Genke, Victor. "The Gottschalk Homepage." The "Primary Sources" section contains original Latin texts of several works translated in the present volume.

http://gregscouch.homestead.com

Johnson, Gregory. "A Bibliographical Review of Historiography on Gottschalk." Paper, Saint Louis University, 1999

http://public.csusm.edu/public/guests/rsclark/brevior.htm

Hanko, Robert. English translation of Gottschalk's *Shorter Confession*.

http://www.dmgh.de/index.html

Monumenta Germaniae Historica. Berlin, Germany: Weidmann, 1877-present.

INDICES

SCRIPTURE

CITATIONS OF EARLIER WRITERS

SUBJECTS

PLACES

MEDIÆVAL PHILOSOPHICAL TEXTS IN TRANSLATION
COMPLETE LIST

UNDER THE EDITORSHIP OF GERARD SMITH, SJ

Grosseteste. *On Light.* Clare Riedl, Tr. ISBN 0-87462-201-8 (Translation No. 1, 1942). 28 pp. $5.

St. Augustine. *Against the Academicians.* Mary Patricia Garvey, R.S.M., Tr. ISBN 0-87462-202-6. (Translation No. 2, 1942). 94 pp. $10

Pico Della Mirandola. *Of Being and Unity.* Victor M. Hamm, Tr. ISBN 0-87462-203-4. (Translation No. 3, 1943). 40 pp. $10

Francis Suarez. *On the Various Kinds of Distinctions.* Cyril Vollert, SJ, Tr. ISBN 0-87462-204-2. (Translation No. 4, 1947). 72 pp. $10

St. Thomas Aquinas. *On Spiritual Creatures.* Mary C. Fitzpatrick, Tr. ISBN 0-87462-205-0. (Translation No. 5, 1949). 144 pp. $15

Guigo. *Meditations of Guigo.* John J. Jolin, SJ, Tr. ISBN 0-87462-206-9. (Translation No. 6, 1951). 96 pp. $10

Giles of Rome. *Theorems on Existence and Essence.* Michael V. Murray, SJ, Tr. ISBN 0-87462-207-7. (Translation No. 7, 1953). 128 pp. $15

John of St. Thomas. *Outlines of Formal Logic.* Francis C. Wade, SJ, Tr. ISBN 0-87462-208-5. (Translation No. 8, 1955). 144 pp. $15

Hugh of St. Victor. *Soliloquy in the Earnest Money of the Soul.* Kevin Herbert, Tr. ISBN 0-87462-209-3. (Translation No. 9, 1956). 48 pp. $5

UNDER THE EDITORSHIP OF JAMES H. ROBB

St. Thomas Aquinas. *On Charity.* Lottie Kendzierski, Tr. ISBN 0-87462-210-7. (Translation No. 10, 1960). 120 pp. $15

Aristotle. *On Interpretation. Commentary by St. Thomas and Cajetan.* Jean T. Oesterle, Tr. ISBN 0-87462-211-5. (Translation No. 11, 1962). 288 pp. $20

Desiderius Erasmus of Rotterdam. *On Copia of Words and Ideas.* Donald B. King and H. David Rix, Tr. ISBN 0-87462-212-3. (Translation No. 12, 1963). 124 pp. $15

Peter of Spain. *Tractatus Syncategorematum and Selected Anonymous Treatises.* Joseph P. Mullally and Roland Houde, Tr. ISBN 0-87462-213-1. (Translation No. 13, 1964). 168 pp. $15

Cajetan. *Commentary on St. Thomas Aquinas' On Being and Essence.* Lottie Kendzierski and Francis C. Wade, SJ, Tr. ISBN 0-87462-214-X. (Translation No. 14, 1965). 366 pp. $20

Suárez. *Disputation VI, On Formal and Universal Unity.* James F. Ross, Tr. ISBN 0-87462-215-8. (Translation. No. 15, 1965). 132 pp. $15

St. Thomas, Siger de Brabant, St. Bonaventure. *On the Eternity of the World.* Cyril Vollert, SJ, Lottie Kendzierski, and Paul Byrne, Tr. ISBN 0-87462-216-6. (Translation No. 16, 1965). 132 pp. $15

Geoffrey of Vinsauf. *Instruction in the Method and Art of Speaking and Versifying.* Roger P. Parr, Tr. ISBN 0-87462-217-4. (Translation No. 17, 1968). 128 pp. $15

Liber De Pomo. *The Apple, or Aristotle's Death.* Mary F. Rousseau, Tr. ISBN 0-87462-218-2. (Translation No. 18, 1968). 96 pp. $5

St. Thomas Aquinas. *On the Unity of the Intellect against the Averroists.* Beatrice H. Zedler, Tr. ISBN 0-87462-219-0. (Translation No. 19, 1969). 96 pp. $10

Nicholas of Autrecourt. *The Universal Treatise.* Leonard L. Kennedy, CSB., Tr. ISBN 0-87462-220-4. (Translation No. 20, 1971). 174 pp. $15

Pseudo-Dionysius Areopagite. *The Divine Names and Mystical Theology*. John D. Jones, Tr. ISBN 0-87462-221-2. (Translation No. 21, 1980). 320 pp. $25

Matthew of Vendome. *Ars Versificatoria*. Roger P. Parr, Tr. ISBN 0-87462-222-0. (Translation No. 22, 1981). 150 pp. $15

Francis Suárez. *On Individuation*. Jorge J.E. Gracia, Tr. ISBN 0-87462-223-9. (Translation No. 23, 1982). 304 pp. $35

Francis Suárez. *On the Essence of Finite Being as Such, on the Existence of That Essence and Their Distinction*. Norman J. Wells, Tr. ISBN 0-87462-224-7. (Translation No. 24, 1983). 248 pp. $20

The Book of Causes (Liber De Causis). Dennis J. Brand, Tr. ISBN 0-87462-225-5. (Translation No. 25, 1984). 56 pp. $5

Giles of Rome. *Errores Philosophorum*. John O. Riedl, Tr. Intro. by Josef Koch. ISBN 0-87462-429-0. (Translation No. 26, 1944). 136 pp. $10

St. Thomas Aquinas. *Questions on the Soul*. James H. Robb, Tr. ISBN 0-87462-226-3. (Translation No. 27, 1984). 285 pp. $25

UNDER THE EDITORSHIP OF RICHARD C. TAYLOR

William of Auvergne. *The Trinity*. Roland J. Teske, SJ and Francis C. Wade, SJ ISBN 0-87462-231-X (Translation No. 28, 1989) 286 pp. $20

UNDER THE EDITORSHIP OF ROLAND J. TESKE, SJ

Hugh of St. Victor. *Practical Geometry*. Frederick A. Homann, SJ, Tr. ISBN 0-87462-232-8 (Translation No. 29, 1991) 92 pp. $10

William of Auvergne. *The Immortality of the Soul*. Roland J. Teske, SJ, Tr. ISBN 0-87462-233-6 (Translation No. 30, 1992) 72 pp. $10

Dietrich of Freiberg. *Treatise of the Intellect and the Intelligible*. M. L. Führer, Tr. ISBN 0-87462-234-4 (Translation No. 31, 1992) 135 pp. $15

Henry of Ghent. *Quodlibetal Questions on Free Will*. Roland J. Teske, SJ, Tr. ISBN 0-87462-234-4 (Translation No. 32, 1993) 135 pp. $15

Francisco Suárez, SJ. *On Beings of Reason. Metaphysical Disputation LIV.* John P. Doyle, Tr. ISBN 0-87462-236-0 (Translation No. 33, 1995) 170 pp. $20

Francisco De Vitoria, OP. *On Homicide*, and *Commentary on Thomas Aquinas. Summa theologiae IIaIIae, 64.* Edited and Translated by John Doyle. ISBN 0-87462-237-9. (Translation No. 34, 1997) 280 pp. $30

William of Auvergne. *The Universe of Creatures*. Edited, Translated, and with an Introduction by Roland J. Teske, SJ .ISBN 0-87462-238-7 (Translation No. 35, 1998) 235 pp. $25

Francis Suarez, SJ. *On the Formal Cause of Substance. Metaphysical Disputation XV.* Translated by John Kronen & Jeremiah Reedy. Introduction & Explanatory Notes by John Kronen. ISBN 0-87462-239-5 (Translation No. 36, 2000) 218 pp. $25

William of Auvergne. *The Soul*. Translated from the Latin with an Introduction and Notes by Roland J. Teske, SJ. ISBN 0-87462-240-9 (Translation No. 37, 2000) 516 pp. $50

The Conimbricenses. Some Questions on Signs. Translated with Introduction and Notes by John P. Doyle. ISBN 0-87462-241-7 (Translation No. 38, 2001) 217 pp. $25

Dominicus Gundissalinus. *The Procession of the World (De processione mundi)*. Translated from the Latin with an Introduction & Notes by John A. Laumakis. ISBN 0-87462-242-5 (Translation No. 39, 2002) 87 pp. $10

Francisco Suárez. *A Commentary on Aristotle's Metaphysics or "A Most Ample Index to the Metaphysics of Aristotle" (Index locupletissimus in Metaphysicam Aristotelis).* Translated with an Introduction & Notes by John P. Doyle. ISBN 0-87462-243-3 (Translation No. 40, 2003) 430 pp. $45

Henry of Ghent. *Quodlibetal Question on Moral Problems.* Translated from the Latin with an Introduction and Notes by Roland J. Teske, SJ ISBN 0-87462-244-1 (Translation No. 41, 2005) 82 pp. $10

Francisco Suárez. *On Real Relation (Disputatio Metaphysica XLVII)* A Translation from the Latin, with an Introduction and Notes by John P. Doyle. ISBN-13: 978-0-87462-244-1. ISBN-10: 0-87462-244-1 (Translation No. 42, 2006) 430 pp. $45

William of Auvergne. *The Providence of God Regarding the Universe. Part Three of the First Principal Part of The Universe of Creatures.* Translated from the Latin with an Introduction and Notes by Roland J. Teske, SJ ISBN 978-0-87462-246-1 (Translation No. 43, 2007) 204 pp. $23

Hervaeus Natalis. *A Treatise of Master Hervaeus Natalis, The Doctor Perspicacissimus, On Second Intentions. Volume One—An English Translation & Volume Two—A Latin Edition* by John P. Doyle. ISBN 978-0-87462-247-8 (Translation No. 44, 2008) 622 pp. $47

William, of Auvergne. *On the Virtues: Part One of On the Virtues and Vices [De virtutibus et vitiis].* Translated from the Latin and with an introduction and notes by Roland J. Teske. ISBN-13: 978-0-87462-248-5 (Translation No. 45, 2009) 310 pp. $30

Albertus, Magnus. *On the Causes of the Properties of the Elements [Liber de causis proprietatum elementorum).* Translated by Irven M. Resnick. ISBN-13: 978-0-87462-249-2 (Translation no. 46, 2010) 132 pp. $15

MEDIÆVAL PHILOSOPHICAL TEXTS IN TRANSLATION

ROLAND J. TESKE, SJ, EDITOR

This series originated at Marquette University in 1942, and with revived interest in Mediæval studies is read internationally with steadily increasing popularity. Available in attractive, durable, colored soft covers. Volumes priced from $5 to $50 each. Complete Set [0-87462-200-X] receives a 40% discount. John Riedl's *A Catalogue of Renaissance Philosophers*, hardbound with red cloth, is an ideal reference companion title (sent free with purchase of complete set). New standing orders receive a 20% discount and a free copy of the Riedl volume. Regular reprinting keeps all volumes available. Recent volumes are also available as ebooks.

See our web page: http://www.marquette.edu/mupress/
Order from:
Marquette University Press
30 Amberwood Parkway
Ashland OH 44805
Tel. 800-247-6553 Fax: 419-281-6883

Editorial Address for **Mediæval Philosophical Texts in Translation:**
Roland J. Teske, SJ, Editor MPTT
Department of Philosophy
Marquette University
Box 1881
Milwaukee WI 53201-1881

Marquette University Press office:
Marquette University Press
Dr. Andrew Tallon, Director
Box 3141
Milwaukee WI 53201-1881
Tel: (414) 288-1564
email: andrew.tallon@marquette.edu.
Web Page: **http://www.marquette.edu/mupress/**